The Taoist MBA

Leading with Softness, Stillness & Silence

Dr. David Leung

BY THE SAME AUTHOR

On a Happy Life: Designing Successful Organisations the Senecan Way

The Finite Advantage: Mastering Time and Leadership the Senecan Way

Bushido Leadership: The Immortal Code of Japan's Warriors

The Golden Mean: Leadership Lessons from Confucius' Doctrine

The Ripple Effect: Leadership Lessons from The Great Learning

Thirty-Six Stratagems: Ancient Chinese Wisdom for Modern Leadership

The Samurai Leader: Management Lessons from The Book of Five Rings

The Resilient Leader: Corporate Wisdom from the Book of Job

The Executive Prince: Adapting Machiavellian Strategies to Modern Leadership

Beyond the Sun: Ecclesiastes' Guide to Modern Leadership

The Hindu Leader: Applying the Bhagavad Gita to Contemporary Management

Wisdom from Proverbs: Biblical Principles for Modern Leadership

The Stoic Leader: Applying Meditations to Modern Management

Enlightened Leadership: Buddhist Principles for Business Success

The Confucian Leader: Transforming Modern Organisations with Classical Philosophy

The Taoist CEO: Navigating Business with Ancient Wisdom

The Art of War for CEOs: Sun Tzu's Timeless Strategies for Modern Business Strategy: A Blueprint for Business Warfare

Inside Accounting: The Sociology of Financial Reporting and Auditing

Research Methods for Accounting & Finance: A Guide to Writing Your Dissertation (ed.)

ABOUT THE AUTHOR

Dr. David Leung is a seasoned university lecturer with over 17 years of teaching experience. He holds a PhD and MSc in Science and Technology Studies from the University of Edinburgh, and an MBA from Durham University.

His journey, however, began far beyond the academic world. Before entering academia, he qualified as a Chartered Global Management Accountant with the Chartered Institute of Management Accountants (CIMA), gaining invaluable business experience across diverse industries—ranging from printing and property management to financial services, biotechnology, and tourism.

In 2024, Dr. Leung founded Dragon Business School (www.DragonBusinessSchool.com). This innovative institution aims to become a beacon of excellence, offering cutting-edge online business management courses designed to empower and inspire the next generation of business leaders.

PREFACE

In the fast-paced, ever-evolving world of modern business, leaders often find themselves grappling with the complexities of decision-making, innovation, and maintaining a harmonious workplace. The wisdom of ancient texts can provide a beacon of clarity amidst this turbulence. Lao Tzu's *Tao Te Ching (dào dé jīng* 道德经/道德經*)*, a timeless piece of philosophical literature, offers profound insights into leading with balance, humility, and integrity.

In my first book, *The Taoist CEO: Navigating Business with Ancient Wisdom*, we delved into the principles of Book 1 (The Book of Tao) of the *Tao Te Ching* (Chapters 1 to 37), exploring how the fundamental truths of the Tao could guide the strategic decisions and leadership styles of modern CEOs. The response to this exploration was overwhelmingly positive, resonating with leaders who sought deeper, more meaningful ways to navigate the complexities of contemporary business landscapes.

The Taoist MBA: Leading with Softness, Stillness & Silence is a continuation of this journey, yet it stands alone as a comprehensive guide to the teachings of Book 2 (The Book of Te) of the *Tao Te Ching* (Chapters 38 to 81). This volume delves into the virtues of softness, stillness, and silence, principles that are crucial for fostering authentic leadership and sustainable success. These teachings emphasise the importance of leading with gentleness and humility, embracing the strength that comes from flexibility, and cultivating an environment of peace and introspection.

Incorporated within these pages is the original translation of Book 2 of the *Tao Te Ching*, providing a direct link to the source of this profound wisdom. Alongside the translations, I offer detailed analyses and interpretations, connecting these ancient principles to modern-day business practices. Through practical examples and thoughtful reflections, this book aims to bridge the gap between ancient philosophy and contemporary leadership, offering actionable insights that can transform the way we lead and manage organisations.

The Taoist MBA encourages leaders to see the value in small, consistent actions, to appreciate the power of subtle influence, and to embrace the paradoxes that often accompany growth and decline. It calls for a shift from traditional, rigid approaches to a more fluid and adaptive style of leadership. By doing so, it helps leaders cultivate environments where innovation can flourish, challenges can be met with resilience, and all members of an organisation can thrive.

Whether you are a seasoned executive, an aspiring leader, or someone interested in the intersection of ancient wisdom and modern business practices, this book offers a fresh perspective on leadership. It invites you to explore the depths of Lao Tzu's teachings and to apply these timeless principles to the ever-changing landscape of the business world.

Thank you for embarking on this journey with me. May the wisdom of the Tao guide you towards a path of balanced, compassionate, and effective leadership.

David Leung
Edinburgh, 28 November 2024

CONTENTS

About the Author 3
Preface 4
Lao Tzu 8
Chapter 38 – Benevolence & Righteousness 12
Chapter 39 – Substance Over Appearance 19
Chapter 40 – Paradox & Contradiction 24
Chapter 41 – Perseverance 27
Chapter 42 – Growth & Decline 34
Chapter 43 – Teaching Without Words 40
Chapter 44 – Contentment 45
Chapter 45 – Action & Stillness 49
Chapter 46 – Peace & Stability 53
Chapter 47 – Introspection 56
Chapter 48 – Unlearning 59
Chapter 49 – Universal Goodwill 62
Chapter 50 – Fearlessness 66
Chapter 51 – Authenticity 70
Chapter 52 – Thoughtfulness 74
Chapter 53 – Boastfulness 80
Chapter 54 – Community 84
Chapter 55 – Innocence 90
Chapter 56 – Silence 97
Chapter 57 – Excessive Control 103

Chapter 58 – Happiness & Misery 107

Chapter 59 – Moderation 112

Chapter 60 – Harmonising Influences 117

Chapter 61 – Service & Support 121

Chapter 62 – Words & Deeds 126

Chapter 63 – Caution & Faith 131

Chapter 64 – Ulterior Motives 136

Chapter 65 – Overuse Of Knowledge 142

Chapter 66 – Leading From Behind 146

Chapter 67 – Economy 151

Chapter 68 – Higher Goals 157

Chapter 69 – Retreat 162

Chapter 70 – Core Principles 167

Chapter 71 – Complacency 172

Chapter 72 – Balance 177

Chapter 73 – Awareness 182

Chapter 74 – Roles 187

Chapter 75 – Excessive Taxation 190

Chapter 76 – Softness 194

Chapter 77 – Arrogance 199

Chapter 78 – Empathy 204

Chapter 79 – Conflict Resolution 209

Chapter 80 – Self-Sufficiency & Empowerment 214

Chapter 81 – Generosity 220

Conclusion 225
Appendix – TAO TE CHING BY LAO TZU 227

LAO TZU

EARLY LIFE

Lao Tzu *(Lǎozǐ* 老子*)* is traditionally believed to have been born around 604 BCE, during the Spring and Autumn period of Chinese history, in a village called Quren, located in the state of Chu. This area corresponds to present-day Luyi in Henan Province. There are various legends about his birth, with some accounts suggesting he was born with white hair, a sign of wisdom and venerability from a young age. His actual name was *Lǐ Ěr (*李耳*)*, and he was later honoured with the title *Lǎozǐ (*老子*)*, meaning 'Old Master.'

Lao Tzu's wisdom and intellectual prowess led him to serve as a royal archivist at the Zhou court in Wangcheng, which is in modern-day Luoyang. In this esteemed position, he had access to a vast array of ancient texts and historical records. His role involved preserving important documents, advising the court, and contributing to the intellectual and cultural life of the Zhou Dynasty. His profound understanding of history, literature, and philosophy made him a respected figure in the court.

Throughout his tenure at the Zhou court, Lao Tzu gained a reputation for his deep wisdom and extensive knowledge. Scholars and officials often sought his counsel on various matters, and he became known for his insightful observations on governance, ethics, and the nature of existence. His philosophical reflections were grounded in his understanding of the Tao *(The Way)*, emphasising harmony, balance, and the natural order of the universe.

Lao Tzu's teachings were characterised by a preference for simplicity, humility, and non-interference, which later became foundational principles of Taoism. His philosophical approach contrasted with the more structured and duty-bound Confucianism, leading to a rich intellectual exchange between followers of these different schools of thought.

ENCOUNTER WITH CONFUCIUS

The reputed encounter between Lao Tzu and Confucius is a legendary event in Chinese philosophical history, symbolising the meeting of two of the most influential thinkers of ancient China. Lao Tzu, the founder of Taoism, and Confucius, the progenitor of Confucianism, represented two distinct yet complementary philosophical traditions. While the historical accuracy of their meeting remains debated, the tale serves to highlight the rich intellectual exchange and the diverse perspectives that shaped Chinese thought.

According to legend, the encounter took place at the Zhou court, where Lao Tzu served as the royal archivist. Confucius, who was then a rising scholar and teacher, visited the court seeking knowledge and wisdom. Drawn by Lao Tzu's reputation for profound insight and learning, Confucius sought an audience with the elder sage.

The meeting between Lao Tzu and Confucius is often depicted as a significant exchange of philosophical ideas. Confucius, known for his teachings on morality, social order, and proper conduct, was reportedly impressed by Lao Tzu's deep understanding of the Tao *(The Way)*. The dialogue between them highlighted their differing yet complementary approaches to life, governance, and human nature.

Lao Tzu's Perspective: Lao Tzu emphasised the importance of living in harmony with the Tao, advocating for simplicity, humility, and naturalness. He stressed the value of non-action *(Wú Wéi*

無為/无为) and the need to let things unfold naturally without forceful intervention. Lao Tzu's philosophy focused on the inherent balance and flow of the universe, encouraging individuals to align themselves with this natural order.

Confucius' Perspective: Confucius, on the other hand, focused on the cultivation of virtue, proper conduct, and the maintenance of social harmony through ethical behaviour and adherence to rituals. His teachings underscored the significance of education, family loyalty, respect for elders, and the importance of moral integrity in governance and personal conduct.

While the details of their conversation are largely speculative, the encounter between Lao Tzu and Confucius is symbolic of the interplay between Taoist and Confucian thought. Their dialogue is said to have left a lasting impression on Confucius, influencing his views on certain aspects of governance and personal conduct.

Lao Tzu's Influence on Confucius: Some accounts suggest that Confucius came away from the meeting with a deeper appreciation for the virtues of humility and simplicity. Lao Tzu's emphasis on non-action and naturalness may have tempered Confucius' more structured and prescriptive approach, leading to a more nuanced understanding of balance and moderation.

Philosophical Divergence and Convergence: Despite their differing approaches, the philosophies of Lao Tzu and Confucius both contributed to the richness of Chinese thought. Taoism and Confucianism offered complementary perspectives that shaped the cultural, spiritual, and social fabric of China. Together, they provided a holistic understanding of life, ethics, and the cosmos.

AUTHORSHIP OF THE *TAO TE CHING*

Lao Tzu is traditionally credited with composing the *Tao Te Ching*. This foundational text of Taoism outlines the principles of living in harmony with the Tao *(The Way)*. The *Tao Te Ching* consists of 81 short chapters, each filled with profound and often paradoxical wisdom that encourages simplicity, humility, and naturalness. It is widely regarded as one of the greatest philosophical works in history, offering timeless insights into the nature of existence, leadership, and the human experience.

While Lao Tzu is traditionally credited with the authorship of the *Tao Te Ching*, modern scholarship suggests that the text may have been the work of multiple authors over time. This perspective is based on several factors:

Linguistic Analysis: Scholars have conducted linguistic analyses of the *Tao Te Ching*, examining the language, style, and terminology used in the text. These analyses suggest that the work may have been composed over an extended period, incorporating contributions from different authors.

Historical Context: The historical context in which the *Tao Te Ching* was written also supports the idea of multiple authorship. The text reflects various philosophical influences and cultural developments that occurred over centuries, indicating that it may have evolved through the collective input of several thinkers.

Manuscript Variations: Variations in ancient manuscripts of the *Tao Te Ching* further support the theory of multiple authorship. Different versions of the text have been discovered, each with slight variations in wording and structure. These differences suggest that the *Tao Te Ching* was a living document, subject to revisions and additions over time.

LATER LIFE

According to traditional accounts, Lao Tzu became increasingly disillusioned with the moral and political decay he observed in the Zhou Dynasty. The corruption and social strife of the time contrasted sharply with his vision of a harmonious life aligned with the Tao. Disheartened by the lack of interest in his teachings and the prevailing chaos, Lao Tzu decided to leave the Zhou court and seek solitude in the western wilderness.

As the legend goes, Lao Tzu embarked on a journey towards the western borders of China, intending to live out his remaining years in seclusion. He rode on an ox, symbolising simplicity and the harmonious relationship with nature that he espoused in his teachings. This journey itself became a metaphor for the Taoist ideal of retreating from worldly concerns to attain inner peace and wisdom.

Upon reaching the western frontier, Lao Tzu encountered a border guard named Yin Xi. Recognising the sage's wisdom, Yin Xi pleaded with Lao Tzu to write down his teachings before departing into seclusion. In response, Lao Tzu composed the *Tao Te Ching* in a single session, distilling his profound insights into the nature of existence, governance, and the Tao into 81 concise chapters. This act of writing down his wisdom ensured that his teachings would endure, even as he retreated from the world.

After completing the *Tao Te Ching*, Lao Tzu handed the manuscript to Yin Xi and continued on his journey, disappearing into the wilderness. The details of his later life remain shrouded in mystery, contributing to his legendary status. The story of his departure underscores the Taoist principles of detachment, simplicity, and the pursuit of harmony with the natural order.

HISTORICAL SIGNIFICANCE

The historical details of Lao Tzu's life remain obscure, largely due to the lack of concrete evidence and the passage of time. Much of what is known about Lao Tzu comes from traditional accounts and legendary narratives. Despite these uncertainties, his philosophical contributions have had a profound and lasting impact on Chinese thought and spirituality.

Lao Tzu's impact on Chinese thought and spirituality is undeniable. His teachings, encapsulated in the *Tao Te Ching*, have shaped the core principles of Taoism, one of the major philosophical and religious traditions in China. The emphasis on living in harmony with the Tao, the natural order of the universe, has resonated deeply with Chinese culture and has influenced various aspects of life, including governance, ethics, and personal conduct.

Taoism: As the foundational text of Taoism, the *Tao Te Ching* provides the philosophical framework for the tradition. Taoism advocates for simplicity, humility, and non-action *(Wú Wéi* 無為/无为*)*, principles that encourage individuals to live in accordance with the natural flow of life. The teachings of Lao Tzu have inspired countless followers and have been integrated into Taoist rituals, meditation practices, and ethical guidelines.

Confucianism: While Taoism and Confucianism are distinct traditions, Lao Tzu's philosophy has also been acknowledged by Confucian scholars. Confucianism, founded by Confucius, focuses on social harmony, ethical behaviour, and the cultivation of virtue. The interplay between these two traditions has enriched Chinese intellectual history, with Confucianism emphasising social order and Taoism advocating for natural harmony and spiritual freedom.

Buddhism: The arrival of Buddhism in China led to the development of Chán (Zen) Buddhism, which incorporates Taoist concepts of naturalness and spontaneity. Lao Tzu's teachings on the Tao and the importance of aligning with the natural order have found parallels in Buddhist thought, contributing to a syncretic blending of philosophical and spiritual ideas.

Lao Tzu is venerated as a philosopher by Confucians and as a saint or deity in popular religion. His wisdom and insights have earned him a revered status in Chinese culture, with many viewing him as a guide to living a balanced and harmonious life. Confucian scholars regard Lao Tzu as a philosopher who offered a unique perspective on life and governance, emphasising humility, simplicity, and non-action, which provides a valuable counterpoint to Confucian ideals of social responsibility and moral rectitude. In popular religion, Lao Tzu is often deified and worshipped as a spiritual figure who embodies the principles of Taoism. Temples dedicated to Lao Tzu can be found across China, serving as places of worship, meditation, and reverence, where people offer prayers and seek guidance from the venerable sage. These cultural and spiritual centres reflect the deep respect for Lao Tzu and his teachings, allowing followers to connect with his wisdom and principles.

During the Tang dynasty (618-907 CE), Lao Tzu was honoured as an imperial ancestor, reflecting the deep respect and admiration for his teachings. The Tang emperors, who claimed descent from Lao Tzu, elevated him to a position of great honour and incorporated Taoist principles into their governance. This recognition by the imperial family underscored the importance of Taoist philosophy in shaping the cultural and political landscape of China. The integration of Taoist principles into governance during the Tang dynasty highlighted the relevance of Lao Tzu's teachings in statecraft, as emperors who embraced Taoist ideals sought to govern with humility, simplicity, and a focus on harmony, aligning their policies with the natural order and the well-being of their subjects.

CHAPTER 38 – BENEVOLENCE & RIGHTEOUSNESS

Chapter 38 of the *Tao Te Ching* explores the different levels of virtue and the natural, unforced way of embodying the Tao. Here's how these teachings can be applied to modern-day strategic management:

EMBRACING GENUINE LEADERSHIP

> *Those who possessed in highest degree the attributes (of the Tao) did not (seek) to show them, and therefore they possessed them (in fullest measure).*

Lao Tzu's Chapter 38 of the *Tao Te Ching* encapsulates the essence of genuine leadership, a concept that is profoundly relevant to modern strategic management. The wisdom here suggests that those who truly embody the highest attributes of leadership do so not for show but because these attributes are an intrinsic part of their being. Genuine leadership is characterised by actions rooted in integrity and consistency, driven by an alignment with core values rather than a desire for external recognition. This authenticity is the cornerstone of trust and respect within an organisation, fostering a cohesive and motivated team.

Authentic leadership begins with a deep self-awareness and a commitment to one's own values. Leaders who embody this principle understand that their actions must consistently reflect their beliefs and principles. This alignment ensures that decisions and behaviours are not merely performative but are genuine expressions of the leader's character. Such authenticity is palpable to team members, who can discern when a leader's actions are sincere versus when they are contrived for appearances. When leaders act with integrity because it is inherently important to them, they naturally inspire trust among their employees. This trust is the foundation upon which strong and resilient teams are built.

Moreover, genuine leadership involves a humility that precludes the need for self-promotion. Authentic leaders do not seek to draw attention to their virtues or achievements; instead, they let their actions speak for themselves. This humility is a powerful leadership trait because it shifts the focus from the leader to the collective efforts of the team. By not seeking the spotlight, authentic leaders create space for their team members to shine, fostering a culture of shared success and mutual support. This approach not only strengthens the bond between the leader and their team but also encourages a spirit of collaboration and collective achievement.

The consistency that defines genuine leadership is crucial for building credibility. When leaders are consistent in their actions and decisions, they create a stable and predictable environment for their team. This reliability allows team members to feel secure, as they know they can count on their leader to act in accordance with their stated values and commitments. Consistency in leadership also sets clear expectations for behaviour and performance within the team. When leaders model integrity and ethical behaviour consistently, it establishes a standard for the entire organisation, promoting a culture of accountability and excellence.

Furthermore, genuine leadership fosters an inclusive environment where all team members feel valued and respected. Authentic leaders recognise that the strength of an organisation lies in its people and that each individual's contribution is vital. By demonstrating respect for diverse perspectives and encouraging open dialogue, leaders can create a culture where employees feel empowered to share their ideas and insights. This inclusivity enhances innovation and problem-solving, as it leverages the collective wisdom of the team. Authentic leaders are also adept at providing support and recognition, ensuring that every team member feels appreciated and motivated to contribute their best.

PRACTISING NATURAL & UNFORCED ACTION

> *Those who possessed in the highest degree those attributes did nothing (with a purpose), and had no need to do anything.*

The chapter offers profound insights into the concept of *Wú Wéi (*無為/无为*)*, or effortless action. This principle suggests that the highest form of action is one that is natural and unforced, where individuals act in harmony with the inherent flow of circumstances rather than through rigid control or excessive effort. In the context of leadership, practising *Wú Wéi* means fostering an environment where processes and decisions unfold smoothly and organically, without the need for constant intervention. By allowing events to progress naturally, leaders can achieve more sustainable and effective outcomes.

Embracing *Wú Wéi* in leadership involves recognising when to act and when to refrain from acting. This discernment is critical, as it allows leaders to avoid unnecessary interventions that could disrupt the natural flow of events. Leaders who practise *Wú Wéi* cultivate patience and trust in the abilities of their team members, understanding that not every problem requires immediate action. By stepping back and allowing space for organic development, leaders create an environment where solutions can emerge naturally. This approach fosters a sense of autonomy and empowerment among employees, who feel trusted and valued for their contributions.

Creating an environment conducive to *Wú Wéi* requires leaders to design systems and processes that are intuitive and self-sustaining. Rather than imposing rigid controls, leaders should focus on establishing clear principles and frameworks that guide actions and decisions. This decentralised approach empowers team members to take initiative and make decisions within the context of their roles. When employees are given the freedom to act independently, they are more likely to find innovative solutions and drive continuous improvement. This empowerment not only enhances productivity but also fosters a culture of ownership and accountability.

Moreover, practising *Wú Wéi* in leadership involves simplifying workflows and eliminating unnecessary complexity. Leaders should strive to streamline processes to ensure that actions can flow naturally and efficiently. This might involve removing bureaucratic hurdles, reducing redundant tasks, and leveraging technology to automate routine activities. By creating a streamlined operational environment, leaders enable their teams to focus on high-value tasks that contribute directly to the organisation's goals. This focus on simplicity and efficiency reduces stress and enhances overall performance, leading to more sustainable outcomes.

The principle of *Wú Wéi* also emphasises the importance of being present and responsive to the current moment. Leaders who practise *Wú Wéi* are attuned to the dynamics of their teams and the external environment, allowing them to respond to emerging opportunities and challenges with agility. This presence and mindfulness enable leaders to make informed decisions that are aligned with the natural flow of events. By staying grounded in the present, leaders can navigate complexities with clarity and calm, fostering a stable and resilient organisational environment.

Furthermore, *Wú Wéi* encourages leaders to develop a deep sense of humility and self-awareness. Recognising that true leadership is not about exerting control but about facilitating growth, leaders who practise *Wú Wéi* prioritise the well-being and development of their team members. This humility allows leaders to listen actively, value diverse perspectives, and promote open dialogue.

By fostering a culture of inclusivity and collaboration, leaders can harness the collective wisdom of their teams, leading to more effective and innovative solutions.

DEMONSTRATING TRUE BENEVOLENCE & RIGHTEOUSNESS

> *Those who possessed the highest benevolence were (always seeking) to carry it out, and had no need to be doing so.*

The chapter delves deeply into the essence of true benevolence and righteousness, emphasising that these qualities are innate and do not require constant demonstration. In the realm of leadership, this principle suggests that the most effective leaders are those who embody genuine care and ethical behaviour naturally, without seeking to make a show of their virtues. This intrinsic approach to benevolence and righteousness fosters a culture of genuine respect and ethical conduct, thereby creating a positive and supportive work environment.

Demonstrating true benevolence in leadership involves acting with a sincere concern for the well-being of others. Leaders who embody this quality prioritise the needs and interests of their team members, making decisions that reflect a deep empathy and compassion. This benevolence is not about grand gestures or public displays of generosity but about consistently showing care and support in everyday interactions. Whether it's through offering guidance, providing resources, or simply being present and attentive, benevolent leaders cultivate a nurturing environment where employees feel valued and supported. This genuine concern for others builds trust and loyalty, as team members recognise that their leader's actions stem from a place of authentic kindness.

Righteousness, in the context of leadership, refers to acting with integrity and fairness. Leaders who practise true righteousness make decisions based on ethical principles, ensuring that their actions are just and equitable. This commitment to ethical behaviour is unwavering, regardless of the circumstances or potential personal gain. Righteous leaders do not seek to broadcast their virtues; instead, they act consistently with their values because it is the right thing to do. This integrity creates a foundation of trust within the organisation, as employees can rely on their leaders to act honourably and transparently. When leaders consistently demonstrate fairness and honesty, it sets a standard for behaviour that permeates the entire organisation.

The principle of acting without the need to show one's virtues underscores the importance of humility in leadership. Humble leaders do not seek recognition or praise for their benevolence and righteousness; they simply act in accordance with their values because it is their natural way of being. This humility is a powerful leadership trait, as it shifts the focus from the leader to the collective effort of the team. By not seeking the spotlight, humble leaders create space for others to shine and contribute, fostering a collaborative and inclusive environment. This approach not only strengthens the bond between the leader and their team but also encourages a culture of shared success and mutual respect.

Moreover, true benevolence and righteousness in leadership contribute to a positive and supportive work environment. When leaders act with genuine care and ethical behaviour, it sets a tone of respect and kindness that influences the entire organisation. Employees feel more comfortable and secure in such an environment, knowing that their leaders will treat them with fairness and compassion. This sense of security enhances job satisfaction and engagement, as team members are more likely to be motivated and committed to their work when they feel valued and respected. A positive work environment also promotes collaboration and teamwork, as individuals are more willing to support each other and work together towards common goals.

AVOIDING SUPERFICIAL PROPRIETY

> *Those who possessed the highest (sense of) propriety were (always seeking) to show it, and when men did not respond to it, they bared the arm and marched up to them.*

The chapter cautions against the pitfalls of superficial propriety, highlighting the importance of genuine relationships and ethical behaviour in leadership. This principle suggests that leaders who are overly concerned with outward displays of propriety may engage in actions that appear virtuous but lack true substance. Such superficial actions can result in disingenuous interactions and erode trust within an organisation. In contrast, by prioritising authenticity over appearances, leaders can cultivate stronger and more meaningful connections with their teams, fostering a culture of trust and integrity.

Superficial propriety in leadership often manifests as an excessive focus on appearances and formalities. Leaders who fall into this trap may prioritise looking good over doing good, engaging in performative actions that are designed to impress rather than to genuinely benefit others. This can create a disconnect between the leader and their team, as employees may sense the lack of sincerity in the leader's actions. Over time, this disingenuous behaviour can erode trust and undermine the leader's credibility. Team members may become cynical and disengaged, feeling that their leader's actions are motivated more by self-interest than by a genuine concern for their well-being.

In contrast, genuine relationships in leadership are built on a foundation of trust and mutual respect. Leaders who prioritise authenticity understand that true connections are formed through honest and ethical behaviour. They engage with their team members in a sincere and transparent manner, valuing their input and showing genuine concern for their needs and aspirations. By acting with integrity and consistency, these leaders create an environment where employees feel valued and respected. This sense of trust fosters a positive and collaborative work atmosphere, where team members are more likely to be engaged, motivated, and committed to their work.

Ethical behaviour is a cornerstone of genuine leadership. Leaders who embody ethical principles make decisions based on what is right and just, rather than what is expedient or superficially appealing. This commitment to ethics requires leaders to be true to their values, even when faced with difficult choices or external pressures. By consistently acting with integrity, ethical leaders set a powerful example for their teams, reinforcing the importance of honesty and accountability. This ethical foundation creates a culture of trust and respect, where employees feel confident that their leaders will do the right thing, even when it is not easy.

Prioritising authenticity over appearances also involves being transparent and honest in communication. Leaders should strive to communicate openly with their teams, sharing information and insights in a straightforward manner. This transparency helps to build trust, as employees feel that they are being kept informed and are part of the decision-making process. Honest communication also involves admitting mistakes and taking responsibility for one's actions. Leaders who are willing to acknowledge their errors and learn from them demonstrate humility and a commitment to continuous improvement. This openness fosters a culture of learning and growth, where employees feel supported in their development.

By avoiding superficial displays of propriety and focusing on genuine relationships and ethical behaviour, leaders can build a more cohesive and motivated organisation. Authentic leaders create an environment where trust and respect are paramount, encouraging team members to collaborate and support one another. This positive culture not only enhances individual and team performance but also contributes to the overall well-being of the organisation. Employees who feel valued and respected are more likely to be engaged and committed to their work, leading to higher levels of productivity and innovation.

FOCUSING ON SUBSTANCE OVER APPEARANCE

Thus it was that when the Tao was lost, its attributes appeared; when its attributes were lost, benevolence appeared; when benevolence was lost, righteousness appeared; and when righteousness was lost, the proprieties appeared.

The chapter offers a compelling critique of the diminishing returns of superficiality, emphasising the necessity of focusing on the substance of actions rather than their appearance. This principle is particularly relevant in the realm of leadership, where the temptation to prioritise external validation can often overshadow genuine values and principles. By emphasising substance over appearance, leaders can ensure that their actions are aligned with the long-term success and well-being of their organisation, fostering a culture of integrity and authenticity.

The essence of focusing on substance over appearance lies in the recognition that true leadership is not about performative gestures but about making meaningful contributions that reflect core values. Leaders who prioritise substance understand that their decisions and actions should be guided by a deep sense of purpose and commitment to their principles. This approach requires a steadfast adherence to ethical standards, even when faced with pressures to conform to superficial expectations. By staying true to their values, leaders can build a foundation of trust and respect, as their actions are seen as sincere and consistent by their team members.

Avoiding the pitfalls of superficiality also involves resisting the allure of quick fixes and shortcuts that prioritise immediate gratification over sustainable success. Leaders who focus on substance recognise that meaningful achievements often require time, effort, and perseverance. They are willing to invest in long-term strategies that may not yield immediate results but are aligned with the organisation's overarching goals. This commitment to long-term thinking fosters a culture of patience and resilience, where team members are encouraged to pursue excellence without succumbing to the pressure of achieving instant recognition. By valuing the process and the journey, leaders create an environment where quality and integrity are paramount.

Focusing on substance over appearance also means engaging in authentic and transparent communication. Leaders who prioritise substance are honest and forthright in their interactions, avoiding the use of flowery language or empty promises to impress others. This transparency builds credibility, as employees appreciate leaders who communicate openly and truthfully. Honest communication also involves acknowledging challenges and setbacks, rather than attempting to obscure or downplay them. By being upfront about difficulties, leaders can foster a culture of accountability and continuous improvement, where team members feel empowered to address issues head-on and learn from their experiences.

Moreover, emphasising substance over appearance requires leaders to model humility and a willingness to learn. Authentic leaders are not afraid to admit their limitations and seek input from others. This openness to feedback and collaboration demonstrates a genuine commitment to growth and development, both for themselves and their organisation. By valuing the contributions and perspectives of their team members, leaders can harness the collective wisdom of the group, leading to more innovative and effective solutions. This collaborative approach reinforces the importance of substance, as decisions are made based on thoughtful deliberation and diverse viewpoints rather than superficial considerations.

The impact of focusing on substance over appearance extends beyond individual leadership to influence the broader organisational culture. When leaders model authenticity and integrity, it sets a standard for behaviour that resonates throughout the organisation. Employees are more likely to emulate these qualities, fostering a culture of trust, respect, and ethical conduct. This positive culture enhances overall organisational performance, as team members are motivated to contribute their best efforts in an environment that values substance and integrity. Additionally, a culture rooted in genuine values and principles attracts and retains top talent, as individuals are drawn to organisations where they feel their contributions are meaningful and respected.

PRIORITISING SOLID FOUNDATIONS

> *Thus it is that the Great man abides by what is solid, and eschews what is flimsy; dwells with the fruit and not with the flower. It is thus that he puts away the one and makes choice of the other.*

The chapter also offers profound insights into the importance of prioritising solid foundations and enduring values in leadership. This principle suggests that effective leaders focus on what is substantial and lasting rather than being swayed by superficial or temporary gains. Leaders who embody this wisdom invest in the long-term health of their organisation, build strong relationships, and create sustainable strategies that ensure stability and resilience. By dwelling with the fruit and not with the flower, leaders emphasise the significance of core values and long-term goals over ephemeral achievements.

Prioritising solid foundations begins with a commitment to core values that guide all actions and decisions. Leaders who focus on enduring principles understand that these values form the bedrock of the organisation, providing direction and stability. This unwavering commitment to core values ensures that decisions are made with integrity and purpose, fostering a culture of trust and consistency. Employees and stakeholders can rely on leaders who demonstrate a steadfast adherence to these values, knowing that their actions are rooted in ethical principles and a long-term vision.

Building strong relationships is another critical aspect of prioritising solid foundations. Effective leaders recognise that the strength of an organisation lies in its people and the quality of the relationships within and outside the organisation. By investing time and effort in developing genuine connections with team members, partners, and stakeholders, leaders create a network of trust and mutual support. These relationships are nurtured through open communication, empathy, and respect, which foster collaboration and loyalty. Strong relationships not only enhance the organisation's ability to navigate challenges but also contribute to a positive and cohesive work environment where individuals feel valued and motivated.

Creating sustainable strategies involves thinking beyond immediate results and focusing on long-term success. Leaders who prioritise sustainability consider the broader impact of their actions on the organisation, the community, and the environment. This forward-thinking approach involves making strategic decisions that balance short-term needs with long-term goals. Sustainable strategies are designed to be adaptable and resilient, allowing the organisation to thrive in changing circumstances. By focusing on sustainability, leaders ensure that the organisation's resources are used wisely and that it remains viable and prosperous for years to come.

Emphasising the importance of substance over appearance means that leaders are not distracted by the allure of quick wins or superficial accolades. Instead, they focus on building a strong foundation that supports sustained growth and success. This approach requires patience and perseverance, as true progress often takes time and effort. Leaders who prioritise solid foundations understand that meaningful achievements are the result of consistent, dedicated work rather than momentary flashes of success. By valuing the process and the underlying principles, leaders create an environment where quality and integrity are paramount.

Moreover, prioritising solid foundations and lasting impact involves fostering a culture of continuous improvement and learning. Leaders who embrace this mindset encourage their teams to seek out opportunities for growth and development. This commitment to lifelong learning ensures that the organisation remains innovative and adaptable, capable of responding to new challenges and opportunities. By investing in the professional and personal development of their team members, leaders create a resilient and skilled workforce that can drive the organisation forward.

CHAPTER 39 – SUBSTANCE OVER APPEARANCE

Chapter 39 of the *Tao Te Ching* emphasises the interconnectedness of all things, the importance of humility, and the strength that arises from acknowledging one's roots. Here's how these teachings can be applied to modern-day strategic management:

EMPHASISING INTERCONNECTEDNESS & UNITY

> *The things which from of old have got the One (the Tao) are—Heaven which by it is bright and pure; Earth rendered thereby firm and sure; Spirits with powers by it supplied; Valleys kept full throughout their void; All creatures which through it do live; Princes and kings who from it get the model which to all they give.*

Lao Tzu's Chapter 39 of the *Tao Te Ching* profoundly underscores the theme of interconnectedness and unity, offering vital insights for contemporary strategic management. The essence of this teaching is that everything within the cosmos is interconnected and derives its existence and function from the Tao, the fundamental principle underlying the universe. This interconnectedness extends to the organisational context, where every department, team, and individual contributes to the overall success of the enterprise. Recognising and fostering this unity is crucial for leaders aiming to create a cohesive and effective organisation.

In the realm of strategic management, leaders must understand that the success of an organisation is not the result of isolated efforts but of the synergistic collaboration between various parts. Each department, whether it's marketing, finance, human resources, or operations, plays an integral role in achieving the organisation's goals. Leaders who appreciate this interconnectedness strive to break down silos that can hinder communication and collaboration. By promoting a holistic view of the organisation, they ensure that all departments work in harmony, leveraging their unique strengths to drive collective success.

Fostering a sense of unity within an organisation begins with the leader's vision and communication. Leaders must clearly articulate the organisation's mission, values, and long-term goals, ensuring that every team member understands how their work contributes to these objectives. This shared understanding creates a sense of purpose and belonging, motivating employees to work together towards common goals. Effective communication is key to this process. Leaders must establish open channels of communication that allow for the free exchange of ideas and information, ensuring that everyone is informed and aligned.

Encouraging teamwork is another essential aspect of emphasising interconnectedness and unity. Leaders should create opportunities for cross-functional collaboration, where employees from different departments can work together on projects and initiatives. This collaboration not only harnesses diverse perspectives and skills but also fosters a sense of camaraderie and mutual respect among team members. By promoting a culture of teamwork, leaders can enhance creativity and innovation, as employees feel empowered to share their ideas and solutions.

Moreover, leaders should recognise and celebrate the contributions of every individual within the organisation. Acknowledging the efforts and achievements of employees fosters a culture of appreciation and respect. When employees feel valued, they are more likely to be engaged and motivated, contributing to a positive and productive work environment. Leaders can reinforce this by providing regular feedback and recognition, ensuring that employees understand their impact on the organisation's success.

Unity and interconnectedness also extend to the way an organisation interacts with external stakeholders. Leaders should cultivate strong relationships with customers, partners, and the community, recognising that these external connections are vital to the organisation's success. By engaging in ethical and transparent practices, leaders can build trust and loyalty, fostering a positive reputation and long-term relationships. This external focus complements the internal emphasis on unity, creating a cohesive and integrated approach to strategic management.

ACKNOWLEDGING THE FOUNDATION OF SUCCESS

> *If heaven were not thus pure, it soon would rend; If earth were not thus sure, 'twould break and bend; Without these powers, the spirits soon would fail; If not so filled, the drought would parch each vale; Without that life, creatures would pass away; Princes and kings, without that moral sway, However grand and high, would all decay.*

The chapter emphasises the importance of acknowledging the foundational elements that underpin success. This wisdom is particularly relevant to modern strategic management, where leaders must recognise that the core values, ethical practices, and well-being of employees are integral to the strength and longevity of an organisation. Without a solid foundation, even the most ambitious strategies can falter. Leaders who prioritise these fundamental principles can maintain the integrity and stability of their organisation, ensuring sustainable growth and success.

Acknowledging the foundational elements begins with a deep commitment to core values. These values act as the guiding principles that shape the organisation's culture and inform decision-making. Leaders must ensure that these values are not just words on paper but are embedded in every aspect of the organisation's operations. This involves consistently demonstrating and reinforcing these values through actions, policies, and communication. When core values are upheld, they create a sense of purpose and direction that aligns the efforts of all team members towards common goals. This alignment fosters a cohesive and motivated workforce, as employees understand the importance of their contributions to the broader mission.

Ethical practices are another critical component of a strong foundation. Leaders who prioritise ethics ensure that their actions and decisions are guided by principles of honesty, fairness, and accountability. This commitment to ethical behaviour builds trust and credibility both within the organisation and with external stakeholders. Ethical leaders serve as role models, setting a standard for behaviour that promotes integrity and respect. By fostering a culture of ethics, leaders can create an environment where employees feel safe and respected, leading to higher levels of engagement and collaboration. Ethical practices also mitigate risks and protect the organisation's reputation, ensuring long-term stability and success.

The well-being of employees is a foundational element that cannot be overlooked. Leaders must recognise that the health and happiness of their team members are essential to the overall success of the organisation. This involves creating a supportive work environment that prioritises work-life balance, mental health, and professional development. Leaders should implement policies and initiatives that promote physical and emotional well-being, such as flexible work arrangements, wellness programmes, and opportunities for career growth. By investing in the well-being of their employees, leaders can enhance productivity, reduce turnover, and foster a positive organisational culture.

Ensuring that actions are aligned with foundational principles requires a proactive and reflective approach. Leaders must continuously evaluate their strategies and decisions to ensure they are consistent with the organisation's values and ethical standards. This involves seeking feedback from employees, stakeholders, and external advisors to identify areas for improvement and address potential misalignments. Leaders should also be willing to make difficult decisions that prioritise long-term integrity and stability over short-term gains. This steadfast commitment to foundational principles builds a resilient organisation that can withstand challenges and adapt to changing circumstances.

The importance of a strong foundation is evident in the ability of an organisation to achieve sustainable success. When leaders prioritise core values, ethical practices, and employee well-being, they create a stable and supportive environment that enables innovation and growth. This foundation supports the organisation through periods of change and uncertainty, providing a sense of continuity and trust. Employees are more likely to stay committed and motivated when they feel that their leaders are dedicated to upholding these principles. This commitment to foundational elements not only drives individual and team performance but also contributes to the overall resilience and sustainability of the organisation.

PRACTISING HUMILITY & GROUNDEDNESS

> *Thus it is that dignity finds its (firm) root in its (previous) meanness, and what is lofty finds its stability in the lowness (from which it rises). Hence princes and kings call themselves 'Orphans,' 'Men of small virtue,' and as 'Carriages without a nave.'*

The chapter profoundly explores the virtues of humility and groundedness, asserting that true dignity and lofty achievements find their stability in humble beginnings. This principle is especially pertinent to effective leadership, where humility is a critical trait that enables leaders to remain grounded and connected to their roots. Leaders who practise humility recognise that their position and success are built on the collective effort and support of their teams. By embracing humility, they can forge stronger, more authentic relationships with their employees, fostering a culture of respect and cooperation where everyone feels valued and motivated to contribute.

Humility in leadership begins with an acknowledgment of one's limitations and the understanding that no leader achieves success in isolation. Effective leaders appreciate the contributions and efforts of their team members, recognising that it is the collective work of the group that drives the organisation forward. This recognition requires leaders to step away from the ego-driven desire for personal glory and instead focus on the broader picture of team success. By doing so, leaders can create an environment where collaboration and mutual support are paramount, and where each team member's role is seen as vital to the organisation's overall achievements.

Practising humility also involves listening actively to others and valuing their perspectives. Leaders who are humble are open to feedback and willing to learn from their team members, regardless of their position or rank. This openness fosters a culture of continuous improvement, where ideas can be freely exchanged and everyone has a voice. By demonstrating that they are not infallible and that they value the input of others, humble leaders build trust and credibility within their teams. This trust is crucial for creating an environment where employees feel safe to express their ideas and take risks, knowing that their contributions are respected and valued.

Remaining grounded as a leader means staying connected to one's roots and the core values that guide one's actions. Leaders who stay grounded do not lose sight of the fundamental principles that have shaped their journey. This grounding helps leaders maintain a sense of purpose and direction, ensuring that their decisions are aligned with the organisation's values and mission. It also provides a sense of stability and consistency that employees can rely on, fostering a sense of security and trust. Grounded leaders are less likely to be swayed by external pressures or fleeting trends, allowing them to stay focused on long-term goals and sustainable success.

Humility and groundedness also play a crucial role in building authentic relationships with employees. Leaders who practise these virtues show genuine care and respect for their team members, treating them as partners rather than subordinates. This authenticity creates a sense of belonging and inclusion, where employees feel that they are part of something larger than themselves. It also encourages loyalty and commitment, as team members are more likely to invest their efforts in an organisation where they feel valued and respected. By building strong, authentic relationships, leaders can enhance team cohesion and create a positive, supportive work environment.

Moreover, humility fosters a culture of respect and cooperation within the organisation. When leaders model humble behaviour, it sets a standard for others to follow, promoting a culture where respect and mutual support are prioritised over competition and individualism. This cooperative environment encourages teamwork and collective problem-solving, as employees are more willing to support each other and work together towards common goals. Respectful interactions also contribute to a positive organisational culture, where conflicts are minimised, and collaboration is enhanced.

VALUING SUBSTANCE OVER APPEARANCE

> *They do not wish to show themselves elegant-looking as jade, but (prefer) to be coarse-looking as an (ordinary) stone.*

The chapter also delves into the profound wisdom of valuing substance over appearance, highlighting the importance of meaningful actions and genuine achievements in leadership. This principle advises leaders to prioritise authenticity and real contributions rather than superficial displays of success. Leaders who embrace this mindset build a more resilient and credible organisation, where the focus is on lasting impact and integrity rather than fleeting recognition and external validation.

In the realm of leadership, focusing on substance over appearance means directing efforts towards actions that truly matter and drive long-term success. Effective leaders understand that the pursuit of external accolades and superficial markers of success can lead to a hollow and unsustainable foundation. Instead, they prioritise initiatives and strategies that align with the core values and mission of the organisation, ensuring that every action taken contributes meaningfully to its overall goals. This approach fosters a culture of authenticity, where team members are encouraged to engage in work that is impactful and aligned with their intrinsic motivations rather than merely seeking to impress or gain approval.

Prioritising meaningful actions requires leaders to cultivate an environment where genuine achievements are recognised and celebrated. This involves setting clear expectations and standards that emphasise the importance of quality, integrity, and sustained effort. Leaders should provide opportunities for employees to take on challenging projects and responsibilities that enable them to grow and develop their skills. By focusing on the substance of their work, employees can derive a sense of fulfillment and purpose from their contributions, which in turn enhances their engagement and commitment to the organisation.

Valuing authenticity is another key aspect of this principle. Leaders who prioritise authenticity demonstrate consistency between their words and actions, maintaining transparency and honesty in all their interactions. This authenticity builds trust within the organisation, as employees can rely on their leaders to be genuine and forthright. Authentic leaders do not seek to project a false image or conform to superficial expectations. Instead, they embrace their true selves and encourage others to do the same. This openness fosters a culture of acceptance and inclusivity, where individuals feel comfortable expressing their unique perspectives and talents.

By focusing on real achievements, leaders also create a more credible organisation. Credibility is built on a foundation of trust, reliability, and demonstrated competence. When leaders prioritise actions that deliver tangible results and uphold ethical standards, they reinforce the organisation's reputation for excellence and integrity. This credibility is crucial for building strong relationships with stakeholders, including customers, partners, and investors, who seek to align themselves with organisations that are trustworthy and principled. Moreover, a credible organisation attracts top talent, as individuals are drawn to environments where their contributions are genuinely valued and where they can make a meaningful impact.

Encouraging employees to focus on genuine contributions rather than seeking external validation is essential for fostering a healthy and productive work culture. Leaders should recognise and reward efforts that align with the organisation's values and contribute to its long-term success. This involves moving away from superficial metrics of success, such as titles and accolades, and instead emphasising the importance of dedication, innovation, and teamwork. By doing so, leaders create an environment where employees are motivated by a sense of purpose and the desire to make a difference rather than by the pursuit of external recognition.

CHAPTER 40 – PARADOX & CONTRADICTION

Chapter 40 of the *Tao Te Ching* explores the concept of movement through opposites and the power of apparent weakness. Here's how these teachings can be applied to modern-day strategic management:

EMBRACING PARADOX & CONTRADICTION

> *The movement of the Tao by contraries proceeds; And weakness marks the course of Tao's mighty deeds.*

Lao Tzu's Chapter 40 of the *Tao Te Ching* highlights the profound wisdom of embracing paradoxes and contradictions, a concept that is highly relevant to strategic management. This principle suggests that true strength often emerges from apparent weakness, and significant progress can arise from seemingly unexpected directions. In the context of leadership and business strategy, this means recognising and accepting the inherent paradoxes within the organisational landscape and remaining open to unconventional approaches that may initially appear counterintuitive. By embracing these paradoxes, leaders can uncover new opportunities for growth and innovation, ultimately leading to more effective and resilient organisations.

One of the central tenets of embracing paradoxes in strategic management is understanding that traditional notions of strength and weakness are not always accurate or absolute. For example, a large, established company might have significant resources and market presence, which are traditionally seen as strengths. However, these attributes can also lead to rigidity, resistance to change, and an inability to quickly adapt to new market conditions. Conversely, a small, agile company might lack the same level of resources and market influence but can leverage its flexibility and innovative spirit to outmanoeuvre larger competitors. By recognising that strength can stem from adaptability and that weakness can drive innovation, leaders can better navigate the complexities of the business environment.

Embracing paradoxes also involves cultivating a mindset that is open to exploring unconventional strategies. Leaders must be willing to challenge conventional wisdom and consider approaches that may seem counterintuitive at first glance. This openness requires a willingness to experiment, take calculated risks, and learn from failures. By adopting a mindset that values curiosity and creativity, leaders can encourage their teams to think outside the box and develop innovative solutions to complex problems. This approach not only drives growth and differentiation but also fosters a culture of continuous improvement and resilience.

The principle of embracing contradictions is also reflected in the dynamic and often unpredictable nature of market forces. Business environments are characterised by constant change and uncertainty, where trends and consumer preferences can shift rapidly. Leaders who recognise and accept this volatility are better equipped to respond proactively rather than reactively. This involves staying attuned to emerging trends, anticipating potential disruptions, and being prepared to pivot when necessary. By embracing the inherent contradictions in the market, leaders can develop more robust and adaptable strategies that position their organisations for long-term success.

Moreover, embracing paradoxes and contradictions requires leaders to balance competing priorities and perspectives. This involves finding harmony between short-term goals and long-term vision, between stability and innovation, and between individual interests and collective success.

Effective leaders understand that these dualities are not mutually exclusive but can coexist and complement each other. By fostering a balanced approach, leaders can create an organisational culture that values both continuity and change, allowing the organisation to thrive in a dynamic environment.

Another important aspect of this principle is the recognition that progress can come from unexpected directions. Innovations and breakthroughs often emerge from the fringes rather than the core of the industry. Leaders must be open to ideas and insights from diverse sources, including employees at all levels, customers, and even competitors. By cultivating an inclusive and collaborative environment, leaders can harness the collective intelligence of their organisation and tap into a wealth of untapped potential. This inclusive approach not only drives innovation but also strengthens the organisation's ability to adapt and grow.

UNDERSTANDING THE VALUE OF HUMILITY

> *All things under heaven sprang from It as existing (and named); that existence sprang from It as non-existent (and not named).*

The chapter also offers a profound meditation on the value of humility, emphasising the concept that all things originate from a state of non-existence. This philosophical insight has powerful implications for leadership, suggesting that true success and influence are deeply rooted in a humble recognition of the interconnected origins and contributions of all components within an organisation. Leaders who embrace humility understand that their achievements are not solely the result of their own efforts, but rather the product of collective endeavour and the foundational principles upon which their organisations are built.

Humility in leadership begins with the acknowledgment that no individual can succeed alone. Leaders must recognise that their positions and accomplishments are made possible by the support, efforts, and talents of their team members. This realisation fosters a sense of gratitude and appreciation for the contributions of others. By embracing humility, leaders create an environment where everyone feels valued and respected, which is essential for building strong, cohesive teams. When leaders openly acknowledge their dependence on their teams, they strengthen the bonds of trust and collaboration, encouraging a culture where mutual support and collective success are prioritised.

Moreover, humility allows leaders to remain grounded and connected to the core values and mission of their organisation. Humble leaders are not swayed by personal ego or the pursuit of power; instead, they stay focused on serving the greater good of the organisation and its stakeholders. This focus on the larger purpose helps leaders make decisions that are in the best interest of the entire organisation, rather than being driven by self-interest. By maintaining this perspective, leaders can navigate challenges and opportunities with a clear sense of direction and integrity, ensuring that their actions are aligned with the foundational principles that underpin their organisation's success.

A culture of mutual respect and collaboration is another critical outcome of humble leadership. When leaders demonstrate humility, they set an example for others to follow. This example encourages employees to treat each other with respect and to collaborate openly and effectively. In such an environment, team members feel comfortable sharing their ideas and insights, knowing that their contributions will be valued and considered. This open exchange of ideas fosters innovation and continuous improvement, as diverse perspectives are brought together to solve problems and develop new strategies. By promoting a culture of respect and collaboration, humble leaders enhance the overall effectiveness and adaptability of their organisation.

Humility also enables leaders to be more receptive to feedback and willing to learn from their experiences. Leaders who are humble understand that they do not have all the answers and that there is always room for growth and improvement. This openness to learning allows them to adapt to changing circumstances and to continuously refine their leadership approach. By seeking input from others and being willing to make adjustments based on feedback, humble leaders create a dynamic and responsive organisation that can thrive in an ever-evolving business landscape.

Furthermore, humility in leadership fosters a sense of shared purpose and unity. When leaders acknowledge their dependence on others and the interconnected nature of their success, they cultivate a sense of collective identity within the organisation. This shared identity helps to align the efforts of all team members towards common goals, creating a cohesive and motivated workforce. By fostering this sense of unity, humble leaders ensure that everyone is working together towards the same objectives, enhancing the overall effectiveness and resilience of the organisation.

CHAPTER 41 - PERSEVERANCE

Chapter 41 of the *Tao Te Ching* highlights the differing reactions to the Tao and the paradoxical nature of its principles. Here's how these teachings can be applied to modern-day strategic management:

EMBRACING & IMPLEMENTING CORE VALUES

Scholars of the highest class, when they hear about the Tao, earnestly carry it into practice.

Lao Tzu's Chapter 41 of the *Tao Te Ching* emphasises the critical importance of embracing and implementing core values. This principle is particularly relevant to strategic management, where the most effective leaders are those who deeply understand their organisation's core values and principles and earnestly carry them into practice. Such leaders do not merely pay lip service to these values but actively embody them in their daily actions and decisions. By doing so, they create a culture of integrity and set a high standard for the entire organisation to follow.

Embracing core values begins with a thorough understanding of what these values are and why they are important. Leaders must internalise the organisation's mission, vision, and values, making them a central part of their leadership philosophy. This deep understanding provides a strong foundation for decision-making and helps leaders navigate complex situations with clarity and purpose. When leaders are guided by clearly defined values, their actions are more likely to be consistent and aligned with the overall goals of the organisation. This consistency fosters trust and confidence among employees, as they can see that their leaders are committed to upholding the principles that define the organisation.

Implementing core values in practice requires leaders to lead by example. This means that leaders must demonstrate their commitment to these values through their behaviour, communication, and decision-making processes. For instance, if one of the organisation's core values is transparency, leaders should practise open and honest communication, sharing information freely and fostering an environment where feedback is encouraged and valued. By embodying these values in their actions, leaders set a powerful example for their team members, showing them what it means to live by the organisation's principles. This approach not only reinforces the importance of these values but also inspires others to follow suit.

The earnest application of core values helps to create a culture of integrity within the organisation. When leaders consistently act in accordance with the organisation's values, it establishes a standard for behaviour that permeates all levels of the organisation. Employees are more likely to adopt these values in their own work, knowing that they are supported and expected by their leaders. This culture of integrity fosters a positive work environment where trust, respect, and ethical behaviour are the norm. In such an environment, team members feel empowered to do their best work, knowing that their efforts are aligned with the organisation's mission and values.

Moreover, implementing core values in practice involves integrating these values into the organisation's policies, procedures, and systems. Leaders should ensure that the organisation's processes are designed to support and reinforce the core values. For example, performance evaluation criteria should reflect the importance of these values, rewarding employees who demonstrate them in their work. Similarly, hiring practices should prioritise candidates who share the organisation's values, ensuring that new team members are aligned with the organisation's culture from the outset. By embedding core values into the fabric of the organisation, leaders can create a cohesive and aligned workforce that is dedicated to achieving the organisation's goals.

The commitment to core values also extends to the way leaders interact with external stakeholders, such as customers, partners, and the community. Leaders who embody the organisation's values in these interactions build trust and credibility, strengthening the organisation's reputation and relationships. This external alignment reinforces the internal culture, as employees see that their leaders are consistent in their actions both within and outside the organisation. This consistency enhances the organisation's brand and fosters long-term loyalty and support from stakeholders.

NAVIGATING CHALLENGES WITH PERSEVERANCE

> *The Tao, when brightest seen, seems light to lack; Who progress in it makes, seems drawing back; Its even way is like a rugged track.*

The chapter sheds light on the intricate and often paradoxical nature of progress, highlighting the significance of perseverance and resilience in leadership. In strategic management, it is crucial for leaders to recognise that the journey toward success is rarely linear or smooth. Instead, true growth frequently involves facing and overcoming significant challenges. The path to achieving long-term goals can be rugged and filled with unexpected obstacles, and at times, progress may even seem to take a step backward. By embracing this reality and maintaining a steadfast commitment to their vision, leaders can effectively navigate these challenges and guide their organisations toward enduring success.

One of the key insights from Lao Tzu's teachings is the understanding that apparent setbacks are often a natural part of the progress. Leaders must develop the ability to view these setbacks not as failures but as valuable learning opportunities that contribute to the overall journey. This perspective requires a mindset shift from focusing solely on immediate outcomes to appreciating the broader, long-term process. By cultivating this outlook, leaders can maintain their motivation and determination, even when faced with difficult situations. This resilience is essential for overcoming challenges and sustaining momentum in the face of adversity.

Resilience is built on the foundation of perseverance, which involves a relentless commitment to one's goals despite obstacles and difficulties. Leaders who exhibit perseverance are unwavering in their pursuit of their vision, demonstrating the tenacity to keep moving forward, regardless of the challenges they encounter. This determination inspires confidence and trust among team members, who are more likely to stay engaged and motivated when they see their leaders' unwavering dedication. Perseverance also fosters a culture of persistence within the organisation, encouraging employees to embrace challenges and continue striving for excellence, even when progress seems slow or uncertain.

The concept of progress appearing as a step backward is particularly relevant in the context of innovation and change. Leaders must recognise that introducing new ideas and implementing transformative strategies often involves periods of disruption and uncertainty. These transitional phases can be challenging, as they may temporarily destabilise established processes and systems. However, it is during these times of upheaval that true innovation and growth occur. Leaders who are able to navigate these periods with patience and resilience can guide their organisations through the complexities of change, ultimately emerging stronger and more competitive.

Effective leadership during challenging times also requires a high degree of adaptability. Leaders must be able to adjust their strategies and approaches in response to evolving circumstances, demonstrating flexibility and a willingness to pivot when necessary. This adaptability is crucial for managing uncertainty and making informed decisions in the face of new information and changing conditions. By being open to change and willing to explore different paths, leaders can navigate the rugged track of progress with greater ease and effectiveness. This adaptability also signals to employees that the organisation is resilient and capable of thriving in dynamic environments.

Additionally, maintaining a focus on long-term goals is essential for navigating challenges with perseverance. Leaders must have a clear vision of their desired outcomes and remain committed to achieving them, even when progress is slow or setbacks occur. This long-term perspective helps to anchor decision-making and provides a sense of direction and purpose, which can be particularly valuable during times of uncertainty. By keeping the end goal in mind, leaders can make strategic decisions that align with their broader vision, ensuring that short-term difficulties do not derail their long-term objectives.

VALUING HUMILITY & SIMPLICITY

> *Its highest virtue from the vale doth rise; Its greatest beauty seems to offend the eyes; And he has most whose lot the least supplies.*

The chapter imparts significant wisdom on valuing humility and simplicity, especially in the context of leadership. These virtues are fundamental for fostering an environment that emphasises the core mission and values of an organisation, steering clear of unnecessary complexity and ostentation. Leaders who embrace humility and simplicity can cultivate an inclusive and focused workplace, ensuring that every team member feels valued and empowered to contribute meaningfully.

Humility in leadership begins with a genuine understanding of one's role and the acknowledgment that leadership is fundamentally about serving others. Leaders who embody humility recognise that their position is not a platform for self-aggrandisement but an opportunity to support and elevate their team members. This perspective fosters a culture of mutual respect and collaboration, as employees feel appreciated and understood. Humble leaders listen actively, value the input of their team members, and are willing to admit their own limitations and mistakes. This openness and self-awareness build trust and credibility, encouraging a more transparent and communicative organisational culture.

Simplicity, as a guiding principle in leadership, involves a focus on clarity and essentialism. Leaders who value simplicity prioritise the organisation's core mission and values, ensuring that all actions and decisions align with these fundamental principles. This approach helps to eliminate unnecessary complexity and distractions that can detract from the organisation's primary goals. By simplifying processes and focusing on what truly matters, leaders can enhance efficiency and effectiveness. This clarity of purpose allows team members to understand their roles and responsibilities better, fostering a sense of direction and cohesion.

Avoiding ostentation is another critical aspect of valuing humility and simplicity. Leaders who shun unnecessary displays of wealth or status set an example of modesty and integrity. This attitude encourages team members to focus on the substance of their work rather than superficial appearances. By creating an environment where achievements are measured by real contributions and impact rather than by outward displays, leaders can foster a culture of genuine accomplishment and pride. This focus on meaningful work and authentic success motivates employees to strive for excellence and innovation, knowing that their efforts are valued for their true worth.

The interplay between humility and simplicity also supports the creation of an inclusive work environment. Leaders who embrace these values are more likely to foster a culture of equity and respect, where diverse perspectives are welcomed and appreciated. This inclusivity ensures that every team member feels seen and heard, contributing to a sense of belonging and empowerment. When employees are encouraged to bring their whole selves to work and their unique talents are recognised, the organisation benefits from a rich tapestry of ideas and experiences. This diversity enhances creativity and problem-solving, driving the organisation forward.

Moreover, valuing humility and simplicity helps leaders navigate challenges with grace and resilience. Simplicity in strategy allows leaders to maintain focus on long-term goals, even amid complexity and uncertainty. Humility enables leaders to seek advice, learn from setbacks, and remain adaptable. By staying grounded in their core values and maintaining a clear sense of purpose, leaders can guide their teams through difficult times with confidence and poise. This steadfastness instills a sense of stability and trust, reinforcing the organisation's ability to overcome obstacles and achieve sustained success.

UNDERSTANDING & EMBRACING PARADOX

> *Its firmest virtue seems but poor and low; Its solid truth seems change to undergo; Its largest square doth yet no corner show.*

The chapter explores the inherent paradoxes and ambiguities in life, offering profound insights that are particularly relevant to contemporary leadership and strategic management. The notion that the firmest virtue may appear poor and low, that solid truth can seem to undergo change, and that the largest square may have no corners reflects the complexity and multifaceted nature of reality. For leaders, this means developing a comfort with paradox and ambiguity, recognising that not everything is as it seems and that effective leadership often involves navigating these complexities with openness and adaptability.

Understanding and embracing paradox in leadership begins with the acceptance that contradictions are a natural part of the organisational landscape. Leaders must recognise that situations often contain opposing elements that are both true and necessary. For instance, an organisation may need to be both stable and innovative, emphasising both efficiency and creativity. Rather than viewing these qualities as mutually exclusive, leaders should see them as complementary aspects that must be balanced. This acceptance allows leaders to make more nuanced and informed decisions, considering the broader context and the interplay of various factors.

Embracing ambiguity requires leaders to be open to different perspectives and interpretations. This openness fosters a culture of diversity and inclusion, where multiple viewpoints are valued and considered. By actively seeking out and listening to diverse perspectives, leaders can gain a deeper understanding of complex issues and make more well-rounded decisions. This approach not only enhances problem-solving but also encourages a collaborative environment where team members feel empowered to contribute their unique insights. The ability to navigate ambiguity with confidence and curiosity is a hallmark of effective leadership, enabling leaders to respond to changing circumstances with agility and creativity.

Remaining adaptable is another crucial aspect of embracing paradox and ambiguity. The business environment is constantly evolving, with new challenges and opportunities emerging regularly. Leaders who are adaptable can respond to these changes with flexibility and resilience, adjusting their strategies and approaches as needed. This adaptability involves being willing to experiment, take risks, and learn from both successes and failures. By fostering a mindset of continuous learning and improvement, leaders can ensure that their organisations remain dynamic and competitive. Adaptable leaders also inspire their teams to embrace change and innovation, creating a culture that is responsive and forward-thinking.

Recognising the inherent paradoxes in leadership and strategy also involves understanding that progress and growth often come from unexpected directions. Leaders must be prepared for the possibility that their initial assumptions and plans may need to be revised in light of new information or shifting circumstances. This willingness to revise and refine strategies is essential for long-term success. It requires humility and a recognition that the path to achieving goals is rarely straightforward. Leaders who can embrace this uncertainty and remain committed to their vision are better equipped to guide their organisations through periods of turbulence and transformation.

The paradoxical nature of leadership extends to the personal qualities that leaders must embody. Effective leaders often possess seemingly contradictory traits, such as being both confident and humble, assertive and empathetic, decisive and reflective. These dualities enable leaders to navigate the complexities of their roles with balance and insight. By integrating these paradoxical qualities, leaders can respond to a wide range of situations with the appropriate blend of strength and sensitivity. This balanced approach enhances their ability to connect with their team members and stakeholders, fostering trust and respect.

FOCUSING ON SUBSTANCE OVER FORM

A vessel great, it is the slowest made; Loud is its sound, but never word it said; A semblance great, the shadow of a shade.

The chapter offers profound insights into the importance of prioritising substance over form, particularly in the realm of leadership and strategic management. The metaphor of a great vessel being the slowest made underscores the value of taking the time to develop meaningful actions and robust strategies. Leaders who focus on substance understand that true success and long-lasting impact stem from thoughtful, deliberate efforts rather than superficial appearances or quick fixes.

In the context of leadership, prioritising substance over form means directing attention to the core principles and objectives that drive the organisation. Leaders must resist the temptation to seek immediate recognition or external validation through flashy but insubstantial efforts. Instead, they should concentrate on building a solid foundation that supports sustainable growth and development. This involves making strategic decisions that may not yield instant results but are aligned with the organisation's long-term vision and goals. By focusing on substance, leaders can ensure that their actions contribute meaningfully to the organisation's mission and overall success.

Developing robust strategies and solutions is a critical component of valuing substance over form. Leaders who prioritise substance invest the necessary time and resources to thoroughly analyse and understand the challenges and opportunities facing their organisation. This comprehensive approach enables them to devise well-considered plans that address underlying issues and leverage the organisation's strengths. These strategies are not just reactive responses to immediate pressures but proactive measures designed to secure the organisation's future. By taking a long-term perspective, leaders can create resilient systems and processes that withstand the test of time.

The commitment to substance over form also involves a focus on genuine actions and results. Leaders who value substance ensure that their efforts are not merely performative but are rooted in authenticity and integrity. This means that they are transparent about their intentions and actions, communicating openly and honestly with their teams and stakeholders. By being forthright and consistent, leaders build trust and credibility, fostering a culture of reliability and accountability. This authenticity is crucial for maintaining the confidence and support of employees, customers, and partners, all of whom are essential for the organisation's sustained success.

Furthermore, prioritising substance over form encourages a culture of continuous improvement and learning. Leaders who emphasise substance understand that growth and development are ongoing processes that require dedication and adaptability. They create an environment where team members are encouraged to learn from their experiences, seek out new knowledge, and strive for excellence. This commitment to continuous improvement not only enhances individual and team performance but also drives innovation and progress within the organisation. By fostering a culture that values learning and development, leaders can ensure that their organisation remains dynamic and competitive.

Valuing substance over form also means recognising and celebrating genuine achievements. Leaders who prioritise substance focus on recognising the hard work and real contributions of their team members, rather than superficial accolades. This recognition fosters a sense of pride and accomplishment, motivating employees to continue striving for excellence. By acknowledging and rewarding meaningful efforts, leaders reinforce the importance of substance and set a standard for the entire organisation. This approach cultivates a culture of meritocracy, where individuals are valued for their true contributions rather than their ability to attract attention.

PROVIDING WHAT IS NEEDED FOR GROWTH

> *The Tao is hidden, and has no name; but it is the Tao which is skilful at imparting (to all things what they need) and making them complete.*

The chapter also highlights the profound importance of effective leadership in providing what is needed for growth. The notion that the Tao, although hidden and unnamed, imparts to all things what they need to become complete, serves as a powerful metaphor for the role of leaders in nurturing and developing their teams. Effective leaders recognise that their primary responsibility is to create an environment in which their employees can thrive and reach their full potential. This involves offering the necessary resources, support, and guidance to ensure their teams are well-equipped to succeed.

Creating such an environment starts with understanding the unique needs and strengths of each team member. Leaders must take the time to get to know their employees, identifying their individual talents, aspirations, and areas for development. This personalised approach enables leaders to provide targeted support that aligns with each team member's specific requirements. By doing so, leaders can help employees build on their strengths and address their challenges, fostering a culture of continuous improvement and growth. This attention to individual needs demonstrates a genuine investment in the well-being and success of team members, which in turn cultivates loyalty and engagement.

Support and guidance are crucial components of effective leadership. Leaders must be accessible and approachable, ready to offer assistance and advice whenever needed. This support can take many forms, including mentoring, coaching, and providing opportunities for professional development. By actively engaging in the growth and development of their teams, leaders can help employees navigate their career paths and achieve their goals. Moreover, this guidance should be coupled with encouragement and positive reinforcement, celebrating achievements and milestones along the way. Recognising and acknowledging employees' hard work and progress boosts morale and motivates them to strive for further success.

In addition to personalised support, effective leaders ensure that their teams have access to the necessary resources to perform their tasks efficiently and effectively. This includes providing adequate tools, technology, training, and other essential materials. Leaders should regularly assess and address any gaps in resources, ensuring that their teams are well-equipped to meet the demands of their roles. By removing obstacles and facilitating access to the right resources, leaders enable employees to focus on their work and deliver high-quality results. This proactive approach to resource management demonstrates a commitment to creating a supportive and productive work environment.

Empowerment is another critical aspect of fostering growth within teams. Leaders who empower their employees encourage them to take ownership of their work and make decisions independently. This empowerment involves delegating responsibilities and trusting team members to carry out their tasks with autonomy. By fostering a sense of ownership and accountability, leaders help employees build confidence in their abilities and develop their problem-solving skills. This empowerment not only enhances individual performance but also drives innovation and creativity, as team members feel more invested in finding effective solutions and improvements.

Furthermore, focusing on the development and well-being of teams extends beyond professional growth to encompass overall well-being. Leaders must recognise the importance of work-life balance and create an environment that supports employees' physical, mental, and emotional health. This can involve implementing flexible work arrangements, promoting wellness initiatives, and encouraging a healthy work culture. By prioritising the holistic well-being of their teams, leaders can reduce stress and burnout, leading to higher levels of job satisfaction and retention. A well-rounded approach to employee well-being contributes to a positive and sustainable organisational culture.

CHAPTER 42 - GROWTH & DECLINE

Chapter 42 of the *Tao Te Ching* delves into the origins of existence, the paradoxical nature of growth and decline, and the consequences of violence and strength. Here's how these teachings can be applied to modern-day strategic management:

UNDERSTANDING THE INTERCONNECTEDNESS OF ALL THINGS

> *The Tao produced One; One produced Two; Two produced Three; Three produced All things.*

Lao Tzu's Chapter 42 of the *Tao Te Ching* delves into the profound concept of interconnectedness, illustrating how the Tao produces unity, duality, and ultimately the multiplicity of all things. This philosophical insight holds significant implications for strategic management, where leaders must recognise the intricate web of interconnections within their organisation. By understanding that every element, from individual roles to departmental functions, is intertwined and contributes to the overall success, leaders can adopt a holistic view that fosters harmony and efficiency within the organisation.

Recognising interconnectedness begins with acknowledging that no part of an organisation operates in isolation. Every role, process, and function is part of a larger system, and changes in one area can have ripple effects throughout the entire organisation. Effective leaders understand this dynamic and strive to create an environment where all parts work together seamlessly. This involves breaking down silos and encouraging cross-functional collaboration, ensuring that communication and cooperation flow freely across all levels and departments. By fostering a culture of interconnectedness, leaders can enhance the organisation's ability to respond to challenges and seize opportunities in a coordinated and efficient manner.

A holistic view of the organisation requires leaders to see beyond the immediate tasks and goals of individual departments and consider the broader impact of their actions. This perspective enables leaders to align the efforts of different teams with the overarching mission and strategic objectives of the organisation. By ensuring that everyone is working towards common goals, leaders can create a sense of unity and purpose that motivates employees and drives collective success. This alignment also helps to optimise resources and reduce redundancies, as teams can collaborate more effectively and leverage each other's strengths.

Understanding the interconnectedness of all things also highlights the importance of systems thinking in strategic management. Leaders must consider how various elements within the organisation interact and influence one another. This approach involves analysing the relationships and dependencies between different functions, identifying potential bottlenecks or inefficiencies, and implementing solutions that address the root causes of problems. By adopting a systems perspective, leaders can develop more comprehensive and sustainable strategies that enhance the organisation's overall performance. This method also fosters innovation, as it encourages leaders to explore how different components can work together in new and creative ways.

Moreover, fostering a holistic view of the organisation involves recognising the value of diversity and inclusion. An interconnected organisation benefits from the unique perspectives and experiences of its members. Leaders should create an inclusive environment where diverse viewpoints are valued and integrated into decision-making processes. This inclusivity enhances the organisation's ability to understand and respond to a wide range of challenges and opportunities. By valuing the contributions of all employees, leaders can build a more resilient and adaptable organisation that is better equipped to navigate the complexities of the modern business landscape.

Leaders who embrace the interconnectedness of all things also prioritise continuous learning and development. They understand that the organisation is a living system that evolves over time, and they invest in the growth and development of their employees to ensure long-term success. This commitment to learning involves providing opportunities for professional development, encouraging experimentation and innovation, and fostering a culture of feedback and improvement. By nurturing the potential of their team members, leaders can create a dynamic and engaged workforce that drives the organisation forward.

EMBRACING CHANGE & TRANSFORMATION

> *All things leave behind them the Obscurity (out of which they have come), and go forward to embrace the Brightness (into which they have emerged), while they are harmonised by the Breath of Vacancy.*

The chapter explores the theme of embracing change and transformation, depicting the journey from obscurity to brightness as a metaphor for innovation and growth. In the context of leadership and strategic management, this principle underscores the importance of recognising change and transformation as integral components of organisational development. Effective leaders understand that progress often requires moving beyond the familiar and stepping into new, unexplored territories. By fostering an environment that welcomes change and encourages continuous improvement, leaders can drive innovation and maintain a dynamic and competitive organisation.

Change is an inevitable part of any organisational landscape. Markets evolve, technologies advance, and consumer preferences shift. Leaders who embrace change are better positioned to navigate these fluctuations and leverage them as opportunities for growth. This mindset involves being open to new ideas and willing to question existing practices. Leaders must cultivate a culture that encourages experimentation and risk-taking, where team members feel empowered to explore innovative solutions without fear of failure. By creating a safe space for innovation, leaders can harness the creative potential of their teams and drive the organisation forward.

Transformation, much like the journey from obscurity to brightness, requires a willingness to let go of outdated methods and embrace new ways of thinking. This process can be challenging, as it often involves disrupting established routines and confronting uncertainty. However, leaders who are committed to transformation understand that it is essential for long-term success. They recognise that clinging to the status quo can hinder progress and limit the organisation's ability to adapt to changing conditions. By embracing transformation, leaders can ensure that their organisations remain agile and responsive, capable of seizing new opportunities as they arise.

Continuous improvement is a cornerstone of embracing change and transformation. Leaders who prioritise continuous improvement foster a culture of ongoing learning and development. This involves regularly assessing processes, identifying areas for enhancement, and implementing changes that drive efficiency and effectiveness. Continuous improvement is not about making drastic changes overnight but about making incremental adjustments that cumulatively lead to significant advancements. By fostering a mindset of continuous improvement, leaders can create an environment where excellence is the norm and where employees are motivated to constantly strive for better results.

Moreover, the journey from obscurity to brightness symbolises the importance of vision and foresight in leadership. Effective leaders have a clear vision of where they want to take their organisation and are adept at communicating this vision to their teams. This vision serves as a guiding light, providing direction and purpose amidst the complexities of change and transformation. Leaders must articulate their vision in a way that inspires and motivates their team members, ensuring that everyone is aligned and committed to the collective goals. By maintaining a strong sense of vision, leaders can navigate the challenges of transformation with confidence and clarity.

The metaphor of being harmonised by the Breath of Vacancy highlights the importance of balance and adaptability in the face of change. Leaders must strike a balance between maintaining stability and fostering innovation. This involves being adaptable and flexible, able to adjust strategies and approaches as circumstances evolve. Leaders who are too rigid may struggle to respond effectively to new challenges, while those who are too fluid may lack the focus needed to achieve long-term objectives. By finding a balance, leaders can create an environment that is both stable and dynamic, capable of navigating the uncertainties of the future while staying true to the organisation's core values.

VALUING HUMILITY & MODESTY

> *What men dislike is to be orphans, to have little virtue, to be as carriages without naves; and yet these are the designations which kings and princes use for themselves.*

The chapter profoundly emphasises the importance of humility and modesty, especially in the context of leadership. The metaphor of kings and princes referring to themselves as orphans or individuals with little virtue illustrates the counterintuitive yet powerful concept that true strength and leadership come from a place of humility. Effective leaders understand that acknowledging their own limitations and vulnerabilities can actually enhance their ability to connect with and lead others. By adopting a modest approach, leaders can build stronger relationships with their teams and create a culture of mutual respect and support.

Humility in leadership involves recognising that success is not solely the result of one's own efforts but is also due to the contributions of others. Leaders who value humility are keenly aware of the collective effort that drives an organisation forward. They attribute success to the team rather than taking personal credit. This perspective fosters a sense of shared achievement and encourages collaboration among team members. When leaders express gratitude and appreciation for their team's hard work, it boosts morale and motivates employees to continue performing at their best. This acknowledgment of collective effort cultivates a supportive and inclusive work environment where everyone feels valued.

Modesty in leadership is about maintaining a grounded and realistic view of oneself. Leaders who practise modesty do not seek to elevate themselves above their team members. Instead, they engage with their employees on a human level, demonstrating genuine interest in their well-being and development. This approach breaks down hierarchical barriers and promotes open communication. By being approachable and relatable, modest leaders create an atmosphere of trust and psychological safety. Employees feel more comfortable sharing their ideas, concerns, and feedback, which can lead to more innovative solutions and improved organisational performance.

Moreover, humility and modesty enable leaders to be more effective listeners and learners. Leaders who understand that they do not have all the answers are more open to seeking advice and learning from others. This openness to learning fosters a culture of continuous improvement, where team members are encouraged to develop their skills and knowledge. Humble leaders create opportunities for professional growth and provide the support needed for employees to thrive. This commitment to development not only enhances individual capabilities but also strengthens the overall capacity of the organisation to adapt and succeed in a changing environment.

Valuing humility and modesty also helps leaders navigate challenges with resilience and grace. Leaders who acknowledge their limitations are more likely to seek out diverse perspectives and collaborate with others to find solutions. This collaborative approach ensures that decisions are well-informed and consider multiple viewpoints. During times of crisis or uncertainty, modest leaders remain calm and composed, focusing on the needs of their team and the organisation rather than their own ego. This ability to stay grounded and focused inspires confidence and trust among employees, reinforcing the leader's credibility and effectiveness.

Furthermore, humility and modesty contribute to ethical and principled leadership. Leaders who are humble are less likely to be driven by personal ambition or self-interest. They prioritise the greater good of the organisation and its stakeholders, making decisions that are fair and just. This ethical grounding builds a culture of integrity, where employees are encouraged to act with honesty and accountability. By setting a positive example, humble leaders reinforce the importance of ethical behaviour and create a strong moral foundation for the organisation.

RECOGNISING THE PARADOX OF GROWTH & DECLINE

> *Some things are increased by being diminished, and others are diminished by being increased.*

The chapter explores the paradoxical relationship between growth and decline, emphasising that sometimes true progress involves reduction rather than expansion. This insight is particularly relevant in the realm of leadership and strategic management, where understanding the delicate balance between growth and decline is crucial for ensuring sustainable success. Leaders must recognise that, paradoxically, scaling back certain aspects of the organisation or reducing complexity can lead to greater overall growth, while attempting to force expansion or overextending resources can precipitate decline. By carefully navigating these dynamics, leaders can cultivate stability and long-term prosperity.

In the context of strategic management, the concept of growth through reduction can manifest in several ways. One approach is streamlining operations to eliminate inefficiencies and redundancies. Leaders who focus on simplifying processes and removing unnecessary layers of complexity can enhance organisational agility and responsiveness. This might involve restructuring teams, consolidating functions, or adopting lean management principles. By reducing complexity, leaders can create a more flexible and efficient organisation that is better equipped to adapt to changing market conditions and capitalise on new opportunities.

Another aspect of this paradox involves the strategic decision to prioritise certain areas over others. Leaders must assess which parts of the organisation contribute most to its core mission and long-term goals, and which areas may be diverting resources and attention without delivering proportional value. This assessment can lead to difficult decisions about scaling back or divesting from non-essential activities, allowing the organisation to focus its efforts and resources on high-impact areas. By concentrating on core competencies and key strategic initiatives, leaders can drive sustainable growth and strengthen the organisation's competitive position.

Conversely, the temptation to force expansion or overextend resources can lead to detrimental outcomes. Rapid growth without proper planning and support can strain the organisation's capabilities and infrastructure. Leaders must be cautious of pursuing aggressive expansion strategies that outpace the organisation's ability to manage and sustain growth. This can result in operational inefficiencies, diminished quality, and a loss of organisational cohesion. Instead, growth should be approached thoughtfully and incrementally, ensuring that each step forward is supported by the necessary resources and infrastructure.

The paradox of growth and decline also highlights the importance of adaptability and resilience. Leaders who embrace this paradox understand that change is a constant and that the ability to pivot and adjust strategies is essential for long-term success. This involves being open to feedback and willing to revisit and refine strategies based on new information and evolving circumstances. By maintaining a flexible and adaptive approach, leaders can navigate the complexities of growth and decline more effectively, positioning their organisations for sustained success.

Moreover, this paradox underscores the value of strategic foresight and prudent resource management. Leaders must anticipate potential challenges and opportunities, planning for both expansion and contraction scenarios. This involves building a resilient organisational structure that can withstand fluctuations and adapting resource allocation to align with strategic priorities. Prudent resource management ensures that the organisation can sustain growth over the long term, avoiding the pitfalls of overextension and resource depletion.

PROMOTING ETHICAL BEHAVIOUR & NON-VIOLENCE

The violent and strong do not die their natural death.

The chapter also underscores the crucial importance of promoting ethical behaviour and non-violence in leadership and organisational management. The assertion that 'the violent and strong do not die their natural death' serves as a poignant reminder that aggressive and coercive tactics ultimately lead to negative outcomes and are unsustainable in the long run. Effective leaders understand that ethical conduct and non-violence are not only moral imperatives but also strategic necessities for achieving enduring success and fostering a positive organisational culture.

Promoting ethical behaviour within an organisation begins with leaders setting a strong example of integrity and ethical decision-making. Leaders must embody the principles of honesty, fairness, and respect in all their actions, serving as role models for their teams. This involves making decisions that are guided by ethical considerations rather than short-term gains or expedient solutions. By prioritising ethical behaviour, leaders can create a culture where employees feel confident that their actions are aligned with the organisation's values and that they are contributing to a greater good. This ethical grounding fosters trust and credibility, both within the organisation and with external stakeholders.

Non-violence, as a leadership principle, extends beyond physical aggression to encompass all forms of coercive and manipulative behaviour. Leaders who promote non-violence recognise the importance of fostering a respectful and supportive work environment where collaboration and mutual respect are the norms. This approach involves actively discouraging behaviours such as intimidation, bullying, and undue pressure, which can erode trust and morale. Instead, leaders should encourage open communication, empathy, and constructive feedback, creating a workplace where employees feel safe and valued. This non-violent approach enhances team cohesion and enables more effective problem-solving and innovation.

Ethical behaviour and non-violence are also essential for building a positive reputation and maintaining strong relationships with stakeholders. Organisations that are known for their ethical conduct and fair treatment of employees, customers, and partners are more likely to earn trust and loyalty. This positive reputation can lead to long-term business success, as stakeholders are more inclined to support and engage with organisations that demonstrate integrity and social responsibility. Additionally, ethical behaviour can mitigate risks and protect the organisation from legal and reputational damage that can arise from unethical practices.

Leaders who focus on ethical decision-making understand that it is a continuous process that requires vigilance and commitment. This involves establishing and upholding clear ethical standards and policies within the organisation. Leaders should provide training and resources to help employees understand and navigate ethical dilemmas, fostering a culture of accountability and transparency. Regularly reviewing and reinforcing ethical standards ensures that they remain relevant and are consistently applied across the organisation. By institutionalising ethical behaviour, leaders can create a resilient organisational culture that withstands external pressures and challenges.

Furthermore, promoting ethical behaviour and non-violence contributes to the overall well-being and satisfaction of employees. When employees feel that they are working in an ethical environment where they are treated with respect and fairness, they are more likely to be engaged and motivated. This positive work environment enhances productivity and reduces turnover, as employees are more committed to staying with an organisation that aligns with their values. By prioritising ethical behaviour and non-violence, leaders can foster a workplace where employees thrive and contribute their best efforts.

CHAPTER 43 – TEACHING WITHOUT WORDS

Chapter 43 of the *Tao Te Ching* emphasises the power of subtlety, softness, and the profound impact of non-action. Here's how these teachings can be applied to modern-day strategic management:

LEVERAGING THE POWER OF SOFTNESS & FLEXIBILITY

The softest thing in the world dashes against and overcomes the hardest.

Lao Tzu's Chapter 43 of the *Tao Te Ching* illuminates the profound power of softness and flexibility, suggesting that these qualities often triumph over hardness and rigidity. In the context of strategic management, this principle underscores the importance of adaptability and openness to change as key drivers of success. Leaders who leverage the power of softness understand that being flexible does not equate to weakness; rather, it signifies resilience and the ability to navigate complex and dynamic environments. By fostering a culture that values adaptability, leaders can position their organisations to respond effectively to challenges and seize opportunities, ultimately overcoming even the most rigid obstacles.

Flexibility in leadership involves a willingness to adjust strategies and approaches in response to changing circumstances. This requires a mindset that is open to new information, diverse perspectives, and innovative solutions. Leaders who embrace flexibility are not wedded to a single way of doing things; instead, they are willing to experiment and adapt based on what works best in a given situation. This adaptability is crucial for staying competitive in fast-paced markets, where conditions can shift rapidly and unpredictably. By being open to change, leaders can make more informed decisions that reflect the current reality and future potential of their organisation.

Creating a culture of adaptability starts with leaders setting the tone and modelling flexible behaviour. This involves demonstrating a willingness to listen to feedback, learn from experiences, and pivot when necessary. Leaders who are open to change encourage their teams to think creatively and explore different approaches to problem-solving. This openness fosters an environment where innovation can flourish, as employees feel empowered to propose and test new ideas without fear of failure. By valuing flexibility, leaders can unlock the full potential of their teams, driving continuous improvement and growth.

Softness, as described by Lao Tzu, is also about resilience and the ability to withstand and adapt to pressure without breaking. In organisational terms, this means building systems and processes that are robust yet adaptable. Leaders should design flexible structures that can accommodate change and support resilience. This might involve decentralising decision-making to empower teams to respond quickly to local conditions or creating cross-functional teams that can collaborate and adapt to new challenges. By embedding flexibility into the organisational structure, leaders can enhance the organisation's ability to navigate uncertainty and thrive in changing environments.

Another critical aspect of leveraging softness and flexibility is the ability to foster a collaborative and supportive work environment. Leaders should encourage open communication and create channels for sharing knowledge and ideas. This collaborative approach ensures that all team members can contribute to and benefit from the collective intelligence of the organisation. By promoting a culture of collaboration, leaders can break down silos and enhance cross-functional teamwork, leading to more effective and innovative solutions. This culture of openness and support strengthens the organisation's ability to respond to challenges and capitalise on opportunities.

Moreover, leaders who value softness and flexibility prioritise the well-being of their employees. They recognise that a resilient and adaptable workforce is essential for long-term success. This involves providing the necessary resources, support, and training to help employees develop their skills and adapt to new roles and responsibilities. Leaders should also promote work-life balance and mental health, ensuring that employees feel supported and valued. By fostering a supportive environment, leaders can enhance employee engagement and retention, contributing to the overall stability and success of the organisation.

EMBRACING SUBTLE INFLUENCE

> *That which has no (substantial) existence enters where there is no crevice.*

The chapter delves into the profound impact of subtle influence, suggesting that often, the most effective force is one that operates gently and without overt exertion. In the realm of leadership, this principle translates into a style that emphasises subtlety, presence, and influence through example rather than through direct commands. Leaders who embrace subtle influence guide their teams with a light touch, allowing initiatives to develop organically and encouraging a more harmonious and responsive work environment.

Subtle influence begins with the art of listening. Leaders who listen attentively to their team members not only gather valuable insights but also demonstrate respect and consideration for their perspectives. This active listening fosters a culture of trust and openness, where employees feel heard and valued. By taking the time to understand the concerns, ideas, and aspirations of their team, leaders can tailor their guidance and support to better meet the needs of their organisation. This approach contrasts sharply with more directive styles of leadership, where commands are issued from the top down without much regard for input from below.

Being present is another crucial element of subtle influence. Leaders who are fully engaged and attentive to their team's dynamics can more effectively nurture a positive work environment. Presence involves more than just physical availability; it requires emotional and cognitive engagement as well. When leaders are present, they can pick up on the nuances of team interactions, recognise underlying issues, and respond with empathy and insight. This attentiveness allows leaders to provide timely and appropriate support, helping their teams navigate challenges and capitalise on opportunities. A leader's presence can be a powerful stabilising force, creating a sense of security and continuity within the organisation.

Influencing through example is a cornerstone of subtle leadership. Leaders who model the behaviours and attitudes they wish to see in their team set a powerful precedent. This form of leadership is not about issuing edicts but about demonstrating through actions what is expected. When leaders consistently exhibit integrity, diligence, and empathy, they inspire their team members to emulate these qualities. This influence through example is often more effective than direct commands because it fosters intrinsic motivation. Employees are more likely to adopt positive behaviours when they see their leaders living those values authentically and consistently.

Allowing initiatives to take root organically is another aspect of leveraging subtle influence. Leaders who practise this approach provide the necessary resources and support but refrain from micromanaging. Instead, they trust their team members to take ownership of projects and to innovate within their roles. This trust empowers employees, fostering a sense of autonomy and accountability. When team members feel that they have the freedom to explore and develop their ideas, they are more likely to be engaged and motivated. This organic growth leads to more sustainable and impactful results, as initiatives are driven by the collective energy and creativity of the team rather than by top-down mandates.

Creating a harmonious and responsive work environment through subtle influence requires a delicate balance. Leaders must know when to step back and let their team take the lead, and when to step in to provide guidance and support. This balance ensures that the team remains cohesive and aligned while also feeling empowered and valued. A harmonious environment is one where team members collaborate effectively, support each other, and work towards common goals with a shared sense of purpose. This responsiveness allows the organisation to adapt to changes and challenges more fluidly, maintaining its agility and resilience in a dynamic landscape.

UNDERSTANDING THE ADVANTAGE OF NON-ACTION

> *I know hereby what advantage belongs to doing nothing (with a purpose).*

The chapter introduces the profound concept of *Wú Wéi (*無為/无为*)*, often translated as non-action, which is essential in the realm of strategic management. The idea of non-action does not imply passivity or inaction; rather, it entails taking purposeful steps to allow things to unfold naturally without unnecessary interference. This subtle yet powerful approach to leadership emphasises trust in one's team and the processes in place, enabling a more organic and effective path to achieving goals.

In strategic management, *Wú Wéi* translates to a leadership style that prioritises the empowerment and autonomy of employees. Leaders who embrace non-action understand the importance of stepping back and giving their teams the freedom to take ownership of their tasks. This trust in the team's capabilities fosters an environment where employees feel valued and confident in their roles. It encourages them to innovate and think creatively, knowing that their leaders support and believe in their potential. By avoiding micromanagement, leaders can create a culture of accountability and self-motivation, which drives higher levels of performance and job satisfaction.

Non-action in leadership also involves recognising the natural flow of processes and allowing them to develop without undue intervention. Leaders should be attuned to the rhythms and dynamics of their organisation, understanding when to act and when to refrain. This awareness helps to prevent disruptions that can arise from overbearing management or forced changes. Instead, leaders should facilitate conditions that enable processes to progress smoothly and organically. By doing so, they can harness the intrinsic momentum of their teams and projects, leading to more sustainable and effective outcomes.

Another aspect of non-action is the strategic use of timing. Leaders must discern the right moments to intervene and the right moments to allow events to unfold. This skill requires patience and a deep understanding of the organisational context. Rushed decisions or premature actions can often lead to setbacks or unintended consequences. Conversely, a well-timed intervention can provide the necessary impetus for progress. Leaders who master this balance of action and inaction can guide their organisations through complex situations with greater finesse and wisdom.

Furthermore, the principle of non-action extends to the cultivation of a supportive environment that nurtures growth and development. Leaders should focus on creating the conditions that enable their teams to thrive. This might involve providing the necessary resources, removing obstacles, and offering guidance and support when needed. By setting up an environment that fosters learning and collaboration, leaders can encourage continuous improvement and adaptability. This proactive yet unobtrusive approach helps teams to build resilience and flexibility, which are crucial for navigating the ever-changing business landscape.

Embracing the concept of *Wú Wéi* also means that leaders must cultivate self-awareness and humility. They must recognise that their role is not to control every aspect of the organisation but to facilitate its natural evolution. This perspective shifts the focus from the leader as the central figure to the collective strength of the team. By acknowledging their limitations and leveraging the diverse talents within the organisation, leaders can foster a more inclusive and effective leadership style. This humility and openness create a culture of mutual respect and collaboration, where everyone is invested in the collective success.

TEACHING WITHOUT WORDS

> There are few in the world who attain to the teaching without words, and the advantage arising from non-action.

The chapter also explores the profound concept of teaching without words, emphasising that actions often speak louder and more effectively than verbal instructions. In the realm of leadership, this principle highlights the power of leading by example. Leaders who embody the principles and values they wish to see within their organisation can inspire and motivate their employees to adopt similar behaviours and attitudes. This form of silent teaching fosters a culture of integrity and authenticity, as employees witness and emulate the behaviours modelled by their leaders.

Leading by example involves more than simply adhering to organisational values; it requires a deep and consistent demonstration of those values in everyday actions. When leaders consistently practise what they preach, they build trust and credibility with their teams. This authenticity is crucial for creating a work environment where employees feel safe and respected. For instance, if a leader emphasises the importance of transparency, they must ensure that their actions reflect this value by communicating openly and honestly with their team. This consistency between words and actions reinforces the leader's commitment to the organisation's values and sets a clear standard for others to follow.

The concept of teaching without words also underscores the importance of subtlety and influence in leadership. Leaders who embody this principle understand that their behaviour is constantly being observed and that their actions can have a powerful impact on their team. By demonstrating qualities such as empathy, diligence, and ethical behaviour, leaders can subtly influence their team's culture and behaviour. This influence is often more effective than direct instructions, as it resonates on a deeper level and encourages employees to internalise the values being modelled. When employees see their leaders handling challenges with integrity and grace, they are more likely to emulate these behaviours in their own work.

Creating a culture of integrity and authenticity through leading by example involves setting clear expectations and providing the support needed for employees to succeed. Leaders should establish a strong ethical foundation and ensure that their actions consistently align with this foundation. This includes making ethical decisions, treating all team members with respect, and fostering an inclusive work environment. By upholding these standards, leaders can build a culture where integrity is valued and practised by all. This ethical culture not only enhances the organisation's reputation but also attracts and retains top talent, as employees are drawn to environments where they can thrive and grow.

Furthermore, the practice of teaching without words requires leaders to be mindful and intentional in their actions. Leaders must be aware of the example they are setting and strive to act in ways that reflect the organisation's values and goals. This mindfulness extends to all interactions, from high-stakes decisions to everyday tasks. By maintaining a consistent and intentional approach, leaders can reinforce the importance of the organisation's values and inspire their team to uphold the same standards. This intentionality also helps to create a cohesive and unified team, as everyone is aligned and working towards common objectives.

The benefits of leading by example extend beyond individual behaviour to influence the overall culture and performance of the organisation. A culture of integrity and authenticity fosters trust, collaboration, and innovation, as employees feel empowered to contribute their best efforts. This positive environment enhances productivity and engagement, leading to better outcomes for the organisation as a whole. Moreover, when leaders model the behaviour they wish to see, they create a self-reinforcing cycle of positive behaviour and mutual support. This cycle strengthens the organisation's foundation and ensures its long-term success.

CHAPTER 44 – CONTENTMENT

Chapter 44 of the *Tao Te Ching* emphasises the importance of prioritising life and contentment over fame and wealth, highlighting the dangers of excess and the value of knowing when to stop. Here's how these teachings can be applied to modern-day strategic management:

PRIORITISING WELL-BEING OVER EXTERNAL REWARDS

Or fame or life, Which do you hold more dear? Or life or wealth, To which would you adhere?

Lao Tzu's Chapter 44 of the *Tao Te Ching* highlights the critical importance of prioritising well-being over external rewards, a principle that holds profound significance in the realm of strategic management. The questions posed about the value of life, wealth, and fame challenge leaders to reflect on what truly matters in their leadership approach and organisational priorities. In modern business practices, this principle suggests that the health and well-being of employees and the overall organisation should take precedence over the pursuit of fame and wealth.

In strategic management, leaders who prioritise well-being understand that a positive and supportive work environment is foundational to success. This means creating a culture where employees feel valued, respected, and empowered to perform at their best. When leaders focus on the well-being of their team, they foster an environment where individuals can thrive, leading to increased productivity, engagement, and job satisfaction. Employees who feel cared for are more likely to be committed, motivated, and loyal to the organisation, which in turn enhances overall organisational performance.

Furthermore, prioritising well-being involves recognising and addressing the various dimensions of employee health, including physical, mental, and emotional aspects. Leaders should implement policies and practices that support work-life balance, provide opportunities for professional development, and create channels for open communication and feedback. By doing so, they can help mitigate stress and burnout, which are common in high-pressure environments. This holistic approach not only benefits the employees but also contributes to the sustainability and resilience of the organisation.

Additionally, by shifting the focus from external rewards like fame and wealth to internal values such as well-being and health, leaders can cultivate a more ethical and socially responsible business culture. This shift can lead to more meaningful and fulfilling work experiences for employees, aligning their personal values with the organisation's mission. When employees see that their leaders are genuinely concerned about their well-being and not solely driven by profit, it builds trust and fosters a sense of community and purpose within the workplace.

Leaders who embody this principle of prioritising well-being set a powerful example for their teams. Their actions and decisions reflect a commitment to the long-term health and success of both their employees and the organisation. This approach requires a conscious effort to balance the demands of business performance with the needs and well-being of the people who make that performance possible. It involves making decisions that may not always align with immediate financial gains but are in the best interest of creating a sustainable and positive work environment.

UNDERSTANDING THE TRUE VALUE OF CONTENTMENT

Who is content Needs fear no shame. Who knows to stop Incurs no blame.

The chapter delves into the profound wisdom of contentment, a concept that holds significant relevance in leadership and organisational management. The essence of this teaching lies in the understanding that true contentment does not come from the relentless pursuit of more but from appreciating and valuing what one already possesses. This principle, when applied to leadership, suggests that leaders who embody contentment can foster a more stable and sustainable organisation.

Contentment in leadership is often an overlooked aspect, yet it is incredibly powerful. Leaders who are content with what they have and who recognise the importance of knowing when to stop can create an environment where stability and sustainability thrive. This approach contrasts sharply with the constant striving for more—be it wealth, power, or recognition—that often characterises modern leadership. By prioritising contentment, leaders can reduce the risk of burnout, both for themselves and for their teams. Burnout is a significant issue in many organisations, leading to decreased productivity, increased turnover, and overall dissatisfaction. Leaders who exemplify contentment can set a tone that values balance and well-being, thereby creating a healthier work environment.

Moreover, a leader who is content and knows when to stop pursuing more can instil a sense of satisfaction and balance within their team. This does not mean complacency or lack of ambition; rather, it means recognising the achievements and progress already made and taking the time to appreciate them. Such leaders encourage their teams to find joy and fulfillment in their work, which can lead to higher levels of engagement and motivation. Employees who feel appreciated and valued are more likely to be committed to their work and loyal to their organisation. This sense of satisfaction can enhance overall productivity and contribute to a positive organisational culture.

In addition, fostering contentment within an organisation can lead to more ethical and responsible decision-making. When leaders are driven solely by the pursuit of external rewards such as fame or wealth, they may be tempted to make decisions that are not in the best interest of the organisation or its employees. Conversely, leaders who value contentment are more likely to prioritise the long-term health and well-being of their organisation. They make decisions that are aligned with the core values and mission of the organisation, leading to sustainable success.

Contentment also allows leaders to be more present and mindful. Instead of being constantly preoccupied with the next big goal or external validation, they can focus on the present moment and the needs of their team. This mindfulness can improve communication, build stronger relationships, and foster a more collaborative and supportive work environment. Leaders who are present and attentive can better understand the challenges and opportunities their team faces, leading to more effective problem-solving and innovation.

AVOIDING THE PITFALLS OF EXCESS

> *Thus we may see, Who cleaves to fame Rejects what is more great; Who loves large stores Gives up the richer state.*

The chapter offers a compelling meditation on the perils of excess and the wisdom of balance. The lesson here is clear: an excessive pursuit of fame, wealth, or unchecked growth can lead to detrimental consequences. This message is particularly pertinent in the realm of strategic management, where leaders often face the temptation to chase after external rewards and rapid expansion without fully considering the long-term implications for their organisation and its people.

Leaders should be keenly aware of the inherent dangers that come with excessive ambition and the unrelenting pursuit of external validation. The desire for fame, for instance, can overshadow more substantial and meaningful goals, leading to superficial achievements that lack depth and sustainability. Similarly, the unbridled accumulation of wealth or resources can divert attention from the richer, more fulfilling aspects of leadership, such as fostering a positive organisational culture, nurturing talent, and contributing to the broader community. These pursuits, while seemingly beneficial in the short term, can ultimately result in a hollow and unstable foundation for the organisation.

Understanding the true value of balance requires leaders to set realistic and achievable goals. Rather than being driven by the allure of rapid growth or external accolades, leaders should focus on the health and well-being of their organisation. This involves prudent resource management, ensuring that financial, human, and material resources are used wisely and sustainably. By adopting a measured approach to growth and expansion, leaders can avoid the pitfalls of overextension, where the pursuit of more can lead to inefficiencies, stress, and burnout among employees.

Moreover, leaders must cultivate an awareness of the broader impact of their decisions. Ethical practices and social responsibility should be at the forefront of strategic planning. This includes considering the environmental, social, and economic implications of business activities. By prioritising ethical considerations and sustainable practices, leaders can build a resilient organisation that not only thrives in the present but also contributes positively to the future. This approach fosters a sense of trust and integrity within the organisation, reinforcing its reputation and solidifying its long-term success.

The principle of avoiding the pitfalls of excess also underscores the importance of self-awareness and self-regulation in leadership. Leaders need to cultivate a sense of contentment and satisfaction with what they have achieved, recognising that more is not always better. This mindset helps to create a culture of gratitude and appreciation within the organisation, where employees feel valued for their contributions rather than constantly pressured to achieve more. By embodying these values, leaders can inspire their teams to adopt a similar attitude, fostering a harmonious and balanced work environment.

RECOGNISING THE LONG-TERM IMPACT OF DECISIONS

From danger free Long live shall he.

The chapter also emphasises the importance of recognising the long-term impact of decisions, a principle that is especially relevant in the field of strategic management. The aphorism serves as a reminder to leaders that prioritising short-term gains at the expense of long-term stability can lead to significant problems down the line. Leaders must cultivate the ability to look beyond immediate benefits and focus on the future health and success of their organisations.

In strategic management, the temptation to prioritise short-term achievements is strong, driven by the pressure of quarterly earnings reports, investor expectations, and market competition. However, leaders who succumb to this pressure may find themselves making decisions that provide quick wins but undermine the sustainability and stability of their organisations. For example, cutting costs by reducing investment in employee development or neglecting innovation may boost short-term profits but can erode the organisation's competitive edge and employee morale over time. Such decisions can lead to a decline in the quality of products or services, loss of customer trust, and ultimately, a weaker market position.

To ensure the longevity and success of an organisation, leaders must adopt a holistic approach to decision-making that balances short-term needs with long-term goals. This involves a careful consideration of the potential consequences of decisions, not just for the immediate future but for years and even decades ahead. Thoughtful, strategic decision-making requires leaders to invest in areas that may not yield immediate returns but are crucial for long-term growth and resilience. These areas include employee training and development, research and innovation, sustainable practices, and building strong customer relationships.

Moreover, leaders who prioritise long-term stability are more likely to foster a culture of trust and loyalty within their organisations. When employees see that their leaders are committed to the long-term health of the organisation, they are more likely to feel secure, valued, and motivated to contribute to its success. This sense of security can lead to higher levels of engagement, productivity, and retention, as employees are more inclined to stay with an organisation that they believe is committed to their future and well-being.

In addition, focusing on the long-term impact of decisions can enhance an organisation's ability to navigate and adapt to changes in the external environment. In a rapidly evolving global market, organisations that are built on a foundation of short-term thinking may struggle to respond effectively to new challenges and opportunities. Conversely, organisations that have invested in building a strong, resilient foundation are better equipped to adapt and thrive in the face of change. This adaptability is essential for maintaining a competitive advantage and achieving sustained success.

Recognising the long-term impact of decisions also aligns with ethical leadership. Leaders who consider the broader implications of their actions are more likely to make decisions that are responsible and beneficial for all stakeholders, including employees, customers, suppliers, and the community. This ethical approach to decision-making can enhance the organisation's reputation and build a strong, positive brand identity, further contributing to its long-term success.

CHAPTER 45 – ACTION & STILLNESS

Chapter 45 of the *Tao Te Ching* emphasises the power of humility, the paradoxical nature of greatness, and the balance between action and stillness. Here's how these teachings can be applied to modern-day strategic management:

EMBRACING HUMILITY & CONTINUOUS IMPROVEMENT

> *Who thinks his great achievements poor shall find his vigour long endure.*

Lao Tzu's wisdom in Chapter 45 of the *Tao Te Ching* encapsulates the essence of humility and continuous improvement in leadership. The idea that one should perceive their great achievements as merely a part of an ongoing journey rather than an endpoint is profoundly significant in the context of strategic management. This perspective encourages leaders to embrace a mindset of continuous learning and development, both personally and organisationally.

Embracing humility requires leaders to acknowledge that no matter how significant their achievements may be, there is always room for growth and improvement. This recognition prevents complacency, a common pitfall in many organisations that have achieved a certain level of success. Leaders who see their accomplishments not as a final destination but as milestones on a longer journey are more likely to remain motivated and driven. This drive, in turn, fuels their commitment to innovation and excellence, ensuring that the organisation continues to evolve and improve over time.

A leader's humility also sets a powerful example for their team. When leaders demonstrate humility, they create an environment where continuous learning is valued and encouraged. Employees are more likely to embrace a growth mindset, understanding that mistakes and challenges are opportunities for development rather than setbacks. This culture of continuous improvement can lead to higher levels of creativity, collaboration, and resilience within the organisation. Team members feel empowered to take risks, experiment with new ideas, and push the boundaries of what is possible, knowing that their efforts are supported and valued by their leaders.

Moreover, the principle of continuous improvement is closely linked to the concept of innovation. In today's rapidly changing business landscape, organisations must constantly adapt and innovate to stay competitive. Leaders who foster a culture of continuous improvement encourage their teams to seek out new ways of doing things, to question the status quo, and to strive for excellence in all aspects of their work. This proactive approach to innovation can lead to the development of new products, services, and processes that drive the organisation forward and enhance its competitive edge.

Humility in leadership also involves recognising and valuing the contributions of others. Leaders who appreciate the collaborative nature of success are more likely to build strong, cohesive teams. They understand that their achievements are not solely the result of their efforts but are the product of collective hard work and dedication. By acknowledging and celebrating the accomplishments of their team members, leaders can foster a sense of pride and ownership within the organisation. This, in turn, boosts morale and motivates employees to continue striving for excellence.

VALUING THE PARADOX OF SIMPLICITY & DEPTH

> *Of greatest fulness, deemed a void, exhaustion ne'er shall stem the tide. Do thou what's straight still crooked deem; thy greatest art still stupid seem, and eloquence a stammering scream.*

The chapter encapsulates the intriguing paradox of simplicity and depth, urging leaders to appreciate the subtle complexity that often underlies seemingly straightforward solutions. This chapter presents the idea that profound wisdom and significant insights may appear simple or even mundane at first glance, yet they possess a depth that can profoundly impact strategic management and leadership.

In the fast-paced world of business, leaders frequently encounter complex problems that require innovative solutions. The paradox of simplicity and depth encourages leaders to look beyond the surface of an idea or a solution and explore its deeper implications. Often, the most effective solutions are those that are elegantly simple, addressing the core of a problem without unnecessary complexity. By valuing simplicity, leaders can streamline processes, reduce inefficiencies, and make more effective decisions. This does not mean oversimplifying problems, but rather distilling them to their essence and addressing the fundamental issues.

Moreover, embracing the paradox of simplicity and depth involves being open to unconventional approaches. Leaders who recognise that the most effective solutions may not always be the most obvious are more likely to foster an environment of creativity and innovation within their organisation. This openness to new ideas can lead to the discovery of unique and effective strategies that may otherwise be overlooked. Encouraging creative thinking allows employees to explore and experiment with different approaches, leading to a more dynamic and adaptable organisation.

The wisdom of valuing simplicity also extends to communication and leadership styles. Leaders who can articulate complex ideas in clear and simple terms are more likely to be understood and followed by their teams. This clarity fosters better communication, reduces misunderstandings, and enhances collaboration. When leaders exemplify the ability to convey profound concepts simply, they set a standard for transparent and effective communication within the organisation.

Furthermore, appreciating the depth in simplicity requires a shift in mindset. Leaders need to cultivate an awareness that what may appear insignificant on the surface can hold substantial value. This perspective encourages a thorough examination of ideas and solutions, looking for the underlying principles and potential long-term benefits. It also fosters humility, as leaders acknowledge that their greatest achievements may seem straightforward yet are underpinned by a deeper understanding and strategic insight.

In the context of organisational culture, the paradox of simplicity and depth promotes a balanced approach to problem-solving and decision-making. By recognising and valuing the simplicity in profound solutions, leaders can create a culture that prioritises efficiency, creativity, and continuous improvement. This approach not only enhances the organisation's adaptability but also its resilience in the face of challenges.

BALANCING ACTION & STILLNESS

> *Constant action overcomes cold; being still overcomes heat. Purity and stillness give the correct law to all under heaven.*

The chapter presents a profound lesson on the balance between action and stillness, a principle that is particularly relevant for effective leadership. The notion that constant action can overcome challenges while stillness can restore and maintain clarity highlights the dual nature of these states. In the context of strategic management and leadership, understanding and practising this balance is crucial for sustaining productivity and overall well-being within an organisation.

Leaders who focus solely on action often drive progress and achieve short-term goals, but this relentless pursuit can lead to burnout and diminished effectiveness over time. Constant activity, while necessary for overcoming immediate obstacles, can create an environment of perpetual stress and urgency, which is not sustainable in the long run. By acknowledging the need for periods of stillness and reflection, leaders can foster a more balanced approach that enhances both individual and organisational performance.

Stillness, in this context, is not merely the absence of action but a deliberate state of mindfulness and introspection. It allows leaders and their teams to pause, reflect on their actions, and gain clarity on their goals and strategies. This reflective practice can lead to deeper insights and more thoughtful decision-making. When leaders encourage their teams to take breaks, step back from their tasks, and recharge, they are not only promoting physical and mental health but also enhancing creativity and innovation. The moments of stillness create a space where new ideas can emerge, and existing challenges can be viewed from fresh perspectives.

Moreover, the balance between action and stillness aligns with the broader principles of sustainability and long-term success. In a fast-paced and often chaotic business environment, the ability to remain calm and focused is a significant asset. Leaders who master this balance are better equipped to handle crises and make strategic decisions that consider both immediate needs and future implications. They create a work culture that values not just the end results but also the processes and well-being of those involved in achieving them.

Encouraging a balance between action and stillness also reflects a deeper understanding of human nature and the rhythms of work. Just as nature operates in cycles of activity and rest, so too should organisations and their teams. By aligning with these natural rhythms, leaders can cultivate a more humane and effective work environment. Employees are more likely to be engaged and motivated when they feel that their leaders respect and support their need for balance.

PROMOTING ETHICAL LEADERSHIP

Purity and stillness give the correct law to all under heaven.

The chapter also emphasises the profound importance of ethical leadership, suggesting that purity and stillness form the foundation for just and effective governance. In the context of modern leadership, this principle underscores the necessity of making decisions grounded in integrity and ethical principles to foster a positive and sustainable organisational culture. Leaders who embody these qualities not only build trust and credibility but also ensure the long-term success and stability of their organisations.

Ethical leadership requires a commitment to transparency and honesty in all actions. When leaders operate with purity, they demonstrate a consistent adherence to ethical standards and values. This means making decisions that are not only legally compliant but also morally sound. By prioritising ethical considerations, leaders set a standard for behaviour within their organisations that others are likely to follow. This establishes a culture of trust, where employees feel confident that their leaders are acting in the best interests of all stakeholders, not just pursuing personal or short-term gains.

Building a positive organisational culture through ethical leadership also involves creating an environment where ethical behaviour is recognised and rewarded. Leaders must model the behaviour they wish to see in their teams, showing through their actions what it means to act with integrity. This might include taking responsibility for mistakes, treating all employees with respect, and being fair and just in decision-making processes. When leaders exemplify these behaviours, they cultivate a culture of mutual respect and accountability, encouraging everyone in the organisation to strive for ethical excellence.

The principle of stillness in Lao Tzu's teaching further complements ethical leadership by advocating for a calm and reflective approach to decision-making. Stillness allows leaders to step back from the immediate pressures and complexities of their roles to consider the broader implications of their actions. This reflective practice helps leaders to maintain clarity and focus, ensuring that their decisions are thoughtful and aligned with their core values. It also provides a space for leaders to engage with their own ethical beliefs, refining their understanding of what it means to lead with integrity.

Moreover, promoting ethical leadership is essential for the long-term viability of any organisation. Trust and credibility are invaluable assets that take time to build but can be quickly eroded by unethical behaviour. Leaders who consistently demonstrate ethical conduct help to safeguard the organisation's reputation, which is crucial for maintaining the confidence of customers, employees, investors, and other stakeholders. Ethical leadership also mitigates risks associated with legal and regulatory compliance, protecting the organisation from potential scandals and legal issues that can arise from unethical practices.

CHAPTER 46 – PEACE & STABILITY

Chapter 46 of the *Tao Te Ching* emphasises the contrast between peace and conflict, the dangers of unchecked ambition, and the value of contentment. Here's how these teachings can be applied to modern-day strategic management:

PRIORITISING PEACE & STABILITY

> When the Tao prevails in the world, they send back their swift horses to (draw) the dung-carts. When the Tao is disregarded in the world, the war-horses breed in the border lands.

Lao Tzu's Chapter 46 of the *Tao Te Ching* presents a profound insight into the importance of peace and stability in leadership and organisational management. The imagery of swift horses being used for mundane tasks when the Tao prevails, versus war-horses breeding in borderlands when the Tao is neglected, serves as a powerful metaphor for the effects of ethical principles and core values on an organisation's harmony and efficiency.

In the realm of strategic management, leaders must prioritise creating a peaceful and stable work environment. This begins with a commitment to core values and ethical principles, which serve as the guiding framework for all organisational activities. When these principles are upheld, there is a natural harmony that pervades the organisation, fostering an atmosphere of trust and collaboration. Employees feel safe and valued, knowing that their well-being is a priority and that they are part of an ethical and fair workplace. This sense of security is crucial for enabling employees to perform at their best, as it reduces anxiety and fosters a positive and supportive culture.

Moreover, prioritising peace and stability involves actively working to maintain a positive and collaborative atmosphere. Leaders play a crucial role in setting the tone for this environment by demonstrating behaviours that promote respect, fairness, and open communication. By engaging with employees transparently and encouraging feedback, leaders can address potential issues before they escalate into conflicts. This proactive approach helps to create a workplace where employees feel heard and valued, which enhances their engagement and motivation.

The benefits of a peaceful and stable work environment extend beyond employee well-being. Such an environment also contributes to increased productivity and efficiency. When employees are not preoccupied with internal conflicts or ethical concerns, they can focus more fully on their work. The resulting boost in productivity can be significant, as employees are able to collaborate more effectively and contribute their best efforts to the organisation's goals. Additionally, a stable environment helps to retain top talent, as employees are more likely to stay with an organisation that prioritises their well-being and operates on ethical principles.

Furthermore, the emphasis on ethical leadership and stability aligns with the broader goals of corporate social responsibility. Organisations that prioritise ethical practices are better positioned to build strong relationships with stakeholders, including customers, investors, and the community. These relationships are founded on trust and mutual respect, which can enhance the organisation's reputation and support its long-term success. By adhering to ethical principles and maintaining a stable work environment, leaders can ensure that their organisation is seen as a responsible and reliable entity.

AVOIDING THE PITFALLS OF EXCESSIVE AMBITION

> *There is no guilt greater than to sanction ambition; no calamity greater than to be discontented with one's lot; no fault greater than the wish to be getting.*

The chapter offers a stark warning against the dangers of unchecked ambition, emphasising the profound impacts it can have on individuals and organisations alike. In the context of leadership and strategic management, this teaching underscores the importance of fostering a balanced approach to ambition and goal-setting. Ambition, when left unchecked, can lead to unethical behaviour, burnout, and widespread dissatisfaction, both for leaders and their teams.

Ambition is often celebrated as a driving force behind progress and achievement. However, when ambition becomes excessive, it can distort judgment and priorities. Leaders who are overly ambitious may resort to unethical practices to achieve their goals, compromising their integrity and the ethical standards of their organisation. This behaviour not only undermines trust and credibility but can also lead to significant legal and reputational risks. The relentless pursuit of more—whether it be power, wealth, or recognition—can cloud a leader's vision, leading them to make decisions that prioritise short-term gains over long-term stability and well-being.

Moreover, excessive ambition can take a severe toll on an individual's mental and physical health. Leaders driven by unbridled ambition often face immense pressure to constantly achieve and outperform, leading to chronic stress and burnout. This relentless drive can result in a lack of balance between professional and personal life, causing further dissatisfaction and potential long-term health issues. Additionally, the culture created by such leadership can permeate throughout the organisation, affecting employees who may feel pressured to keep up with unrealistic expectations, ultimately leading to a toxic work environment.

To mitigate these dangers, leaders must encourage a balanced approach to goal-setting. This begins with setting realistic and achievable targets that align with the organisation's core values and long-term objectives. By focusing on attainable goals, leaders can foster a sense of accomplishment and progress, which is crucial for maintaining motivation and engagement among employees. It is equally important for leaders to recognise and celebrate these achievements, no matter how small they may seem. Acknowledging progress helps build a culture of appreciation and contentment, where employees feel valued and recognised for their contributions.

Furthermore, leaders should cultivate a mindset of contentment and gratitude within their organisations. This involves encouraging employees to appreciate what they have accomplished and to find satisfaction in their work. By fostering a culture that values balance and well-being over relentless pursuit, leaders can create an environment where employees feel supported and motivated to perform at their best. This approach not only enhances overall satisfaction but also contributes to the long-term sustainability and resilience of the organisation.

In addition, fostering a balanced approach to ambition requires self-awareness and continuous reflection. Leaders must regularly assess their motivations and the impact of their actions on their teams and the broader organisation. This reflective practice helps them stay grounded and aligned with their ethical principles and organisational values. By promoting a culture of ethical ambition— one that seeks to achieve great things without compromising integrity or well-being—leaders can guide their organisations towards sustainable success and fulfillment.

EMBRACING CONTENTMENT & SUSTAINABILITY

> *Therefore the sufficiency of contentment is an enduring and unchanging sufficiency.*

The chapter also imparts the timeless wisdom of contentment and sustainability as essential elements for achieving long-term success. This teaching underscores the importance of fostering a culture where employees are encouraged to derive satisfaction from their work and personal accomplishments. Leaders play a critical role in promoting this culture by recognising and valuing the principles of balance, well-being, and ethical practices.

Contentment, as highlighted by Lao Tzu, is a state of being where individuals feel sufficient and satisfied with what they have. In the context of organisational leadership, this principle translates to creating an environment where employees can find genuine fulfillment in their roles. This involves acknowledging their efforts and celebrating their achievements, no matter how small. When employees feel appreciated and recognised, it fosters a sense of belonging and purpose. This intrinsic motivation not only enhances their performance but also contributes to a positive and supportive workplace atmosphere.

Promoting sustainability goes hand-in-hand with fostering contentment. Leaders must focus on sustainable growth, which means setting realistic goals that ensure the long-term health and viability of the organisation. This approach requires a shift from short-term gains to long-term value creation. Sustainable growth is achieved by investing in practices that balance economic success with environmental stewardship and social responsibility. By prioritising ethical decision-making, leaders can build a resilient organisation that withstands challenges and adapts to changing circumstances.

Ethical practices are the backbone of sustainable leadership. Leaders must consistently make decisions that are not only profitable but also align with moral and ethical standards. This includes fair treatment of employees, responsible resource management, and transparent communication. By doing so, leaders build trust and credibility, both internally and externally. An organisation that operates with integrity is more likely to gain the loyalty of its employees and the trust of its customers and stakeholders.

Furthermore, the value of balance and well-being cannot be overstated. Leaders should actively promote work-life balance, encouraging employees to take breaks and engage in activities that recharge them. This holistic approach to well-being ensures that employees are not overworked and can maintain their mental and physical health. A balanced work environment reduces burnout and turnover, leading to a more stable and engaged workforce.

Incorporating the principles of contentment and sustainability into organisational practices requires a strategic and mindful approach. Leaders need to cultivate a culture where these values are deeply embedded in the daily operations and decision-making processes. This can be achieved through continuous education, open dialogue, and leading by example. When leaders themselves embody these principles, it sets a powerful precedent for the entire organisation to follow.

CHAPTER 47 – INTROSPECTION

Chapter 47 of the *Tao Te Ching* highlights the concept of inner knowledge and the power of introspection, suggesting that true understanding and wisdom come from within. Here's how these teachings can be applied to modern-day strategic management:

LEVERAGING THE POWER OF INTROSPECTION

> *Without going outside his door, one understands (all that takes place) under the sky; without looking out from his window, one sees the Tao of Heaven.*

Lao Tzu's Chapter 47 of the *Tao Te Ching* illuminates the profound power of introspection and self-reflection in leadership and strategic management. The principle that one can understand the broader world without stepping outside one's door emphasises the importance of looking inward to gain deep insights and wisdom. For leaders, this means recognising that true understanding and effective decision-making often come from a place of inner reflection and self-awareness.

In the context of strategic management, the practice of introspection allows leaders to pause and thoughtfully consider their experiences, thoughts, and emotions. By doing so, they can uncover deeper insights into their organisation's dynamics and operational intricacies. This reflective process helps leaders to identify patterns, understand underlying issues, and gain a clearer perspective on their actions and their impact on the organisation. When leaders take the time to introspect, they cultivate a heightened sense of self-awareness, which is crucial for making informed and effective decisions.

Furthermore, introspection aids in fostering emotional intelligence, an essential trait for effective leadership. By reflecting on their own emotional responses and understanding their motivations, leaders can develop greater empathy and connect more authentically with their team members. This emotional attunement enhances their ability to lead with compassion and understanding, creating a supportive and inclusive work environment. Leaders who practise self-reflection are better equipped to manage conflicts, navigate challenges, and build strong, trusting relationships within their organisation.

Introspection also encourages leaders to internalise their learning experiences, allowing them to grow and evolve continually. Rather than relying solely on external feedback and validation, introspective leaders draw from their own experiences and insights to guide their decisions. This self-reliance fosters a sense of confidence and independence, enabling leaders to act decisively and with conviction. Additionally, this internal process of reflection can lead to innovative thinking and creative problem-solving, as leaders are able to see beyond immediate circumstances and consider broader, more holistic solutions.

Moreover, the value of introspection extends to strategic visioning and planning. Leaders who regularly reflect on their goals and strategies are more likely to align their actions with the long-term mission and values of the organisation. This alignment ensures that decisions are not made in isolation but are connected to a larger vision that guides the organisation's trajectory. Introspective leaders are thus able to maintain a balance between short-term objectives and long-term aspirations, navigating the complexities of the business landscape with clarity and purpose.

EMPHASISING INTERNAL WISDOM OVER EXTERNAL NOISE

> *The farther that one goes out (from himself), the less he knows.*

The chapter offers a profound reminder about the importance of internal wisdom and intuition in leadership. In today's world, where information is overwhelmingly abundant and easily accessible, it is easy for leaders to become distracted by the constant influx of external inputs. The essence of Lao Tzu's teaching is that the farther one goes out from oneself, the more one loses touch with their inner understanding and true knowledge. For leaders, this emphasises the critical need to prioritise internal wisdom and the collective intuition of their team over the noise of external trends and opinions.

In strategic management, leaders often face the temptation to chase after the latest trends, technologies, or market predictions in an effort to stay ahead. While staying informed is certainly important, it should not come at the expense of a leader's own judgment and the core values of the organisation. When leaders place too much weight on external sources, they risk making decisions that are not fully aligned with the unique needs and goals of their organisation. Instead, leaders should cultivate a deep sense of internal awareness, drawing on their own experiences, insights, and the collective wisdom of their team to guide their strategic decisions.

This focus on internal wisdom does not mean ignoring external information altogether but rather integrating it thoughtfully. Leaders should filter external inputs through the lens of their organisation's values, mission, and long-term vision. By doing so, they can ensure that any external influences serve to complement and enhance their internal strategies rather than dictate them. This balanced approach helps leaders maintain clarity and purpose, making decisions that are both innovative and true to the essence of their organisation.

Moreover, trusting in one's own judgment and the collective intuition of the team fosters a culture of confidence and empowerment. When leaders demonstrate faith in their own decision-making abilities and those of their team members, it encourages a sense of ownership and responsibility among employees. This trust empowers team members to contribute their ideas and insights, knowing that their perspectives are valued and considered. As a result, the organisation benefits from a diverse range of viewpoints and a more robust decision-making process.

Emphasising internal wisdom also aligns with the principles of mindful leadership. Leaders who practise mindfulness are more attuned to their inner state and the present moment, allowing them to respond to challenges with greater clarity and composure. This heightened awareness helps leaders navigate the complexities of their roles with a calm and focused mindset, avoiding the pitfalls of reactive or impulsive decision-making. By cultivating a habit of introspection and reflection, leaders can strengthen their connection to their inner wisdom and intuition, enhancing their overall effectiveness.

Furthermore, focusing on internal strengths and values helps organisations remain resilient and adaptable in the face of change. External trends and market conditions are often unpredictable and beyond a leader's control. However, by staying grounded in their core principles, leaders can guide their organisations through uncertainty with confidence and stability. This resilience is rooted in a strong sense of identity and purpose, which provides a solid foundation for navigating the evolving business landscape.

SIMPLIFYING PROCESSES & REDUCING OVER-COMPLICATION

> Therefore the sages got their knowledge without travelling; gave their (right) names to things without seeing them; and accomplished their ends without any purpose of doing so.

The chapter also teaches a profound lesson about the virtues of simplicity and clarity in leadership. The imagery of sages gaining knowledge without traveling and naming things without seeing them speaks to the essence of wisdom and efficiency that comes from understanding and focusing on the core elements. For leaders, this translates into the strategic simplification of processes and the reduction of unnecessary complexities within their organisations.

In the modern business environment, it is easy for organisations to become entangled in overly complex processes and bureaucratic procedures. These complexities can lead to inefficiencies, confusion, and a lack of focus on the essential goals. Leaders who embrace Lao Tzu's wisdom understand that by simplifying operations and eliminating unnecessary steps, they can create a more efficient and effective organisation. This begins with identifying the core objectives and ensuring that all processes and strategies are aligned with these fundamental goals.

Simplifying processes involves streamlining workflows and removing redundant or non-essential tasks. This can be achieved through careful analysis and evaluation of existing procedures to determine what adds value and what does not. By cutting out the extraneous, leaders can reduce waste and focus resources on activities that directly contribute to the organisation's success. This approach not only improves operational efficiency but also clarifies roles and responsibilities, reducing the potential for confusion and errors.

Furthermore, simplifying processes enhances decision-making. When leaders and their teams are not bogged down by complexity, they can make quicker and more informed decisions. Clear, straightforward strategies allow for better communication and understanding across the organisation. Employees are more likely to be engaged and motivated when they have a clear sense of direction and know how their work contributes to the overarching goals. This clarity fosters a sense of purpose and alignment, driving higher levels of productivity and satisfaction.

Another critical aspect of simplifying processes is the adoption of straightforward and transparent communication practices. Leaders should prioritise clear and concise communication, ensuring that information is easily accessible and understood by all members of the organisation. This helps to build a culture of openness and trust, where employees feel informed and valued. Effective communication is essential for maintaining alignment and coherence within the organisation, particularly during times of change or uncertainty.

Leaders must also be vigilant about avoiding the trap of overcomplicating tasks and initiatives. This can often occur when there is a tendency to over-engineer solutions or when too many layers of approval and oversight are added. By focusing on the essential elements and maintaining a disciplined approach to simplicity, leaders can prevent unnecessary complications that hinder progress and innovation. This disciplined approach requires a constant reassessment of processes and a willingness to adapt and streamline as needed.

CHAPTER 48 – UNLEARNING

Chapter 48 of the *Tao Te Ching* explores the concepts of learning through accumulation and the power of diminishing actions, ultimately reaching a state of effortless accomplishment. Here's how these teachings can be applied to modern-day strategic management:

BALANCING LEARNING & UNLEARNING

> *He who devotes himself to learning (seeks) from day to day to increase (his knowledge); he who devotes himself to the Tao (seeks) from day to day to diminish (his doing).*

Lao Tzu's Chapter 48 of the *Tao Te Ching* offers a profound exploration of the delicate balance between learning and unlearning, a concept that is particularly relevant in the field of strategic management. The wisdom conveyed here suggests that while the pursuit of knowledge is vital for growth and innovation, it is equally important to engage in the process of unlearning—letting go of outdated habits and practices that no longer serve the organisation. This dual approach can help leaders streamline operations, enhance efficiency, and focus on what truly matters.

In the modern business environment, the accumulation of knowledge is often emphasised as the cornerstone of success. Continuous learning is indeed essential, as it enables leaders and their teams to stay informed about industry trends, technological advancements, and best practices. It fosters innovation, drives competitive advantage, and supports personal and professional development. However, the relentless pursuit of knowledge can sometimes lead to an overload of information and a clutter of outdated practices that hinder progress. This is where the concept of unlearning becomes crucial.

Unlearning involves critically examining existing processes, habits, and beliefs to identify what is no longer relevant or effective. It requires a willingness to challenge the status quo and a readiness to embrace change. For leaders, this means recognising that some strategies, tools, or approaches that once brought success may now be obsolete. By letting go of these outdated practices, leaders can create space for new ideas and approaches that better align with the current organisational goals and market conditions.

The process of unlearning is not about discarding all past knowledge but about discerning which elements are still valuable and which need to be modified or abandoned. This selective process ensures that the organisation remains agile and adaptable, ready to respond to new challenges and opportunities. Leaders who master the art of unlearning can prevent stagnation and maintain a dynamic and forward-thinking organisational culture.

Balancing learning and unlearning also involves fostering an environment where both processes are encouraged and supported. Leaders should promote a culture of continuous improvement, where employees feel empowered to question existing practices and suggest new ideas. This can be achieved through regular training and development programmes, open communication channels, and a supportive atmosphere that values experimentation and learning from mistakes. By nurturing this culture, leaders can harness the collective intelligence of their teams, driving innovation and efficiency.

Moreover, focusing on what truly matters means prioritising the core values and strategic objectives of the organisation. Leaders should ensure that their efforts and resources are directed towards activities that align with these priorities. This targeted approach helps to eliminate unnecessary complexities and distractions, allowing the organisation to operate more efficiently and effectively. It also fosters a sense of clarity and purpose among employees, who can see how their contributions directly impact the organisation's success.

EMBRACING THE POWER OF NON-ACTION

> *He diminishes it and again diminishes it, till he arrives at doing nothing (on purpose). Having arrived at this point of non-action, there is nothing which he does not do.*

The chapter delves into the profound concept of *Wú Wéi (*無為/无为*)*, often translated as non-action or effortless action. This principle, though seemingly paradoxical, holds significant relevance in the realm of leadership and strategic management. The idea of non-action emphasises creating an environment where processes flow naturally and goals are achieved without undue force or intervention. For leaders, this means fostering a culture where empowerment and creativity are paramount, allowing the organisation to thrive organically.

The essence of *Wú Wéi* lies in the notion that sometimes the best way to achieve results is by stepping back and allowing things to unfold naturally. In leadership, this translates to trusting one's team to take ownership of their tasks and make decisions independently. By providing the necessary support and resources, leaders can enable their teams to operate with autonomy and confidence. This trust not only empowers employees but also encourages them to innovate and take initiative, leading to a more dynamic and adaptable organisation.

Creating an environment that embraces the power of non-action requires a shift in mindset. Leaders must move away from micromanagement and excessive control, recognising that such approaches can stifle creativity and hinder progress. Instead, they should focus on establishing clear goals and guidelines, then allow their teams the freedom to determine the best ways to achieve these objectives. This approach fosters a sense of ownership and responsibility among employees, as they feel trusted and valued for their contributions. It also reduces the pressure on leaders, who can then concentrate on strategic visioning and long-term planning rather than being bogged down by day-to-day operations.

Moreover, the principle of non-action is closely tied to the idea of efficiency and effectiveness. When leaders refrain from unnecessary interference, they allow for a smoother and more efficient workflow. Employees are not burdened by constant supervision or approval processes, which can often slow down progress and create bottlenecks. By trusting their teams and focusing on the bigger picture, leaders can streamline operations and enhance overall productivity. This approach aligns with the concept of doing less but achieving more, as it minimises wasted effort and maximises the impact of each action taken.

In addition, embracing non-action can lead to a more harmonious and balanced organisational culture. When leaders demonstrate a willingness to step back and let their teams lead, it fosters a sense of mutual respect and collaboration. Employees are more likely to support and help one another, as they feel part of a cohesive and empowered team. This sense of community and shared purpose can boost morale and engagement, leading to higher levels of satisfaction and retention within the organisation.

RECOGNISING THE VALUE OF SIMPLICITY

> *He who gets as his own all under heaven does so by giving himself no trouble (with that end). If one take trouble (with that end), he is not equal to getting as his own all under heaven.*

The chapter also highlights the profound value of simplicity in leadership and strategic management. This teaching underscores the idea that achieving great results often does not require complex and intricate strategies but rather a clear, straightforward approach. Leaders who recognise the importance of simplicity can streamline operations, reduce unnecessary stress, and enhance overall productivity by focusing on essential goals and trusting their teams to find the best paths to success.

In the modern business landscape, it is easy for organisations to become entangled in layers of complexity, whether through overcomplicated processes, excessive micromanagement, or convoluted strategic plans. While these complexities might stem from a desire to cover all bases or to ensure thoroughness, they can often backfire, creating more obstacles and inefficiencies. Leaders who embrace simplicity understand that clarity and focus are paramount. By setting simple, clear objectives, they can provide a roadmap that is easy for everyone in the organisation to follow. This clarity reduces ambiguity and confusion, enabling employees to align their efforts more effectively with the organisation's goals.

Simplicity in leadership also involves trusting teams to take ownership of their work and make decisions independently. Micromanaging can stifle creativity and innovation, as employees feel constrained and less empowered to think outside the box. When leaders step back and allow their teams the autonomy to determine the best approaches to achieving objectives, it fosters a culture of trust and empowerment. Employees are more likely to take initiative and be proactive when they feel trusted and valued for their expertise. This autonomy not only boosts morale but also drives higher levels of engagement and productivity.

Moreover, simplifying processes can lead to significant improvements in efficiency. By eliminating unnecessary steps and focusing on what truly matters, leaders can streamline workflows and reduce bottlenecks. This approach minimises wasted time and resources, allowing the organisation to operate more smoothly and effectively. Simplified processes are easier to understand and follow, reducing the likelihood of errors and misunderstandings. This operational efficiency translates into better outcomes and a more agile organisation that can quickly adapt to changes and challenges.

The principle of simplicity also extends to communication within the organisation. Leaders should strive to communicate clearly and concisely, ensuring that messages are easily understood by all employees. Clear communication helps to align everyone with the organisation's vision and goals, fostering a sense of unity and shared purpose. It also facilitates better collaboration, as team members can more easily coordinate their efforts when they have a clear understanding of expectations and objectives.

Furthermore, recognising the value of simplicity involves continuous reflection and assessment. Leaders must regularly evaluate their strategies and processes to ensure they remain relevant and effective. This ongoing assessment allows for the identification and removal of any elements that add unnecessary complexity. By maintaining a focus on simplicity, leaders can ensure that their organisations remain nimble and responsive, capable of navigating the complexities of the business environment with ease.

CHAPTER 49 – UNIVERSAL GOODWILL

Chapter 49 of the *Tao Te Ching* emphasises the sage's ability to align with the people, practise universal goodwill, and maintain an open and unbiased mind. Here's how these teachings can be applied to modern-day strategic management:

ALIGNING WITH THE TEAM

The sage has no invariable mind of his own; he makes the mind of the people his mind.

Lao Tzu's Chapter 49 of the *Tao Te Ching* profoundly underscores the importance of aligning leadership with the collective mindset of the team. In strategic management, this principle emphasises the need for leaders to adopt a flexible and empathetic approach, recognising that effective leadership is not about rigidly imposing one's own ideas but about harmonising with the perspectives and needs of the team. Leaders who embody this principle can foster a collaborative and unified organisational culture, where decisions are made with a deep understanding of the collective mindset.

Understanding and aligning with the team begins with active listening. Leaders must prioritise creating open channels of communication where employees feel heard and valued. This involves more than just soliciting feedback; it requires genuinely engaging with the insights and concerns of team members. By actively listening, leaders can gain a nuanced understanding of the team's dynamics, challenges, and aspirations. This deeper connection allows leaders to tailor their strategies and decisions in ways that are more resonant and impactful. Employees are more likely to be motivated and committed when they feel that their voices influence organisational direction and decision-making.

Gathering feedback is another critical aspect of aligning with the team. Leaders should implement structured processes for regular feedback collection, such as surveys, focus groups, and one-on-one meetings. This systematic approach ensures that diverse perspectives are considered and that the decision-making process is informed by a broad range of inputs. Leaders who actively seek and incorporate feedback demonstrate humility and a willingness to adapt, qualities that build trust and respect within the team. This inclusivity fosters a sense of ownership and accountability among employees, as they see their contributions shaping the organisation's path forward.

Adaptability is essential for leaders who aim to align with the collective mindset. The modern business environment is characterised by rapid change and uncertainty, and leaders must be agile in responding to evolving circumstances. This requires a flexible approach to leadership, where strategies and plans can be adjusted based on new information and shifting team dynamics. Leaders who are adaptable can pivot effectively, ensuring that the organisation remains aligned with its core values while navigating external changes. This adaptability also empowers employees to innovate and take initiative, knowing that their leaders are supportive and responsive to their needs and ideas.

Aligning with the team also means fostering a culture of collaboration and unity. Leaders should encourage cross-functional teamwork and create opportunities for employees to work together on shared goals. This collaborative spirit breaks down silos and enhances the flow of information across the organisation. When leaders facilitate collaboration, they not only harness the diverse strengths and expertise of their team but also build a cohesive and supportive work environment. This unity drives collective success, as employees are more likely to support each other and work towards common objectives.

PRACTISING UNIVERSAL GOODWILL & SINCERITY

> *To those who are good (to me), I am good; and to those who are not good (to me), I am also good; — and thus (all) get to be good. To those who are sincere (with me), I am sincere; and to those who are not sincere (with me), I am also sincere; — and thus (all) get to be sincere.*

The chapter offers a profound lesson on the power of universal goodwill and sincerity in leadership. This teaching emphasises the importance of treating all individuals with kindness and integrity, regardless of their behaviour or attitude. In the context of strategic management, leaders who practise this approach can cultivate a positive and inclusive work environment, fostering a culture where every employee feels valued and respected.

Practising universal goodwill involves extending kindness and understanding to all team members, even those who may not reciprocate these behaviours initially. This principle challenges leaders to rise above negative interactions and maintain a consistent standard of ethical and respectful behaviour. By doing so, leaders set a powerful example for their teams, demonstrating that respect and decency are not conditional but fundamental to the organisation's values. This unwavering commitment to kindness can gradually influence the overall workplace culture, encouraging employees to adopt similar attitudes and behaviours.

Sincerity in leadership is equally crucial. It entails being genuine and transparent in all interactions, ensuring that actions and words align with true intentions. When leaders are sincere, they build trust and credibility, as team members can see that their leaders' actions are motivated by honesty and integrity. This transparency fosters an atmosphere of openness and trust, where employees feel safe to express their thoughts and concerns. Sincere leaders are also more likely to receive candid feedback from their teams, which is invaluable for continuous improvement and organisational growth.

The practice of universal goodwill and sincerity creates a ripple effect within the organisation. When employees experience consistent kindness and integrity from their leaders, they are more likely to mirror these behaviours in their interactions with colleagues and clients. This positive cycle enhances collaboration, reduces conflicts, and builds stronger interpersonal relationships within the team. Employees who feel respected and valued are also more likely to be engaged and motivated, contributing to higher levels of productivity and job satisfaction.

Moreover, leaders who embody these principles are better equipped to navigate challenges and conflicts. By approaching difficult situations with empathy and sincerity, leaders can de-escalate tensions and find constructive solutions that address the underlying issues. This approach not only resolves conflicts more effectively but also strengthens the sense of unity and cooperation within the team. Employees learn that challenges can be managed respectfully and collaboratively, reinforcing the culture of mutual respect and trust.

In the long term, practising universal goodwill and sincerity contributes to the organisation's reputation and success. An organisation known for its ethical leadership and positive work environment is more likely to attract and retain top talent. Prospective employees are drawn to workplaces where they know they will be treated with respect and integrity. Similarly, clients and partners are more inclined to engage with organisations that demonstrate ethical practices and a commitment to genuine, positive interactions.

MAINTAINING AN OPEN & UNBIASED MIND

> *The sage has in the world an appearance of indecision, and keeps his mind in a state of indifference to all.*

The chapter illuminates the value of maintaining an open and unbiased mind in leadership. In the realm of strategic management, this principle emphasises the importance of avoiding snap judgments and being receptive to a wide array of perspectives. Leaders who embody this open-mindedness can make more balanced and fair decisions, fostering an environment of inclusivity and encouraging innovation and creativity within their teams.

Maintaining an open and unbiased mind begins with the practice of active listening and withholding immediate judgment. Leaders should approach each interaction and piece of information with curiosity rather than preconceived notions. This attitude allows them to fully understand the various viewpoints and ideas presented by their team members. By genuinely considering diverse perspectives, leaders can uncover insights and solutions that might otherwise be overlooked. This comprehensive approach to decision-making not only enhances the quality of outcomes but also demonstrates respect for the contributions of all team members.

Fostering an environment of inclusivity and openness is crucial for tapping into the collective intelligence of the organisation. When leaders create a culture where all voices are heard and valued, they encourage employees to share their unique ideas and experiences. This diversity of thought drives innovation, as team members feel empowered to propose creative solutions and challenge the status quo. Inclusive leadership ensures that the organisation benefits from a wide range of talents and viewpoints, enhancing its ability to adapt and thrive in a rapidly changing business landscape.

The appearance of indecision mentioned by Lao Tzu reflects the deliberate and thoughtful nature of an open-minded leader. Rather than rushing to conclusions, such leaders take the time to weigh all options and consider the broader implications of their decisions. This reflective process might be perceived as indecision, but it is actually a sign of careful deliberation and a commitment to fairness. By thoroughly analysing the information available and seeking input from various sources, leaders can make informed decisions that are in the best interest of the organisation and its stakeholders.

An open and unbiased mind also helps leaders build stronger, more trusting relationships with their teams. When employees see that their leaders are open to different ideas and willing to change their minds in light of new evidence, it fosters a culture of trust and mutual respect. Team members are more likely to engage openly and honestly when they believe that their perspectives will be considered seriously. This trust is a foundational element of effective teamwork and collaboration, driving higher levels of engagement and commitment.

Moreover, leaders who maintain an open mind are better equipped to navigate the complexities of the modern business environment. The ability to adapt and respond to new information and changing circumstances is critical for long-term success. By remaining flexible and receptive, leaders can steer their organisations through uncertainty with resilience and agility. This adaptability not only enhances organisational performance but also ensures that the team remains aligned with its core values and mission amidst evolving challenges and opportunities.

BEING A COMPASSIONATE & APPROACHABLE LEADER

> *The people all keep their eyes and ears directed to him, and he deals with them all as his children.*

The chapter also extols the virtues of compassionate and approachable leadership, likening a sage leader to a parental figure who treats all people as his children. This analogy highlights the importance of genuine care and concern for the well-being of employees in leadership. In strategic management, this principle translates into leaders being available for support, offering guidance, and treating each team member with empathy and respect. Leaders who practise compassion and approachability can foster a cohesive and motivated team, creating a positive and productive organisational culture.

Compassionate leadership begins with a genuine interest in the well-being of employees. Leaders must go beyond mere professional interactions and take the time to understand the personal and professional aspirations, challenges, and needs of their team members. This requires active listening and a willingness to engage with employees on a human level. By showing empathy and understanding, leaders can build trust and rapport, making employees feel valued and appreciated. This sense of being cared for can significantly enhance employee morale and engagement, as team members are more likely to be motivated and committed to their work when they feel supported by their leaders.

Approachability is another crucial aspect of compassionate leadership. Leaders should cultivate an open-door policy where employees feel comfortable approaching them with concerns, ideas, or questions. This openness fosters a culture of transparency and trust, where employees do not fear judgment or repercussions for speaking up. When leaders are approachable, they create a safe space for open dialogue and collaboration, which can lead to more innovative and effective problem-solving. An approachable leader is seen as accessible and willing to help, which encourages a more inclusive and communicative work environment.

Providing support and guidance is an essential function of compassionate leadership. Leaders should be proactive in offering assistance and resources to help employees succeed. This may include providing regular feedback, mentoring, and professional development opportunities. By investing in the growth and development of their team members, leaders not only enhance the capabilities of their workforce but also demonstrate a commitment to their long-term success. This support can empower employees to reach their full potential, fostering a culture of continuous improvement and excellence within the organisation.

Treating employees with empathy involves recognising and respecting their individuality and unique contributions. Leaders should be attuned to the diverse backgrounds and perspectives of their team members, appreciating the value that each person brings to the organisation. This empathy fosters an inclusive culture where all employees feel respected and valued for who they are. By embracing diversity and encouraging different viewpoints, leaders can drive creativity and innovation, as diverse teams are better equipped to generate novel ideas and solutions.

Building strong, supportive relationships with employees is fundamental to creating a cohesive and motivated team. When leaders demonstrate genuine care and concern, they inspire loyalty and dedication among their team members. This sense of connection and shared purpose can significantly enhance teamwork and collaboration, as employees are more likely to support and help one another. A cohesive team is more resilient in the face of challenges and more capable of achieving collective goals.

CHAPTER 50 - FEARLESSNESS

Chapter 50 of the *Tao Te Ching* discusses the cyclical nature of life and death, the impact of excessive efforts to control life, and the idea of living skillfully and fearlessly. Here's how these teachings can be applied to modern-day strategic management:

EMBRACING THE NATURAL CYCLES & UNCERTAINTY

> *Men come forth and live; they enter (again) and die.*

Lao Tzu's Chapter 49 of the *Tao Te Ching* imparts the wisdom of recognising and embracing the natural cycles and inherent uncertainties of life. This perspective is particularly relevant in the context of strategic management, where leaders must navigate the ebbs and flows of organisational growth, change, and decline. Understanding these cycles as intrinsic elements of business life enables leaders to remain resilient and adaptable, effectively guiding their organisations through various phases and challenges.

In strategic management, acknowledging the natural cycles of an organisation—its periods of growth, stability, and decline—is crucial for long-term success. Leaders who recognise that these phases are inevitable can better prepare their teams to adapt to change and seize opportunities as they arise. This acceptance fosters a proactive approach to management, where leaders anticipate potential challenges and develop strategies to mitigate their impact. By embracing the natural rhythms of business, leaders can create a more dynamic and responsive organisation that is better equipped to thrive in an ever-changing environment.

Embracing uncertainty is another key aspect of effective leadership. The business world is inherently unpredictable, and leaders who understand this can cultivate a mindset of flexibility and preparedness. Rather than fearing the unknown, these leaders view uncertainty as an opportunity for innovation and growth. This perspective allows them to remain calm and focused in the face of unexpected changes, making more thoughtful and strategic decisions. By accepting that not everything can be controlled or predicted, leaders can foster a culture of resilience and adaptability within their organisations.

A critical component of navigating natural cycles and uncertainty is fostering a culture of continuous learning and improvement. Leaders should encourage their teams to embrace change and view it as an opportunity for development. This involves creating an environment where experimentation and calculated risk-taking are supported, and where failures are seen as valuable learning experiences rather than setbacks. By promoting a growth mindset, leaders can help their organisations remain agile and responsive to changing conditions, ensuring long-term sustainability.

Additionally, effective leaders understand the importance of balance during periods of growth and decline. In times of expansion, it is vital to maintain a focus on core values and strategic objectives, ensuring that growth is sustainable and aligned with the organisation's long-term vision. Conversely, during periods of contraction or difficulty, leaders must prioritise the well-being of their teams and manage resources wisely to stabilise the organisation. This balanced approach helps to navigate the cyclical nature of business while maintaining a steady course toward long-term goals.

Moreover, embracing natural cycles and uncertainty involves building strong, supportive relationships within the organisation. Leaders should foster open communication and collaboration, ensuring that team members feel supported and valued during times of change. By creating a culture of trust and mutual respect, leaders can enhance the collective resilience of their teams, enabling them to weather challenges more effectively. Strong relationships also facilitate the sharing of ideas and resources, driving innovation and problem-solving in uncertain times.

BALANCING EFFORTS & AVOIDING EXCESSIVE CONTROL

> *Of every ten three are ministers of life (to themselves); and three are ministers of death. There are also three in every ten whose aim is to live, but whose movements tend to the land (or place) of death. And for what reason? Because of their excessive endeavours to perpetuate life.*

The chapter conveys a critical lesson on the necessity for leaders to balance their efforts and avoid the pitfalls of excessive control. This principle underscores the understanding that overextending efforts to control every aspect of an organisation can have detrimental effects, such as burnout, inefficiency, and overall negative outcomes. Leaders who attempt to micromanage every detail often find themselves overwhelmed and disconnected from the strategic vision that should guide their leadership. This approach can stifle creativity, reduce morale, and hinder the overall productivity of the team.

Effective leadership requires a balance between guidance and autonomy. Leaders should recognise the importance of empowering their teams, fostering an environment where employees feel trusted and capable of handling their responsibilities. Empowerment involves delegating tasks and responsibilities appropriately, ensuring that team members have the autonomy to make decisions and execute their duties without constant oversight. This trust in employees' abilities encourages a sense of ownership and accountability, motivating them to perform at their best and contribute meaningfully to the organisation's success.

Delegating responsibilities is not only about distributing tasks but also about recognising and utilising the unique strengths and skills of each team member. Leaders who understand their team's capabilities can assign tasks that align with individual strengths, promoting efficiency and job satisfaction. This strategic delegation helps to distribute the workload evenly, preventing burnout and ensuring that no single individual is overwhelmed. By trusting their team members, leaders can focus on higher-level strategic planning and vision, rather than being bogged down by day-to-day operations.

Furthermore, avoiding excessive control means fostering a culture of continuous improvement and learning. Leaders should encourage their teams to experiment, take risks, and learn from failures. This approach cultivates an innovative mindset where employees are not afraid to propose new ideas and solutions. When leaders provide the freedom to explore and innovate, they tap into the collective creativity of the team, driving progress and adaptation in an ever-changing business environment.

A balanced approach to leadership also involves maintaining open lines of communication. Leaders should be approachable and available for support, offering guidance when needed but refraining from unnecessary interference. This open communication ensures that team members feel supported and valued, knowing that they can seek advice and feedback without fear of judgment. Regular check-ins and feedback sessions can help leaders stay informed about the team's progress and challenges, allowing for timely interventions and adjustments without resorting to micromanagement.

Moreover, creating a sustainable and healthy work environment requires leaders to model the behaviour they wish to see in their teams. This includes demonstrating a balanced approach to work and life, setting realistic expectations, and promoting well-being. Leaders who prioritise their own health and balance set a positive example for their employees, encouraging them to do the same. This holistic approach to leadership helps to build a resilient and motivated team, capable of sustaining long-term success.

PRACTISING SKILLFUL MANAGEMENT & FEARLESSNESS

> But I have heard that he who is skilful in managing the life entrusted to him for a time travels on the land without having to shun rhinoceros or tiger, and enters a host without having to avoid buff coat or sharp weapon.

The chapter also presents a vivid metaphor for the qualities of effective leadership, highlighting the importance of skillful management and fearlessness. In strategic management, leaders who embody these qualities navigate their organisations through complexities with confidence and poise. This involves making thoughtful decisions, maintaining composure under pressure, and approaching challenges with a positive attitude. Such leaders inspire their teams and foster a culture of resilience and determination.

Skillful management in leadership is about more than just having the right strategies and plans in place. It involves a deep understanding of the organisation's dynamics, recognising both its strengths and areas for improvement. Effective leaders are adept at leveraging the talents and capabilities of their team members, aligning their efforts towards common goals. They ensure that resources are allocated efficiently and that the organisation's activities are coherent and directed towards achieving its strategic objectives. This requires continuous learning and adaptation, as leaders must stay informed about industry trends and adjust their approaches as needed to maintain competitiveness.

Fearlessness in leadership is not about the absence of fear but about the ability to face challenges head-on with confidence and resolve. Leaders who exhibit fearlessness do not shy away from making difficult decisions or confronting obstacles. Instead, they approach problems with a proactive and solution-oriented mindset. This attitude is contagious; when team members see their leaders tackling challenges with courage and optimism, they are more likely to adopt the same mindset. Fearless leaders foster a culture where employees feel empowered to take risks and innovate, knowing that their efforts are supported and valued.

Maintaining composure under pressure is a hallmark of effective leadership. In times of crisis or uncertainty, leaders who remain calm and focused can provide the stability and direction that their teams need. This composure helps to mitigate panic and confusion, allowing for more rational and effective responses to challenges. By demonstrating calmness and clarity, leaders can instil confidence in their teams, reassuring them that the situation is under control and that there is a clear plan moving forward.

Approaching challenges with a positive attitude is also crucial for fostering a resilient organisational culture. Leaders who frame challenges as opportunities for growth and improvement can shift the team's perspective from one of defeat to one of possibility. This positive outlook encourages creative problem-solving and helps to build a resilient mindset among team members. When employees view setbacks as temporary and surmountable, they are more likely to persevere and continue striving towards their goals.

Building a culture of resilience and determination requires consistent effort and intentionality from leaders. It involves creating an environment where employees feel safe to express their ideas and take risks. Leaders should provide regular feedback and recognition, celebrating successes and learning from failures. This supportive environment nurtures confidence and encourages continuous improvement. Additionally, leaders should be transparent about the challenges the organisation faces and involve the team in developing solutions. This collaborative approach fosters a sense of ownership and commitment, driving collective resilience and determination.

CHAPTER 51 – AUTHENTICITY

Chapter 51 of the *Tao Te Ching* highlights the Tao's nurturing and selfless nature, emphasising the process of growth and development without claiming possession or control. Here's how these teachings can be applied to modern-day strategic management:

NURTURING GROWTH & DEVELOPMENT

> *All things are produced by the Tao, and nourished by its outflowing operation. They receive their forms according to the nature of each, and are completed according to the circumstances of their condition.*

Lao Tzu's Chapter 51 of the *Tao Te Ching* delves into the art of nurturing growth and development, illustrating the natural way in which all things are produced and nourished by the Tao. This metaphor can be directly applied to leadership in the context of strategic management, where the primary role of a leader is to foster an environment that promotes the growth and development of their teams and the organisation as a whole. Leaders must ensure that their employees have access to the necessary resources, support, and conditions that enable them to thrive.

Effective leadership begins with the recognition that each team member possesses unique strengths and needs. This understanding allows leaders to tailor their approach to support individual development effectively. By identifying and acknowledging these individual qualities, leaders can provide personalised guidance and opportunities that align with each employee's potential. This customised support not only aids in the personal growth of the employees but also contributes to the collective strength of the team, as everyone is working in roles and on tasks that best suit their skills and interests.

Providing the necessary resources is a fundamental aspect of nurturing growth. Leaders must ensure that their teams have the tools, information, and training required to perform their tasks efficiently. This involves investing in technology, professional development programmes, and continuous learning opportunities that keep employees up-to-date with industry trends and enhance their skill sets. By equipping employees with the right resources, leaders empower them to excel in their roles and contribute more effectively to the organisation's objectives.

Support from leadership is equally crucial in fostering a thriving work environment. Leaders should be approachable and available to offer guidance, feedback, and encouragement. Regular one-on-one meetings, mentorship programmes, and open-door policies can help leaders stay connected with their teams and understand their challenges and aspirations. This ongoing support builds a strong foundation of trust and collaboration, where employees feel valued and confident in seeking assistance and sharing their ideas.

Creating a conducive environment for growth also involves fostering a culture that encourages innovation and creativity. Leaders should cultivate an atmosphere where employees feel safe to experiment, take risks, and learn from failures. This involves promoting a growth mindset, where mistakes are viewed as learning opportunities rather than setbacks. By encouraging this mindset, leaders can inspire their teams to push boundaries, explore new ideas, and continuously improve their processes and outcomes.

Furthermore, recognising and celebrating achievements is an essential part of nurturing development. Leaders should acknowledge the hard work and accomplishments of their team members, both publicly and privately. This recognition not only boosts morale but also reinforces positive behaviours and motivates employees to strive for excellence. Celebrating milestones and successes fosters a sense of pride and belonging within the team, driving higher levels of engagement and commitment.

ENCOURAGING AUTHENTIC & SPONTANEOUS RECOGNITION

> *Therefore all things without exception honour the Tao, and exalt its outflowing operation. This honouring of the Tao and exalting of its operation is not the result of any ordination, but always a spontaneous tribute.*

The chapter emphasises the importance of authentic and spontaneous recognition in fostering a positive and motivating work environment. In the realm of leadership and strategic management, this principle encourages leaders to cultivate a culture where appreciation and gratitude are naturally expressed, rather than relying solely on formal recognition programmes. When recognition arises organically, it carries a sense of genuineness and sincerity that formalised processes may lack.

Authentic and spontaneous recognition begins with leaders demonstrating genuine appreciation for their team members' efforts and contributions. This involves being attuned to the daily work and achievements of employees and taking the time to acknowledge them in real-time. A simple 'thank you' or a few words of praise can go a long way in making employees feel valued and appreciated. When recognition is given spontaneously and from the heart, it resonates more deeply with employees, enhancing their sense of belonging and motivation.

Creating a culture of spontaneous recognition requires leaders to model the behaviour they wish to see in their teams. Leaders should regularly express gratitude and appreciation, setting the tone for others to follow. By consistently recognising and celebrating successes, leaders can inspire a ripple effect throughout the organisation, where employees feel encouraged to acknowledge and support one another. This culture of mutual appreciation fosters stronger relationships and a more cohesive team dynamic.

Moreover, spontaneous recognition is often more timely and relevant than scheduled recognition programmes. When recognition is given immediately after a job well done, it reinforces positive behaviours and encourages continued high performance. Employees can see the direct correlation between their efforts and the appreciation they receive, which boosts their morale and engagement. This immediacy and relevance make spontaneous recognition a powerful tool for maintaining a motivated and productive workforce.

Leaders can also encourage spontaneous recognition by creating an environment where employees feel comfortable expressing appreciation for their colleagues. This can be achieved through open communication channels, regular team meetings, and a supportive atmosphere where recognition is a natural part of the organisational culture. Encouraging peer-to-peer recognition further enhances this environment, as employees feel empowered to acknowledge each other's contributions. This collective approach to recognition builds a sense of community and shared purpose within the team.

In addition, authentic recognition should be personalised to reflect the unique contributions and preferences of each employee. Leaders should make an effort to understand what forms of recognition are most meaningful to their team members. For some, public acknowledgment in a team meeting may be highly motivating, while others may prefer a private word of thanks or a handwritten note. By tailoring recognition to individual preferences, leaders can ensure that their appreciation feels sincere and impactful.

LEADING SELFLESSLY & WITHOUT CLAIM

> *It produces them and makes no claim to the possession of them; it carries them through their processes and does not vaunt its ability in doing so.*

The chapter underscores the essence of selfless leadership, highlighting the principle that true leadership lies in focusing on the success and well-being of the team rather than seeking personal glory. This philosophy is particularly pertinent in the context of modern leadership, where the ability to support and empower others without claiming credit is a hallmark of effective management. Leaders who embrace selflessness create a positive, collaborative, and empowering environment that fosters trust and respect within their teams.

At the heart of selfless leadership is the commitment to the growth and development of team members. This involves providing guidance, resources, and support to help employees reach their full potential. Leaders should act as mentors, offering constructive feedback and encouragement while allowing team members the autonomy to learn and grow from their experiences. By doing so, leaders create a nurturing environment where employees feel valued and motivated to contribute their best efforts. This approach not only enhances individual performance but also strengthens the overall capabilities of the team.

Selfless leadership also entails recognising and celebrating the achievements of others without seeking personal recognition. Leaders should make it a point to acknowledge and credit the contributions of their team members publicly. This practice fosters a sense of pride and ownership among employees, boosting their confidence and engagement. When team members feel that their efforts are appreciated and recognised, they are more likely to be motivated and committed to their work. Moreover, by attributing success to the team rather than oneself, leaders can build a culture of mutual respect and shared accomplishment.

Another key aspect of selfless leadership is the ability to remain humble and refrain from boasting about one's abilities. Effective leaders understand that their role is to facilitate the success of others rather than to highlight their own achievements. This humility creates an environment of equality and respect, where all team members feel valued regardless of their position or status. By leading with humility, leaders can inspire their teams to work collaboratively and support one another, fostering a strong sense of unity and cohesion.

Additionally, selfless leadership involves making decisions that prioritise the well-being and interests of the team and the organisation as a whole. This means considering the long-term impact of decisions and actions, rather than seeking immediate personal gain. Leaders should strive to create a positive and sustainable work environment, where the needs and aspirations of employees are taken into account. This approach not only enhances employee satisfaction and retention but also contributes to the overall health and success of the organisation.

Furthermore, selfless leaders are approachable and accessible, creating open channels of communication with their team members. They actively seek input and feedback, valuing the perspectives and ideas of others. This openness fosters a culture of transparency and trust, where employees feel comfortable sharing their thoughts and concerns. By listening to and addressing the needs of their team, selfless leaders can build strong, supportive relationships that enhance collaboration and innovation.

ALLOWING NATURAL PROCESSES & AUTONOMY

> *It brings them to maturity and exercises no control over them; — this is called its mysterious operation.*

The chapter also offers profound insights into the importance of allowing natural processes and granting autonomy within leadership. This concept emphasises that leaders should trust their teams, providing them with the freedom to explore and grow without excessive interference. The analogy of nurturing without control encapsulates the essence of fostering an environment where employees can reach their full potential through their own efforts and ingenuity.

Effective leadership involves creating conditions where team members are empowered to take ownership of their responsibilities and navigate their roles independently. By allowing natural processes to unfold, leaders enable employees to develop their skills and capabilities organically. This autonomy is crucial for fostering creativity and innovation, as it gives individuals the space to experiment and take risks without the fear of constant oversight. When employees feel trusted and valued, they are more likely to engage deeply with their work, bringing fresh ideas and perspectives to the table.

Micromanagement, on the other hand, can stifle this natural growth. When leaders excessively control every aspect of their team's work, it can lead to a stifling environment where creativity and initiative are suppressed. Employees may become overly reliant on directives from their leaders, losing the confidence to make independent decisions. This dependence not only hampers personal and professional growth but also limits the organisation's capacity for innovation. By stepping back and exercising restraint, leaders can create a more dynamic and responsive team capable of adapting to new challenges and opportunities.

Autonomy also plays a critical role in building accountability within teams. When employees are given the freedom to manage their tasks, they develop a sense of ownership over their work. This ownership cultivates a strong sense of responsibility, as individuals understand that their contributions directly impact the organisation's success. This intrinsic motivation is far more powerful than external supervision, driving higher levels of productivity and engagement. Employees who feel accountable for their work are more likely to invest their best efforts and strive for excellence.

Moreover, allowing natural processes and autonomy fosters a culture of trust and respect. When leaders demonstrate trust in their team's abilities, it reinforces the belief that each member is competent and capable. This trust-building is reciprocal; as employees experience trust from their leaders, they, in turn, develop greater trust and respect for their leaders. This mutual trust creates a cohesive and supportive work environment, where collaboration and open communication flourish. Teams that operate on a foundation of trust are better equipped to navigate conflicts and work together towards shared goals.

Additionally, autonomy encourages continuous learning and adaptation. In a rapidly changing business landscape, the ability to learn and adapt is essential for long-term success. When employees are allowed to explore new ideas and approaches, they gain valuable insights and experiences that contribute to their growth. This iterative process of learning and improvement keeps the organisation agile and forward-thinking. Leaders who support this environment of continuous learning position their teams to thrive amidst uncertainty and change.

CHAPTER 52 – THOUGHTFULNESS

Chapter 52 of the *Tao Te Ching* discusses the origins of all things, the importance of preserving one's core values, the power of silence and simplicity, and the significance of perceiving small details and guarding softness. Here's how these teachings can be applied to modern-day strategic management:

RECOGNISING CORE VALUES & PRINCIPLES

> *(The Tao) which originated all under the sky is to be considered as the mother of them all.*

Lao Tzu's Chapter 52 of the *Tao Te Ching* emphasises the importance of recognising and honouring the core values and principles that serve as the foundation of an organisation. These core values are akin to the 'mother' that gives birth to and nurtures the organisation, guiding its direction and ensuring its long-term success and integrity. In the realm of strategic management, leaders must remain steadfast in their commitment to these foundational values, understanding that they are the bedrock upon which the organisation is built.

Core values and principles are the essence of an organisation's identity. They define its purpose, shape its culture, and influence its decision-making processes. Leaders who recognise the significance of these values can create a strong, cohesive organisational culture that aligns with the company's mission and vision. This alignment fosters a sense of unity and purpose among employees, as they understand how their individual roles contribute to the broader goals of the organisation. When leaders consistently uphold these values, they set a clear example for their teams, reinforcing the importance of integrity and ethical behaviour.

Honouring core values also involves integrating them into all aspects of the organisation's operations. This means embedding these principles into the strategic planning process, ensuring that every decision, policy, and action aligns with the core values. By doing so, leaders can create a consistent and authentic organisational identity that resonates with employees, customers, and stakeholders. This authenticity builds trust and credibility, as the organisation is seen as staying true to its principles, regardless of external pressures or challenges.

Moreover, core values serve as a guiding compass during times of uncertainty and change. In a constantly evolving business landscape, leaders must navigate numerous challenges and make difficult decisions. By grounding their actions in the organisation's core values, leaders can maintain a steady course and make decisions that are in line with the organisation's long-term goals and ethical standards. This steadfastness helps to protect the organisation from veering off track and ensures that it remains focused on its mission.

Leaders must also recognise that honouring core values requires regular reflection and assessment. This involves continuously evaluating the organisation's practices and strategies to ensure they remain aligned with its foundational principles. When discrepancies arise, leaders must be willing to make adjustments and realign their actions with the core values. This proactive approach helps to maintain the integrity of the organisation and fosters a culture of continuous improvement.

Creating a supportive environment where core values are celebrated and upheld is essential for fostering employee engagement and loyalty. Leaders should actively communicate the importance of these values and encourage employees to embody them in their daily work. This can be achieved through regular training, open discussions, and recognition of behaviours that exemplify the core values. By reinforcing these principles, leaders can create a positive and motivating work environment where employees feel a strong connection to the organisation's mission.

Furthermore, leaders should recognise the evolving nature of core values and be open to adapting them as the organisation grows and changes. While the fundamental principles may remain constant, the way they are expressed and implemented may need to evolve to meet new challenges and opportunities. Leaders who are flexible and responsive to these changes can ensure that the core values continue to serve as a relevant and powerful guide for the organisation.

PRESERVING CORE QUALITIES & VALUES

> *When the mother is found, we know what her children should be. When one knows that he is his mother's child, and proceeds to guard (the qualities of) the mother that belong to him, to the end of his life he will be free from all peril.*

The chapter emphasises the importance of preserving and protecting the core qualities and values that define an organisation. These values serve as the bedrock upon which the organisation is built, akin to a mother nurturing her children. Leaders who understand and embrace this principle recognise the necessity of consistently aligning their actions and decisions with these fundamental principles. This steadfast commitment to core values not only ensures stability and cohesion within the organisation but also enhances its resilience in the face of challenges.

In the realm of strategic management, the preservation of core qualities and values is paramount. These values act as a compass, guiding the organisation through periods of growth, change, and adversity. Leaders who anchor their decisions and strategies in these core values can maintain a clear and consistent direction, even amidst the turbulence of the business environment. This consistency builds a strong organisational culture where employees understand and share a common set of beliefs and principles. It fosters unity and purpose, as everyone within the organisation works towards the same goals, grounded in the same foundational values.

The act of preserving core qualities requires a deep understanding and articulation of what these values are. Leaders must take the time to define and communicate these principles clearly to all members of the organisation. This involves integrating these values into every aspect of the organisational framework, from strategic planning and policy-making to daily operations and employee interactions. By embedding these values deeply into the organisational DNA, leaders ensure that they permeate every action and decision, creating a coherent and aligned operational ethos.

Moreover, preserving core values involves actively guarding against actions and decisions that could undermine these principles. This vigilance requires leaders to regularly evaluate their practices and strategies, ensuring they remain true to the organisation's foundational values. When faced with decisions that could potentially compromise these values, leaders must have the courage and conviction to choose the path that aligns with their principles, even if it is more challenging or less immediately rewarding. This integrity builds trust and credibility, both within the organisation and with external stakeholders, as it demonstrates a steadfast commitment to ethical conduct and long-term sustainability.

A key aspect of protecting core values is fostering a culture of accountability and transparency. Leaders should encourage open dialogue and feedback, allowing team members to voice concerns and provide input on how the organisation is living up to its values. This inclusive approach ensures that everyone is engaged in the process of preserving and upholding the core principles. It also enables the identification of any discrepancies between the stated values and actual practices, providing opportunities for correction and improvement. By maintaining this culture of accountability, leaders reinforce the importance of core values and ensure they remain a central focus of the organisational identity.

Additionally, the preservation of core qualities and values contributes to the organisation's resilience. In times of crisis or change, these values provide a stable foundation that can withstand external pressures. They offer a sense of continuity and reliability, reassuring employees and stakeholders that the organisation remains true to its principles. This resilience is further strengthened by the trust and cohesion built through consistent adherence to core values, enabling the organisation to navigate challenges with confidence and solidarity.

THE POWER OF SILENCE & THOUGHTFULNESS

> *Let him keep his mouth closed, and shut up the portals (of his nostrils), and all his life he will be exempt from laborious exertion. Let him keep his mouth open, and (spend his breath) in the promotion of his affairs, and all his life there will be no safety for him.*

The chapter underscores the significant impact of silence and thoughtfulness in leadership. This principle highlights the power of restraint and the profound benefits that come from mindful communication and reflective decision-making. Leaders who understand the value of silence and thoughtfulness can navigate complex organisational dynamics more effectively, fostering a more harmonious and productive work environment.

In the realm of strategic management, the ability to listen more and speak less is a critical skill. Leaders who embrace silence as a tool for understanding can gain deeper insights into the thoughts, feelings, and motivations of their team members. By taking the time to listen actively, leaders can better grasp the nuances of situations and make more informed decisions. This practice not only enhances the quality of decision-making but also builds trust and respect among team members, who feel heard and valued.

Thoughtfulness in leadership involves carefully considering the impact of one's words and actions before taking them. This means weighing the potential consequences and ensuring that communication is clear, concise, and purposeful. Thoughtful leaders avoid speaking impulsively or making hasty decisions that could lead to misunderstandings or conflicts. Instead, they take the time to reflect on the best course of action, considering all perspectives and possible outcomes. This reflective approach helps to prevent unnecessary disruptions and fosters a culture of deliberate and effective problem-solving.

Moreover, the power of silence can be particularly effective in diffusing tense situations. When conflicts arise, a leader's ability to remain calm and composed, listening to all parties involved before responding, can help to de-escalate tensions and find mutually acceptable solutions. Silence allows for a pause in the conversation, providing space for emotions to settle and for thoughtful responses to emerge. This practice of mindfulness can lead to more constructive and harmonious interactions, fostering a more positive and collaborative work environment.

Quality over quantity is a principle that applies not only to communication but also to decision-making. Leaders who focus on making fewer, but more impactful, decisions can drive greater results than those who spread themselves too thin. By prioritising the most critical issues and addressing them with careful consideration, leaders can ensure that their actions have the desired effect without causing unintended consequences. This strategic focus allows for more efficient use of resources and energy, leading to better outcomes for the organisation.

Additionally, the practice of thoughtful silence can enhance a leader's ability to observe and understand the dynamics within the team and the organisation as a whole. By stepping back and observing, leaders can identify patterns and trends that may not be immediately apparent. This awareness can inform more strategic decisions and interventions, helping to address underlying issues and capitalise on emerging opportunities. Leaders who cultivate this observational skill can maintain a broader perspective, ensuring that their actions are aligned with the long-term goals and values of the organisation.

VALUING SMALL DETAILS & SOFTNESS

> *The perception of what is small is (the secret of) clear-sightedness; the guarding of what is soft and tender is (the secret of) strength.*

The chapter elucidates the profound importance of valuing small details and embracing softness in leadership. The principle that clear-sightedness comes from perceiving what is small and strength from guarding what is soft holds significant implications for strategic management. Leaders who pay attention to the subtle nuances within their organisation can gain greater clarity and make more informed decisions. Additionally, by valuing softness and flexibility, leaders can cultivate a resilient and adaptable organisation capable of thriving amidst changing circumstances.

Focusing on small details involves being meticulous and observant, recognising that even the slightest elements can have substantial impacts on the organisation's overall functioning. Leaders who practise this kind of attentiveness can identify emerging issues before they escalate, address minor problems that could potentially disrupt operations, and capitalise on small opportunities that others might overlook. This level of detail-oriented observation requires a disciplined and patient approach, as it often involves looking beyond the obvious and delving into the intricacies of daily operations. By understanding the significance of these smaller elements, leaders can fine-tune their strategies and optimise their processes for better efficiency and effectiveness.

Valuing softness and flexibility, on the other hand, highlights the strength found in adaptability and openness. Traditional notions of strength often emphasise rigidity and control, but Lao Tzu's teachings suggest that true strength lies in the ability to bend and adapt. Leaders who embrace this principle are more likely to respond effectively to unexpected challenges and shifting market conditions. This adaptability ensures that the organisation remains resilient, capable of pivoting strategies and operations to meet new demands. Flexibility also fosters a culture of innovation, as employees feel empowered to explore creative solutions without fear of rigid constraints.

Embracing softness in leadership also translates to adopting a compassionate and empathetic approach towards team members. By being attentive to the emotional and psychological needs of employees, leaders can build a supportive and inclusive work environment. This approach encourages open communication, trust, and collaboration, as team members feel respected and valued. Softness, in this context, does not imply weakness; rather, it signifies an understanding and accommodating leadership style that recognises the human aspects of the workplace. This empathetic approach can lead to higher levels of employee satisfaction, engagement, and loyalty.

Furthermore, the combination of attentiveness to small details and flexibility can enhance strategic decision-making. Leaders who are both detail-oriented and adaptable can balance long-term vision with the agility needed to navigate immediate challenges. They can make strategic adjustments based on a deep understanding of the organisation's operations and the broader external environment. This balanced approach helps to mitigate risks and seize opportunities in a timely manner, ensuring sustained growth and success.

Leaders who incorporate these teachings into their management practices can foster a dynamic and resilient organisational culture. By paying attention to the finer details, they can maintain a clear vision of their operational landscape and make precise, well-informed decisions. Simultaneously, by valuing softness and flexibility, they can create an environment that supports innovation, adaptability, and emotional well-being. This holistic approach to leadership not only enhances organisational performance but also contributes to a more harmonious and productive workplace.

EMBRACING SIMPLICITY & INNER STRENGTH

> Who uses well his light, reverting to its (source so) bright, will from his body ward all blight, and hides the unchanging from men's sight.

The chapter also encapsulates the profound wisdom of embracing simplicity and inner strength in leadership. This principle advocates for leaders to focus on their core purpose and values, using these foundational principles as a guiding light. By returning to and upholding these essential tenets, leaders can navigate challenges with a clarity and resilience that inspires confidence within their teams.

Simplicity in leadership is about stripping away unnecessary complexities and focusing on what truly matters. In the fast-paced world of modern business, it is easy for leaders to become overwhelmed by myriad details and distractions. However, those who prioritise simplicity are able to maintain a clear vision of their objectives, ensuring that their actions and decisions remain aligned with the organisation's core mission. This clarity of purpose enables leaders to act decisively and effectively, avoiding the pitfalls of overcomplication and maintaining a steady course towards their goals.

Embracing simplicity also means fostering an environment where straightforward, transparent communication is valued. Leaders who practise clear and open communication can build trust and cohesion within their teams. By conveying messages succinctly and ensuring that everyone understands the organisation's direction and priorities, leaders can prevent misunderstandings and keep everyone focused on their shared objectives. This approach not only enhances operational efficiency but also promotes a sense of unity and purpose among team members.

Inner strength, as highlighted by Lao Tzu, is derived from a deep connection to one's core values and principles. Leaders who cultivate this inner strength possess the resilience needed to face challenges and uncertainties with confidence. This resilience is not about being impervious to difficulties but about having the fortitude to remain steadfast and composed in the face of adversity. Leaders with inner strength can inspire their teams by demonstrating calm and poise, even in the most trying circumstances. This demeanour reassures team members and encourages them to remain focused and determined, knowing that their leader is unwaveringly committed to guiding them through challenges.

Moreover, inner strength is closely linked to self-awareness and emotional intelligence. Leaders who are attuned to their own strengths and weaknesses can better understand their impact on others and navigate interpersonal dynamics with greater skill. This self-awareness enables leaders to build strong, supportive relationships within their teams, fostering a culture of mutual respect and collaboration. Emotional intelligence also allows leaders to respond empathetically to the needs and concerns of their team members, creating a positive and inclusive work environment.

Embracing simplicity and inner strength requires leaders to be authentic and true to themselves. This authenticity builds credibility and trust, as team members can see that their leader's actions are guided by a genuine commitment to the organisation's values. Authentic leaders are transparent about their intentions and consistent in their behaviour, which helps to create a stable and predictable environment where employees feel secure and valued. This stability is crucial for fostering long-term engagement and loyalty among team members.

Additionally, simplicity and inner strength in leadership involve a continuous process of reflection and renewal. Leaders must regularly revisit their core values and principles, ensuring that they remain aligned with their actions and decisions. This ongoing reflection helps leaders to stay grounded and maintain their focus on what truly matters, even as external circumstances change. By continually drawing strength from their foundational principles, leaders can navigate the complexities of the business environment with confidence and clarity.

CHAPTER 53 - BOASTFULNESS

Chapter 53 of the *Tao Te Ching* emphasises the dangers of boastfulness and superficiality, the simplicity of the Tao, and the pitfalls of prioritising appearance over substance. Here's how these teachings can be applied to modern-day strategic management:

AVOIDING BOASTFULNESS & SUPERFICIAL DISPLAYS

> If I were suddenly to become known, and (put into a position to) conduct (a government) according to the Great Tao, what I should be most afraid of would be a boastful display.

Lao Tzu's Chapter 53 of the *Tao Te Ching* offers profound guidance on the dangers of boastfulness and superficial displays, especially in positions of leadership. Lao Tzu emphasises that true leadership is not about seeking attention and recognition through ostentatious displays, but rather about focusing on genuine achievements and the well-being of one's team. This wisdom is particularly relevant in the context of modern organisational management, where the allure of superficial success can often overshadow the importance of substantive accomplishments.

In leadership, the temptation to engage in boastfulness and superficial displays can be strong, especially in a society that frequently rewards and idolises outward success. However, such behaviours can be detrimental to the long-term health of an organisation. When leaders prioritise appearance over substance, they risk creating a culture where image is valued more highly than integrity and hard work. This can lead to an environment where employees feel pressured to focus on short-term gains and external validations rather than on meaningful contributions and personal growth.

A leader who avoids boastfulness fosters an atmosphere of humility and authenticity. By not seeking personal glory, leaders can direct their energy towards supporting their team and achieving the organisation's true goals. This selfless approach encourages team members to emulate similar behaviours, fostering a collaborative and supportive work environment. When leaders recognise and celebrate the genuine achievements of their teams without claiming the spotlight for themselves, it builds a strong sense of trust and respect. Employees are more likely to feel valued and appreciated for their contributions, which can significantly boost morale and engagement.

Moreover, focusing on genuine achievements rather than superficial displays cultivates a culture of integrity. Leaders who prioritise substance over appearance demonstrate a commitment to ethical principles and long-term success. This integrity can permeate throughout the organisation, influencing employees to adhere to high standards of conduct in their own work. When integrity is at the forefront, it enhances the organisation's reputation and builds lasting relationships with stakeholders, clients, and the broader community.

Leaders who avoid boastfulness also promote a culture of continuous improvement and learning. By acknowledging that there is always room for growth and development, these leaders set an example of humility and openness. They encourage their teams to seek out new knowledge, embrace challenges, and learn from their experiences. This mindset fosters innovation and resilience, as employees feel empowered to take risks and pursue excellence without the fear of failure or the need to maintain a facade of perfection.

Furthermore, avoiding superficial displays helps to mitigate the risk of complacency. When leaders are constantly striving for genuine progress and improvement, they are less likely to become content with merely maintaining appearances. This proactive approach ensures that the organisation remains dynamic and adaptable, continually evolving to meet new challenges and opportunities. By focusing on real accomplishments, leaders can drive sustainable growth and foster a culture of excellence that endures over time.

EMBRACING SIMPLICITY & CLARITY

The great Tao (or way) is very level and easy; but people love the by-ways.

The chapter offers a compelling lesson on the virtues of simplicity and clarity, particularly within the context of leadership and strategic management. The Tao, as described by Lao Tzu, represents a path that is straightforward and easy to follow, yet humans often complicate their journeys by straying into convoluted by-ways. This wisdom is profoundly applicable to modern organisational dynamics, where leaders frequently grapple with the complexities of management and decision-making.

In the realm of strategic management, embracing simplicity involves stripping away unnecessary layers of complexity to focus on what truly matters. This means identifying the core mission and values of the organisation and ensuring that all actions and decisions align with these foundational principles. By clarifying goals and streamlining processes, leaders can create a more efficient and effective organisational structure. This approach not only enhances productivity but also fosters a sense of purpose and direction among team members.

Simplicity in leadership also entails clear and direct communication. Leaders must articulate their vision and objectives in a manner that is easily understood by everyone in the organisation. This clarity ensures that all team members are on the same page, working towards common goals. When communication is clear, there is less room for misunderstandings and confusion, allowing teams to function more cohesively and efficiently. Furthermore, clear communication promotes transparency and trust, as employees feel informed and valued when they understand the bigger picture.

Additionally, simplicity involves prioritising tasks and initiatives that have the greatest impact on the organisation's success. Leaders should focus on a few key strategic priorities rather than spreading resources too thin across numerous projects. This concentrated effort enables deeper engagement and better results, as teams can dedicate their full attention and energy to achieving specific objectives. By avoiding the temptation to pursue every opportunity and instead honing in on the most critical areas, leaders can drive significant progress and innovation.

The principle of clarity also applies to the delegation of responsibilities. Effective leaders understand the importance of entrusting their team members with clear and well-defined roles. By delineating responsibilities and setting clear expectations, leaders empower their teams to take ownership of their work. This autonomy not only boosts morale and motivation but also encourages accountability and initiative. When team members know exactly what is expected of them, they can perform their tasks with greater confidence and competence.

Embracing simplicity and clarity is also about fostering a culture that values straightforwardness and authenticity. Leaders should encourage an environment where feedback is direct and constructive, and where problems are addressed openly and honestly. This approach minimises the potential for miscommunication and ensures that issues are resolved efficiently. A culture of simplicity and clarity helps to build strong relationships within the team, characterised by mutual respect and understanding.

Moreover, simplicity and clarity can enhance decision-making processes. Leaders who cut through the noise and focus on the essential elements of a situation are better equipped to make informed and effective decisions. By avoiding unnecessary complexity, they can evaluate options more clearly and choose the best course of action with confidence. This decisiveness is crucial for navigating the dynamic and often unpredictable landscape of modern business.

PRIORITISING SUBSTANCE OVER APPEARANCE

> Their court(-yards and buildings) shall be well kept, but their fields shall be ill-cultivated, and their granaries very empty. They shall wear elegant and ornamented robes, carry a sharp sword at their girdle, pamper themselves in eating and drinking, and have a superabundance of property and wealth;—such (princes) may be called robbers and boasters. This is contrary to the Tao surely!

The chapter also offers profound wisdom on the importance of prioritising substance over appearance in leadership. The critique of leaders who focus on external show rather than genuine achievements underscores a timeless principle: true success lies in the maintenance and enhancement of an organisation's core functions and values. In the realm of strategic management, this means that leaders should invest in the essential aspects of the business, such as employee development, customer satisfaction, and operational efficiency, rather than creating an illusion of success through superficial displays.

Effective leadership requires a focus on long-term health and sustainability rather than short-term gains. Leaders who prioritise substance understand that the real value of an organisation is built over time through consistent and meaningful efforts. This involves cultivating a work environment that emphasises continuous improvement, innovation, and ethical practices. By focusing on these core elements, leaders can ensure that their organisations remain robust and resilient in the face of challenges.

One of the key areas where substance must be prioritised is in employee development. Investing in the growth and well-being of employees is fundamental to the success of any organisation. This includes providing opportunities for professional development, fostering a culture of collaboration and support, and ensuring that employees feel valued and appreciated. When employees are empowered and engaged, they are more likely to contribute positively to the organisation's goals and objectives. This intrinsic motivation drives higher levels of performance and productivity, which are essential for long-term success.

Customer satisfaction is another critical area that requires substantive focus. Leaders must prioritise the needs and expectations of their customers, ensuring that the products and services offered are of high quality and meet the demands of the market. This involves listening to customer feedback, continuously improving offerings, and maintaining a commitment to excellence. By building strong relationships with customers and consistently delivering value, organisations can enhance their reputation and secure customer loyalty.

Operational efficiency is also vital for sustaining an organisation's success. Leaders should strive to streamline processes, reduce waste, and optimise resources to achieve the best possible outcomes. This requires a deep understanding of the organisation's operations and a commitment to implementing best practices. By focusing on efficiency, leaders can ensure that the organisation operates smoothly and effectively, reducing costs and increasing profitability.

In contrast, leaders who prioritise appearance over substance may achieve short-term gains, but these are often unsustainable. Superficial displays of success, such as extravagant spending on appearances or focusing on image rather than substance, can create a false sense of achievement. This approach can lead to neglect of the organisation's core functions and values, ultimately resulting in a weakened foundation. Over time, the lack of genuine investment in the essential aspects of the business can lead to declining performance and diminished trust from employees, customers, and stakeholders.

CHAPTER 54 - COMMUNITY

Chapter 54 of the *Tao Te Ching* emphasises the enduring power of the Tao when it is deeply rooted and nurtured, and its positive effects on individuals, families, communities, and states. Here's how these teachings can be applied to modern-day strategic management:

CULTIVATING STRONG FOUNDATIONS

> *What (Tao's) skilful planter plants can never be uptorn; What his skilful arms enfold, From him can ne'er be borne.*

Lao Tzu's Chapter 53 of the *Tao Te Ching* delves into the importance of cultivating strong foundations, both in personal practice and within leadership. The idea that what a skilful planter plants can never be uprooted emphasises the enduring nature of well-established roots, whether they be in personal virtues or organisational values. In the context of strategic management, this principle translates into the necessity of leaders focusing on building and nurturing foundational elements within their organisations. These elements include core values, principles, and practices that must be deeply embedded within the organisational culture. By establishing a robust foundation, leaders can ensure that their organisations remain resilient and capable of withstanding various challenges.

A strong foundation in an organisation is akin to the roots of a tree that anchor it firmly in the ground, enabling it to withstand storms and adverse conditions. Leaders who prioritise the cultivation of these foundational elements understand that the long-term health and sustainability of their organisations depend on the solidity of these roots. This process begins with clearly defining and communicating the core values and principles that the organisation stands for. These values serve as guiding lights for decision-making and behaviour, ensuring consistency and integrity in all actions. When these values are deeply ingrained in the organisational culture, they create a unified sense of purpose and direction among employees.

Nurturing these foundations involves more than just defining values; it requires ongoing effort to reinforce and embody them in everyday operations. Leaders must lead by example, demonstrating their commitment to these principles through their actions and decisions. This includes creating policies and practices that align with these values, providing training and development opportunities that emphasise their importance, and recognising and rewarding behaviours that exemplify them. By doing so, leaders foster an environment where these values become second nature to all employees, guiding their interactions and contributions.

In addition to core values, cultivating strong foundations also involves investing in essential organisational practices that support sustainable growth. This includes building effective systems for communication, decision-making, and performance management. Leaders should ensure that these systems are transparent, fair, and aligned with the organisation's goals. By creating efficient and reliable processes, leaders can enhance the organisation's operational capabilities, enabling it to adapt and thrive in a dynamic environment.

Moreover, a strong foundation in an organisation is built on the development and empowerment of its people. Leaders should focus on nurturing the talents and potential of their employees, providing them with the resources and opportunities they need to grow and excel. This involves creating a supportive and inclusive work environment where employees feel valued and motivated. When employees are engaged and invested in the organisation's success, they contribute to building a strong and resilient foundation that supports long-term growth.

Leaders must also recognise the importance of adaptability in maintaining a strong foundation. While core values and principles provide stability, the organisation must remain flexible and responsive to changing circumstances. This requires a continuous process of reflection and adaptation, where leaders regularly assess the effectiveness of their practices and make necessary adjustments. By staying attuned to the evolving needs of the organisation and its environment, leaders can ensure that their foundational elements remain relevant and robust.

NURTURING PERSONAL DEVELOPMENT

Tao when nursed within one's self, His vigour will make true;

The chapter emphasises the profound impact of nurturing personal development, both in oneself and within an organisation. The idea that the Tao's vigour, when cultivated within an individual, brings true strength and vitality highlights the importance of continuous self-improvement and well-being. For leaders, prioritising personal development is not just about enhancing their own capabilities but also about fostering the growth and development of their team members. This dual focus on personal and collective growth can significantly elevate overall organisational performance and drive long-term success.

Leaders who commit to personal development set a powerful example for their teams. By demonstrating a dedication to learning and self-improvement, they inspire others to pursue their own growth journeys. This commitment can manifest in various ways, such as engaging in professional training, seeking mentorship, and reflecting on personal and professional experiences. When leaders actively work on their own development, they model the values of curiosity, resilience, and continuous improvement, which can permeate the organisational culture. This creates an environment where learning is valued, and individuals are encouraged to seek opportunities for growth and advancement.

Encouraging personal development among team members is equally crucial. Leaders can create a supportive environment that promotes continuous learning by providing resources and opportunities for skill development. This can include offering access to educational programmes, workshops, and professional development courses, as well as fostering a culture of mentorship and collaboration. By investing in their team's development, leaders help individuals enhance their competencies and confidence, which can lead to greater job satisfaction and engagement. A motivated and skilled workforce is more likely to contribute effectively to the organisation's goals, driving innovation and productivity.

The focus on well-being is also a critical aspect of nurturing personal development. Leaders should recognise that the well-being of their team members directly impacts their performance and overall organisational health. This means supporting not only the professional growth of employees but also their physical, mental, and emotional well-being. Leaders can promote well-being by encouraging work-life balance, providing access to wellness programmes, and creating a supportive and inclusive work environment. When employees feel cared for and valued, they are more likely to be engaged and committed to their work, which can enhance overall performance and reduce turnover.

Furthermore, nurturing personal development contributes to building a resilient organisation. Individuals who are encouraged to grow and develop are better equipped to adapt to changes and challenges. They can bring fresh perspectives and innovative solutions to the table, helping the organisation navigate complex and dynamic environments. By fostering a culture of continuous improvement, leaders can ensure that their teams remain agile and responsive, capable of addressing emerging opportunities and threats with confidence.

FOSTERING A POSITIVE CULTURE

And where the family it rules, What riches will accrue! The neighbourhood where it prevails in thriving will abound;

The chapter emphasises the transformative power of nurturing a positive culture within an organisation. The metaphor of a family thriving under sound principles extending their benefits to the larger neighbourhood underscores the broad impact that a positive organisational culture can have. For leaders, fostering such a culture means creating an environment that prioritises collaboration, respect, and mutual support, ultimately leading to enhanced employee satisfaction and engagement.

A positive organisational culture is foundational to the success of any enterprise. When leaders cultivate an environment that promotes respect and mutual support, they lay the groundwork for a collaborative and cohesive team. In such a culture, employees feel valued and appreciated, which boosts their morale and encourages them to contribute their best efforts. This environment of mutual respect fosters open communication and trust, allowing team members to share ideas, provide feedback, and work together towards common goals. The resulting synergy not only enhances productivity but also sparks innovation as individuals are encouraged to think creatively and collaboratively.

Furthermore, a culture that aligns with core organisational values is crucial for long-term prosperity. When the organisational culture reflects its fundamental principles, it creates a sense of purpose and direction for employees. This alignment ensures that all actions and decisions are guided by the same values, leading to consistency and integrity in the organisation's operations. Employees who understand and believe in the organisation's core values are more likely to be engaged and committed to their work. This commitment translates into higher levels of performance and a stronger sense of loyalty to the organisation.

Leaders play a pivotal role in shaping and maintaining a positive culture. They must lead by example, embodying the values and behaviours they wish to see in their team. This means demonstrating respect, integrity, and support in their interactions, and making decisions that reflect these principles. By modelling the desired culture, leaders set the standard for others to follow, reinforcing the importance of these values throughout the organisation. Additionally, leaders should actively recognise and celebrate behaviours that exemplify the organisation's values, further encouraging a culture of positivity and alignment.

Investing in the development and well-being of employees is another critical aspect of fostering a positive culture. Leaders should provide opportunities for professional growth, such as training programmes, mentoring, and career development initiatives. Supporting employees in their personal development not only enhances their skills and capabilities but also shows that the organisation values their contributions and is committed to their success. This investment in employees' growth fosters a sense of belonging and motivation, driving higher levels of engagement and performance.

A positive organisational culture also thrives on inclusivity and diversity. Leaders should strive to create an inclusive environment where all employees feel respected and valued, regardless of their backgrounds or perspectives. Embracing diversity in all its forms brings a wealth of ideas and experiences to the organisation, fuelling innovation and creativity. By fostering an inclusive culture, leaders can tap into the full potential of their workforce, driving the organisation towards greater success and sustainability.

PROMOTING COMMUNITY & STATEWIDE IMPACT

And when 'tis seen throughout the state, Good fortune will be found. Employ it the kingdom o'er, And men thrive all around.

The chapter poignantly addresses the expansive influence that leaders and their organisations can exert on the broader community and society at large. The idea that the positive practices and principles employed within an organisation can bring about good fortune throughout the state and even the entire kingdom underscores the far-reaching impact of ethical leadership and responsible organisational behaviour. Leaders who recognise this broader influence understand that their actions do not occur in a vacuum; rather, they reverberate through the community and beyond, creating ripples of positive change.

Promoting community and statewide impact begins with the adoption of ethical practices that prioritise social good. Organisations that embed ethical considerations into their operations make a conscious effort to ensure that their activities benefit not just their bottom line but also the welfare of society. This involves making decisions that reflect a commitment to fairness, transparency, and sustainability. By conducting business in a manner that respects ethical standards, organisations can build trust with their stakeholders, including employees, customers, suppliers, and the community at large.

Contributing to social good means going beyond mere compliance with legal and regulatory requirements; it involves proactive engagement in initiatives that enhance societal well-being. Organisations can do this through various means, such as corporate social responsibility (CSR) programmes, philanthropic efforts, and community involvement. These activities can range from supporting local charities and volunteering in community projects to implementing environmentally friendly practices and advocating for social justice. By actively participating in efforts that address social and environmental issues, organisations can demonstrate their commitment to making a positive impact.

Leaders play a crucial role in fostering a sense of responsibility and purpose within their organisations. By setting a clear vision that includes a commitment to social good, leaders can inspire their teams to embrace these values and integrate them into their daily work. This sense of purpose can enhance employee engagement and motivation, as individuals feel that their work contributes to something greater than themselves. When employees see that their organisation is dedicated to ethical practices and social good, they are more likely to take pride in their work and feel a deeper connection to the organisation's mission.

The broader impact of such practices is seen in the way they enhance the organisation's reputation and foster goodwill among stakeholders. A strong reputation for ethical behaviour and social responsibility can differentiate an organisation in a competitive market, attracting customers who value these principles. It can also build stronger relationships with suppliers and partners who share similar values, creating a network of support and collaboration. Furthermore, regulatory bodies and policymakers may view ethically responsible organisations more favourably, potentially easing regulatory scrutiny and fostering a more conducive business environment.

The ripple effects of promoting community and statewide impact can be profound. As organisations demonstrate their commitment to ethical practices and social good, they can influence other businesses and leaders to adopt similar approaches. This collective effort can lead to broader societal changes, as more organisations contribute to addressing pressing social and environmental challenges. The cumulative impact of these efforts can result in significant improvements in the quality of life within communities and the overall health of the state and beyond.

OBSERVING & LEARNING FROM DIFFERENT LEVELS

In this way the effect will be seen in the person, by the observation of different cases; in the family; in the neighbourhood; in the state; and in the kingdom.

The chapter highlights the profound importance of observing and learning from the effects of actions across different levels, from the individual to the kingdom. This principle is a testament to the interconnectedness of all aspects of leadership and governance, emphasising that the impact of decisions and practices can ripple through various layers of society. For leaders, this means that a comprehensive perspective is essential to ensure that strategies are effective and beneficial at every level.

Understanding the effects of actions at the individual level is the foundation of informed leadership. Leaders must begin by considering how their decisions impact themselves and their immediate circle. Personal growth, ethical integrity, and emotional intelligence are crucial components of this introspective observation. By nurturing their development and leading by example, leaders can inspire those around them and foster a culture of continuous improvement and self-awareness. This personal vigilance sets the tone for the broader organisational environment, establishing a standard of conduct that others can follow.

At the team level, leaders should observe how their actions and policies influence the dynamics within their immediate groups. Effective communication, collaboration, and mutual support are vital elements that determine a team's success. Leaders who pay attention to these dynamics can identify areas for improvement and address any issues that may hinder team performance. By fostering an environment of trust and respect, leaders can enhance team cohesion and productivity, ensuring that everyone works harmoniously towards shared goals.

Moving to the organisational level, leaders must consider how their decisions affect the overall structure and function of the entire entity. This involves evaluating operational efficiency, resource allocation, and strategic alignment with the organisation's core mission and values. Leaders who take a holistic approach to organisational management are better equipped to identify potential areas of risk and opportunity. They can implement policies that support sustainable growth and innovation, creating a resilient and adaptable organisation capable of thriving in a dynamic environment.

At the societal level, the actions of an organisation can have far-reaching consequences. Leaders should recognise their responsibility to contribute positively to the community and broader society. This means adopting ethical practices that prioritise social good, environmental sustainability, and economic equity. Organisations that engage in corporate social responsibility initiatives and community involvement can build strong relationships with stakeholders and foster goodwill. By understanding and addressing the broader impact of their actions, leaders can ensure that their organisations are not only successful but also contribute to the well-being of society as a whole.

Finally, at the level of governance or the state, the principles of effective leadership extend to the broader context of public administration and policy-making. Leaders in these positions must consider how their decisions affect the entire population and the functioning of the state. This requires a deep understanding of the interconnectedness of various social, economic, and political systems. By making informed and equitable decisions, leaders can promote stability, prosperity, and justice for all citizens.

ENSURING SUSTAINABILITY & CONTINUITY

Sons shall bring in lengthening line, Sacrifices to his shrine.

The chapter also speaks volumes about the importance of sustainability and continuity, especially in the realm of leadership and organisational management. The metaphor of sons continuing to honour their ancestors symbolises the enduring impact of well-laid plans and the long-lasting benefits of thoughtful leadership. For leaders, this means that ensuring sustainability and continuity is not merely about maintaining the status quo but about actively planning and implementing strategies that secure the organisation's future health and success.

Sustainability in an organisation requires a strategic approach that considers long-term impacts rather than short-term gains. Leaders must cultivate practices that promote resilience and adaptability, ensuring that the organisation can withstand and thrive amidst various challenges. This involves a thorough understanding of the organisation's core values and mission, which should serve as the guiding principles for all decision-making processes. By aligning strategies with these foundational elements, leaders can maintain a clear direction and purpose, which is crucial for sustainable growth.

Succession planning is a critical aspect of ensuring continuity. Leaders must identify and develop potential successors who can carry forward the organisation's mission and values. This process involves mentoring and providing opportunities for emerging leaders to gain experience and skills necessary for their future roles. Effective succession planning not only secures the organisation's future leadership but also fosters a culture of growth and development. When team members see clear pathways for advancement, it enhances their commitment and engagement, contributing to a stable and motivated workforce.

Preserving institutional knowledge is another essential component of sustainability. Organisations accumulate valuable insights, skills, and experiences over time, which are crucial for informed decision-making and strategic planning. Leaders should implement systems to document and share this knowledge, ensuring that it is accessible to current and future team members. This can involve creating comprehensive databases, encouraging collaborative learning, and fostering an environment where knowledge sharing is valued and rewarded. By safeguarding institutional knowledge, leaders prevent the loss of critical information and enable the organisation to build on its past successes.

Maintaining a focus on long-term goals is also vital for sustainability and continuity. Leaders should regularly revisit and reassess these goals to ensure they remain relevant and achievable in light of changing circumstances. This requires a dynamic approach to strategic planning, where flexibility and adaptability are integrated into the organisation's operations. By keeping the long-term vision in sight while remaining responsive to immediate needs, leaders can navigate the complexities of the business environment effectively, ensuring that the organisation continues to move forward.

Furthermore, sustainability extends to ethical and environmental considerations. Leaders have a responsibility to ensure that their organisations operate in ways that are socially responsible and environmentally sustainable. This means adopting practices that minimise negative impacts on the environment and contribute positively to the community. By committing to sustainable practices, organisations can enhance their reputation, build trust with stakeholders, and secure their long-term viability.

CHAPTER 55 - INNOCENCE

Chapter 55 of the *Tao Te Ching* offers insights into the qualities of the Tao, likening them to an infant's purity and harmony, and warning against the pitfalls of striving for excessive strength. Here's how these teachings can be applied to modern-day strategic management:

EMBRACING PURITY & INNOCENCE

He who has in himself abundantly the attributes (of the Tao) is like an infant.

Lao Tzu's Chapter 55 of the *Tao Te Ching* underscores the profound wisdom in embracing purity and innocence in one's approach to life and leadership. The analogy of being like an infant, who naturally embodies the attributes of the Tao, highlights the importance of maintaining a sense of openness, curiosity, and an unprejudiced perspective. In the context of strategic management, leaders can derive significant benefits from adopting these qualities. By maintaining a mindset of continuous learning and adaptability, leaders can more effectively navigate the complexities of the modern business environment and uncover innovative solutions to challenges.

Embracing purity and innocence in leadership begins with cultivating an openness to new ideas and experiences. Much like an infant who approaches the world with wonder and a sense of discovery, leaders should strive to remain receptive to diverse perspectives and novel approaches. This openness allows them to recognise opportunities that might otherwise be overlooked and to respond creatively to emerging issues. In an ever-changing business landscape, the ability to adapt and innovate is critical for staying ahead. Leaders who embrace a learning mindset are more likely to experiment with new strategies and solutions, fostering an environment where innovation thrives.

Curiosity is another key aspect of this approach. An inquisitive mindset drives leaders to question the status quo and seek deeper understanding. By continuously asking questions and exploring new possibilities, leaders can gain insights that lead to more informed and effective decision-making. This curiosity can also inspire and motivate team members, encouraging them to take initiative and contribute their ideas. When leaders demonstrate a genuine interest in learning and improvement, it sets a positive example for the entire organisation, promoting a culture of intellectual curiosity and growth.

Willingness to learn is essential for personal and professional development. Leaders who are committed to their own growth are better equipped to guide their teams and navigate the complexities of their roles. This commitment involves being open to feedback, acknowledging mistakes, and viewing challenges as opportunities for learning. By modelling this behaviour, leaders can create a supportive environment where employees feel safe to take risks and learn from their experiences. This collective learning process enhances the organisation's capacity to adapt and innovate, driving long-term success.

Innocence, in this context, also implies approaching situations without preconceived biases or rigid expectations. Leaders who can look at challenges with a fresh perspective are more likely to identify unique solutions and opportunities. This unbiased approach enables them to see the potential in unconventional ideas and to collaborate more effectively with diverse teams. By valuing each team member's contributions and fostering an inclusive atmosphere, leaders can harness the full range of talents and perspectives within the organisation.

The principles of purity and innocence also extend to ethical leadership. Maintaining these qualities involves acting with integrity and honesty, upholding the organisation's values, and treating others with respect and fairness. Leaders who exemplify these virtues build trust and credibility, both within their teams and with external stakeholders. This trust forms the foundation for strong, collaborative relationships, which are crucial for achieving organisational goals. By leading with authenticity and ethical principles, leaders can inspire loyalty and commitment, creating a positive and supportive work environment.

VALUING FLEXIBILITY & RESILIENCE

(The infant's) bones are weak and its sinews soft, but yet its grasp is firm.

The chapter eloquently illustrates the significance of flexibility and resilience through the metaphor of an infant whose seemingly fragile form possesses a surprisingly firm grasp. This imagery underscores the strength that lies in flexibility and the resilience required to adapt and thrive in varying conditions. In the realm of strategic management, these qualities are indispensable. Leaders who recognise and cultivate flexibility within their organisations can better navigate the complexities and uncertainties of the business world, ensuring stability and fostering long-term success.

Flexibility in an organisation begins with the willingness to adapt strategies and operations in response to changing circumstances. This requires a mindset that embraces change and views it as an opportunity for growth rather than a threat. Leaders who foster this mindset encourage their teams to be open to new ideas and approaches, enabling the organisation to pivot when necessary. This adaptability is crucial in a dynamic business environment where market conditions, technologies, and consumer preferences can shift rapidly. By remaining flexible, organisations can respond swiftly to new opportunities and challenges, maintaining their competitive edge.

Resilience, on the other hand, is about the capacity to withstand and recover from setbacks. It involves building systems and processes that are robust enough to handle disruptions and continue functioning effectively. Resilient organisations are those that can absorb shocks, learn from adversity, and emerge stronger. This resilience is built on a foundation of strong leadership, effective communication, and a culture that values learning and improvement. Leaders play a pivotal role in cultivating resilience by promoting a positive attitude towards challenges and setbacks, encouraging their teams to view failures as learning experiences and opportunities for growth.

The metaphor of the infant also highlights the importance of maintaining core strengths even in the face of flexibility. Just as an infant's grasp is firm despite its soft sinews, organisations must hold onto their core values and mission while being flexible in their strategies and operations. This balance ensures that the organisation remains true to its identity and purpose while navigating change. Leaders must be clear about the organisation's foundational principles and ensure that all decisions and actions align with these core values. This clarity provides a stable anchor amidst the turbulence of change, guiding the organisation towards sustainable success.

Flexibility and resilience also extend to organisational culture. A culture that values these qualities is one where employees feel empowered to take initiative, experiment with new ideas, and learn from their experiences. Leaders can cultivate such a culture by recognising and rewarding adaptability and innovation, providing opportunities for continuous learning and development, and fostering an environment of psychological safety where team members feel comfortable taking risks. This cultural resilience enhances the organisation's ability to thrive in a rapidly evolving business landscape.

Moreover, flexible and resilient organisations are better positioned to seize new opportunities and drive innovation. By maintaining an open and adaptive approach, these organisations can explore new markets, adopt emerging technologies, and develop innovative products and services that meet changing consumer needs. This proactive stance not only ensures survival in the face of disruption but also positions the organisation as a leader in its industry.

MAINTAINING HARMONY & BALANCE

(The infant) shows the harmony (in its constitution).

The chapter poetically illustrates the concept of harmony through the image of an infant, whose natural state exemplifies balance and tranquility. This metaphor offers profound insights for leaders in the context of organisational management. In a modern workplace, harmony and balance are crucial for sustaining organisational health and achieving long-term success. Leaders must endeavour to create an environment where employees feel supported, valued, and motivated. This involves fostering a culture characterised by collaboration, open communication, and mutual respect, which are essential elements for enhancing overall productivity and employee satisfaction.

Creating a balanced work environment starts with recognising the diverse needs and contributions of all employees. Leaders should strive to ensure that everyone feels included and appreciated, regardless of their role or background. This requires a commitment to equity and inclusivity, where opportunities for growth and advancement are accessible to all. By promoting a culture that values diversity, leaders can harness a wide range of perspectives and experiences, leading to more innovative and effective solutions to organisational challenges. Additionally, when employees feel that their unique contributions are recognised and valued, they are more likely to be engaged and committed to their work.

Fostering collaboration is another key aspect of maintaining harmony within an organisation. Leaders should encourage teamwork and the sharing of ideas, creating an environment where employees feel comfortable working together towards common goals. This can be achieved through team-building activities, collaborative projects, and a physical workspace designed to facilitate interaction. By breaking down silos and promoting cross-functional collaboration, leaders can ensure that knowledge and expertise are shared across the organisation, leading to more cohesive and integrated efforts. Effective collaboration not only enhances productivity but also strengthens the sense of community and camaraderie among employees.

Open communication is also critical for maintaining organisational harmony. Leaders must establish transparent and honest communication channels that allow for the free flow of information and feedback. This involves regularly updating employees on organisational developments, providing clear instructions and expectations, and actively listening to their concerns and suggestions. When employees feel informed and heard, they are more likely to trust their leaders and feel a sense of ownership over their work. This trust is the foundation of a harmonious work environment, where conflicts can be resolved constructively and everyone feels aligned with the organisation's mission and goals.

Mutual respect is fundamental to creating a supportive and positive workplace culture. Leaders should model respectful behaviour in all interactions and set clear expectations for how employees should treat one another. This includes recognising and celebrating achievements, addressing issues of disrespect or harassment promptly, and fostering an environment where everyone feels safe and valued. When mutual respect is ingrained in the organisational culture, employees are more likely to feel psychologically safe, enabling them to take risks, share ideas, and fully engage in their work.

Maintaining harmony and balance also involves recognising and supporting the well-being of employees. Leaders should prioritise work-life balance, ensuring that employees have the flexibility and resources needed to manage their professional and personal responsibilities. This can include offering flexible work arrangements, providing access to wellness programmes, and creating a supportive environment that recognises the importance of mental and physical health. By caring for the holistic well-being of employees, leaders can enhance job satisfaction and reduce burnout, leading to a more sustainable and productive workforce.

UNDERSTANDING THE LIMITS OF STRENGTH

All life-increasing arts to evil turn; Where the mind makes the vital breath to burn, (False) is the strength, (and o'er it we should mourn.)

The chapter offers a poignant reflection on the nature of strength and the perils of excessive ambition. The admonition against unchecked growth and the pursuit of power serves as a powerful reminder for leaders to be mindful of the limits of strength. The essence of this wisdom lies in recognising that true strength does not stem from force or relentless ambition but from balance, harmony, and sustainable growth. In the realm of strategic management, this perspective is crucial for fostering an environment where both individuals and organisations can thrive without succumbing to the detrimental effects of overexertion and undue pressure.

Understanding the limits of strength involves acknowledging the inherent risks associated with overambition. Leaders who relentlessly strive for constant growth and power may inadvertently push their teams towards burnout and exhaustion. This pursuit often leads to a work culture that prioritises results over well-being, where employees feel compelled to overextend themselves to meet increasingly demanding expectations. Such an environment not only diminishes morale but also reduces overall productivity and creativity. By recognising these dangers, leaders can take proactive steps to create a more balanced and supportive work environment that values the health and well-being of its members.

Sustainable growth is a key component of effective leadership. Rather than focusing solely on short-term gains and rapid expansion, leaders should prioritise long-term stability and resilience. This involves setting realistic goals that are achievable without compromising the well-being of the team. Sustainable growth is about pacing development in a manner that allows the organisation to evolve organically, ensuring that resources are utilised efficiently and that the foundations of the business remain strong. By fostering a culture that values sustainable practices, leaders can ensure that their organisations are built to endure and prosper over time.

Moreover, leaders must cultivate a mindset of balance and harmony within their organisations. This means creating policies and practices that support a healthy work-life balance for employees. Encouraging regular breaks, promoting flexible work arrangements, and providing access to wellness resources are all ways to support the physical and mental health of the team. When employees feel that their well-being is prioritised, they are more likely to be engaged, motivated, and committed to their work. This, in turn, enhances overall productivity and fosters a positive and supportive organisational culture.

Recognising the limits of strength also entails understanding the importance of resilience. While ambition drives progress, resilience ensures that the organisation can withstand challenges and recover from setbacks. Leaders should focus on building resilient systems and teams that can adapt to changing circumstances and bounce back from adversity. This involves fostering a culture of continuous learning and improvement, where failures are viewed as opportunities for growth rather than setbacks. By cultivating resilience, leaders can ensure that their organisations remain flexible and capable of navigating the complexities of the modern business landscape.

Furthermore, true strength in leadership comes from a commitment to ethical practices and integrity. Leaders who prioritise honesty, transparency, and fairness build trust within their teams and with external stakeholders. This trust forms the foundation of strong and lasting relationships, which are crucial for long-term success. By maintaining high ethical standards and leading by example, leaders can inspire their teams to uphold the same values, creating a culture of integrity that permeates all aspects of the organisation.

EMBRACING NATURAL PROCESSES & CYCLES

> *When things have become strong, they (then) become old, which may be said to be contrary to the Tao. Whatever is contrary to the Tao soon ends.*

The chapter deeply explores the notion of embracing natural processes and cycles, illustrating the inevitable transformations that all entities undergo. The insight that strength can lead to aging, a state contrary to the Tao, emphasises the transient nature of all things and the importance of aligning with these natural rhythms. For leaders, understanding and embracing these cycles within their organisations can significantly enhance decision-making and management effectiveness. Recognising that periods of growth and decline are intrinsic to any organisational life cycle helps leaders navigate transitions more smoothly and maintain a resilient, adaptable enterprise.

In strategic management, acknowledging the natural ebb and flow of growth and decline is crucial for sustainable leadership. Every organisation, like any living entity, will experience phases of expansion, peak performance, and subsequent decline. These phases are part of a broader cycle that, if embraced rather than resisted, can provide valuable insights into effective management. Leaders who understand this can prepare for and manage these transitions more effectively. For instance, during periods of growth, they can capitalise on momentum, invest in innovation, and strengthen core capabilities. Conversely, during downturns, they can focus on efficiency, consolidation, and strategic planning for future growth.

Embracing natural cycles requires a shift in perspective from viewing decline as failure to recognising it as a phase that can be managed and learned from. This mindset allows leaders to make informed decisions that are aligned with the organisation's long-term health. Instead of overextending resources in an attempt to avoid decline, leaders can focus on building a robust foundation that supports resilience. This includes maintaining a flexible approach to strategy, being open to change, and fostering an organisational culture that is adaptable and forward-thinking.

Leaders can also benefit from integrating an awareness of natural cycles into their strategic planning processes. This means developing contingency plans that anticipate potential downturns and having strategies in place to mitigate their impact. By planning for these cycles, leaders can ensure that the organisation is better prepared to handle challenges without resorting to drastic measures that could destabilise operations. This proactive approach to management helps sustain organisational stability and continuity, even during difficult times.

Furthermore, aligning with natural cycles involves recognising the importance of timing and pacing in organisational activities. Just as natural processes follow rhythms and patterns, organisational initiatives should be timed and paced according to the internal and external environment. Leaders who understand this can better gauge when to launch new projects, enter new markets, or implement significant changes. This timing is crucial for maximising impact and ensuring that efforts are synchronised with broader organisational goals and market conditions.

Maintaining organisational resilience through alignment with natural cycles also involves fostering a culture of continuous learning and adaptation. Leaders should encourage their teams to view challenges and transitions as opportunities for growth and innovation. By promoting a mindset that embraces change and values learning, leaders can cultivate a workforce that is resilient and capable of navigating uncertainties. This cultural resilience is a key asset in ensuring the organisation's long-term success and adaptability.

LEADING WITH WISDOM & INSIGHT

> *To him by whom this harmony is known, (The secret of) the unchanging (Tao) is shown, And in the knowledge wisdom finds its throne.*

The chapter also profoundly articulates the virtues of wisdom and insight, portraying these qualities as the foundation of effective leadership. The notion that understanding harmony reveals the unchanging Tao, and in this knowledge, wisdom finds its throne, is a timeless reminder of the depth and nuance required for true leadership. To lead with wisdom and insight means more than just the accumulation of knowledge or the implementation of effective strategies; it entails a deep, intuitive understanding of the fundamental principles that govern both the organisation and the broader environment in which it operates.

For leaders, seeking to understand these deeper principles is crucial. This understanding begins with a clear grasp of the organisation's core values, mission, and vision. These elements serve as the guiding stars, ensuring that every decision and action aligns with the organisation's fundamental purpose. Leaders who internalise these principles can navigate their organisations through complex and uncertain terrains with a sense of clarity and purpose. This alignment not only fosters coherence within the organisation but also builds trust among employees, stakeholders, and customers, as it demonstrates a commitment to consistent and principled leadership.

Wisdom in leadership also involves the ability to perceive and anticipate the subtleties and dynamics of the external environment. This requires a continuous effort to stay informed about industry trends, market shifts, and broader socio-economic changes. Insightful leaders are adept at connecting the dots between seemingly disparate pieces of information, identifying patterns, and discerning underlying causes and potential outcomes. This foresight enables them to make proactive, rather than reactive, decisions, positioning their organisations to capitalise on emerging opportunities and mitigate risks.

Moreover, leading with wisdom and insight means fostering a culture of continuous learning and adaptability within the organisation. Leaders must encourage a mindset that values curiosity, experimentation, and learning from both successes and failures. This involves creating an environment where employees feel safe to express their ideas, take risks, and innovate. By promoting a culture that embraces learning, leaders ensure that their organisations remain agile and resilient in the face of change. This adaptability is critical for long-term success, as it allows the organisation to evolve and thrive in an ever-changing landscape.

Another essential aspect of wise leadership is the ability to balance short-term demands with long-term goals. While it is necessary to address immediate challenges and opportunities, leaders must also keep an eye on the future, ensuring that current actions do not compromise the organisation's long-term health and sustainability. This balance requires a strategic vision that integrates both immediate needs and future aspirations, guiding the organisation towards sustainable growth and development. Wise leaders are those who can maintain this dual focus, making decisions that serve the organisation's best interests both now and in the future.

Furthermore, wisdom and insight in leadership involve emotional intelligence and empathy. Effective leaders are not only intellectually adept but also attuned to the emotions and needs of their team members. They understand that leadership is fundamentally about people and relationships. By demonstrating empathy, listening actively, and showing genuine concern for their employees' well-being, leaders can build strong, cohesive teams. This emotional intelligence fosters a supportive and collaborative work environment, where individuals feel valued and motivated to contribute their best efforts.

CHAPTER 56 – SILENCE

Chapter 56 of the *Tao Te Ching* delves into the nature of true knowledge, the power of silence, and the profound impact of harmonising with others. Here's how these teachings can be applied to modern-day strategic management:

EMBRACING THE POWER OF SILENCE

> *He who knows (the Tao) does not (care to) speak (about it); he who is (ever ready to) speak about it does not know it.*

Lao Tzu's Chapter 56 of the *Tao Te Ching* highlights the profound concept of embracing silence as a vehicle for wisdom. The wisdom embedded in this passage underscores a key tenet of effective leadership: the understanding that true knowledge often manifests through actions rather than words. In the realm of strategic management, this principle becomes particularly significant. Leaders who grasp the power of silence and thoughtfulness can profoundly influence their organisations, cultivating a culture of respect, mindfulness, and deliberate action.

The first aspect of embracing the power of silence involves recognising the value of listening. Effective leaders understand that listening is not a passive activity but an active engagement with their surroundings and team members. By truly listening, leaders can gain deeper insights into the needs, concerns, and ideas of their employees. This attentive approach allows leaders to gather essential information that can inform strategic decisions and foster a more inclusive and responsive organisational environment. When leaders prioritise listening, they demonstrate respect for their team members, validating their contributions and creating a sense of belonging and value within the organisation.

Observing is another crucial element of this approach. Leaders who take the time to observe the dynamics within their organisation can identify patterns and trends that may not be immediately apparent. This observational skill allows leaders to understand the underlying currents that influence organisational behaviour, enabling them to address issues proactively and strategically. By being observant, leaders can also recognise the strengths and potential of their team members, which can be nurtured and developed to enhance overall performance and innovation. This mindful observation helps leaders stay attuned to the pulse of the organisation, ensuring that they can respond effectively to both challenges and opportunities.

Acting with intention is the third pillar of embracing silence and thoughtfulness. Leaders who act deliberately and thoughtfully set a powerful example for their teams. Rather than making hasty or reactive decisions, these leaders take the time to consider the long-term implications of their actions. This thoughtful approach fosters a culture of careful planning and strategic thinking within the organisation. By acting with intention, leaders demonstrate that they value substance over show, prioritising meaningful impact over superficial gestures. This focus on deliberate action cultivates a sense of trust and reliability among team members, who are more likely to feel confident in their leaders' decisions.

The power of silence also lies in its ability to create space for reflection and introspection. In the fast-paced world of business, it is easy for leaders to become consumed by the constant need to communicate and perform. However, moments of silence provide an opportunity for leaders to step back and reflect on their actions, goals, and strategies. This reflective practice allows leaders to gain clarity and perspective, enabling them to make more informed and balanced decisions. By integrating periods of silence into their routines, leaders can maintain a sense of calm and focus amidst the demands of their roles.

Furthermore, a culture that values silence and thoughtfulness encourages employees to engage in deep thinking and problem-solving. When leaders model these behaviours, they create an environment where team members feel empowered to take their time in considering solutions and strategies. This thoughtful approach to problem-solving can lead to more innovative and effective outcomes, as employees are encouraged to explore different perspectives and ideas without the pressure of immediate responses. The emphasis on thoughtful action over constant verbalisation can enhance the quality of decision-making and foster a more thoughtful and deliberate organisational culture.

PRACTISING THOUGHTFUL COMMUNICATION

He (who knows it) will keep his mouth shut and close the portals (of his nostrils).

The chapter underscores the profound wisdom in practising thoughtful communication. The idea that true understanding leads one to speak less and listen more highlights the essence of effective leadership. In the realm of strategic management, thoughtful communication is not merely a skill but a fundamental principle that enhances a leader's ability to connect with their team, make informed decisions, and foster a collaborative environment.

Practising thoughtful communication begins with the recognition that words carry significant weight and impact. Leaders must be mindful of their language, ensuring that their words are purposeful, considerate, and aligned with their intentions. This mindfulness requires a heightened awareness of the effects of one's communication on others. By speaking less, leaders avoid the pitfalls of impulsive or unnecessary remarks that can cause confusion or misunderstanding. Instead, they focus on delivering clear, concise, and meaningful messages that advance the organisation's goals and resonate with their audience.

A critical component of thoughtful communication is the art of listening. Effective leaders understand that listening is an active process that involves more than just hearing words. It requires attention, empathy, and an open mind. By truly listening to their team members, leaders can gain a deeper understanding of their needs, concerns, and aspirations. This understanding enables leaders to respond more effectively and make decisions that are informed by the insights and perspectives of those they lead. Listening fosters an environment of inclusivity, where everyone feels heard and valued, contributing to a more cohesive and motivated team.

Thoughtful communication also plays a pivotal role in conflict resolution. Leaders who practise mindful communication can navigate conflicts with greater ease and effectiveness. By approaching disputes with a calm and composed demeanour, they can de-escalate tensions and facilitate constructive dialogue. This approach involves acknowledging the emotions and viewpoints of all parties involved and seeking common ground. Thoughtful leaders use their words to bridge gaps, clarify misunderstandings, and build consensus. This not only resolves conflicts but also strengthens relationships and trust within the team.

Building stronger relationships through thoughtful communication requires leaders to be genuinely present in their interactions. This means engaging with team members in a manner that shows respect and appreciation for their contributions. Thoughtful leaders make time for one-on-one conversations, provide feedback that is constructive and supportive, and express gratitude for the efforts of their team. These practices help to cultivate a positive and inclusive work culture where individuals feel valued and motivated to perform at their best.

Moreover, thoughtful communication extends beyond verbal interactions. Leaders must also be mindful of non-verbal cues such as body language, facial expressions, and tone of voice. These elements can convey just as much, if not more, than words themselves. By being aware of and controlling their non-verbal communication, leaders can ensure that their messages are received as intended and reinforce a sense of openness and approachability.

SIMPLIFYING & HARMONISING

> *He will blunt his sharp points and unravel the complications of things; he will attemper his brightness, and bring himself into agreement with the obscurity (of others).*

The chapter elegantly captures the importance of simplifying and harmonising in leadership. The metaphor of blunting sharp points and unraveling complications speaks to the necessity of reducing unnecessary complexities within an organisation. Leaders who prioritise simplification can significantly enhance the efficiency and effectiveness of their operations. By stripping away the excess and focusing on what truly matters, they create a streamlined environment where resources are optimally utilised, and processes run smoothly. This approach not only increases productivity but also alleviates stress and confusion among team members, enabling them to concentrate on their core responsibilities with clarity and purpose.

Simplification in leadership involves a keen eye for identifying and eliminating redundant or convoluted procedures. This requires a commitment to continuous improvement and a willingness to challenge the status quo. Leaders must actively seek feedback from their teams to uncover inefficiencies and areas for enhancement. By engaging in open dialogue and encouraging suggestions for improvement, leaders can foster a culture of innovation and collective problem-solving. This participatory approach not only unravels complexities but also empowers employees, making them feel valued and integral to the organisation's success.

Harmonising with one's team is another critical aspect of effective leadership. It entails aligning one's actions and decisions with the needs and perspectives of others, creating a sense of unity and cooperation. Leaders who practise harmony prioritise the collective well-being of their team over individual agendas. This involves being attuned to the emotional and psychological states of team members and addressing their concerns with empathy and compassion. By understanding and supporting their team's needs, leaders can build strong, trust-based relationships that foster loyalty and commitment.

Harmonisation also means being adaptable and open to different viewpoints. Leaders must recognise that diversity of thought is a valuable asset that can drive innovation and growth. By creating an inclusive environment where all voices are heard and respected, leaders can harness the full potential of their team. This involves actively seeking out and considering diverse perspectives, even if they challenge conventional thinking. Embracing this diversity requires humility and a willingness to learn from others, acknowledging that wisdom can come from any level within the organisation.

In practice, harmonising with others might involve adjusting one's leadership style to better suit the team's dynamics. For example, some situations may require a more directive approach, while others may benefit from a collaborative or democratic style. Effective leaders are flexible and can seamlessly transition between these styles based on the context and needs of their team. This adaptability not only enhances team performance but also reinforces the leader's credibility and influence.

A harmonious organisational culture is characterised by mutual respect and collaboration. Leaders play a pivotal role in cultivating this culture by modelling respectful behaviour and setting clear expectations for how team members should interact. This involves addressing conflicts constructively, celebrating achievements collectively, and recognising the contributions of each individual. By fostering a collaborative environment, leaders can inspire a shared sense of purpose and drive, motivating their teams to work together towards common goals.

BEING BEYOND SELF-INTEREST

> *(Such an one) cannot be treated familiarly or distantly; he is beyond all consideration of profit or injury; of nobility or meanness.*

The chapter deeply explores the concept of transcending self-interest in leadership, emphasising the importance of making decisions for the greater good rather than personal gain. This profound wisdom highlights the notion that a truly effective leader is one who is beyond considerations of profit or injury, nobility or meanness, and treats everyone with fairness and integrity. In the realm of strategic management, this principle is not only ethical but also practical, as it fosters a culture of trust, credibility, and long-term commitment within the organisation.

Leaders who transcend self-interest prioritise the well-being of their organisation and stakeholders above their personal ambitions. This selflessness is not about neglecting one's own needs but about understanding that the true measure of success lies in the collective prosperity of the team and the organisation. When leaders consistently make decisions that benefit the broader group, they demonstrate a commitment to shared goals and values. This approach builds a solid foundation of trust, as employees and stakeholders recognise that the leader's actions are motivated by integrity and fairness rather than self-serving motives.

The absence of self-interest in leadership enhances credibility. When leaders are perceived as impartial and dedicated to the common good, their decisions carry more weight and are more likely to be accepted and respected by others. This credibility is essential for effective leadership, as it enables leaders to influence and guide their teams more effectively. Employees are more likely to follow leaders they trust and respect, leading to a more cohesive and motivated workforce. Furthermore, stakeholders, such as clients, partners, and investors, are more inclined to support organisations led by individuals who consistently demonstrate ethical and fair practices.

Being beyond self-interest also involves fostering a culture of mutual respect and collaboration. Leaders who embody this principle create an environment where all team members feel valued and heard. This inclusivity encourages open communication and the sharing of diverse perspectives, which can lead to more innovative and effective solutions. When team members see that their contributions are recognised and that decisions are made with the organisation's best interests in mind, they are more likely to be engaged and committed to their work. This collective commitment drives higher levels of performance and productivity, contributing to the organisation's overall success.

Additionally, focusing on the greater good requires leaders to be adaptable and open to different viewpoints. This adaptability is crucial in a constantly changing business landscape, where flexibility and responsiveness are key to navigating challenges and seizing opportunities. Leaders who are beyond self-interest are willing to adjust their strategies and actions based on input from their teams and changing circumstances. This openness to change fosters a culture of continuous improvement and resilience, ensuring that the organisation can thrive in the face of uncertainty.

The principle of being beyond self-interest also extends to long-term strategic planning. Leaders who prioritise the well-being of the organisation and its stakeholders are more likely to make decisions that ensure sustainable growth and stability. This long-term perspective involves considering the impact of decisions on future generations and the overall health of the organisation. By avoiding short-sighted actions driven by personal gain, leaders can create a legacy of integrity and success that endures over time.

DEMONSTRATING TRUE NOBILITY

He is the noblest man under heaven.

The chapter also provides a profound exploration of what it means to demonstrate true nobility in leadership. This concept is deeply rooted in the qualities of humility, wisdom, and a dedication to the collective well-being. True nobility, as described by Lao Tzu, transcends titles and superficial markers of status; it is reflected in the character and actions of a leader who prioritises the greater good above personal ambition. Leaders who embody these noble qualities set a powerful example for their teams, fostering a positive and inspiring organisational culture that motivates everyone to contribute their best.

Humility is a cornerstone of noble leadership. Leaders who approach their roles with humility understand that their position is not about exerting power over others but about serving and empowering their team. This humility is manifested in a willingness to listen, to acknowledge the contributions of others, and to admit one's own limitations and mistakes. Humble leaders do not seek the spotlight for themselves but are quick to shine it on their team members, recognising and celebrating their achievements. This humility creates a culture of respect and appreciation, where everyone feels valued and motivated to excel.

Wisdom is another essential attribute of true nobility in leadership. Wise leaders possess a deep understanding of the principles that guide their organisation and the broader context in which it operates. They are adept at seeing the bigger picture and making decisions that are informed by long-term considerations rather than short-term gains. This wisdom allows them to navigate complex situations with clarity and insight, balancing the needs of various stakeholders and anticipating potential challenges and opportunities. By leading with wisdom, these leaders inspire confidence and trust, as their decisions are seen as thoughtful, fair, and well-considered.

A focus on the collective well-being is the third pillar of noble leadership. True noble leaders prioritise the health and success of their organisation and its members above their personal interests. They are committed to creating an environment where everyone can thrive, both professionally and personally. This involves fostering a culture of collaboration, support, and mutual respect, where team members feel empowered to share their ideas and work together towards common goals. Noble leaders recognise that their success is intrinsically linked to the success of their team, and they invest in the development and well-being of their people. This selfless dedication to the collective good builds a strong sense of loyalty and commitment within the organisation.

The impact of demonstrating true nobility in leadership extends beyond the immediate team to the broader organisational culture. When leaders embody humility, wisdom, and a focus on collective well-being, they set a powerful example that others are inspired to follow. This creates a ripple effect throughout the organisation, fostering a culture where these values are deeply embedded and consistently practised. Employees who see their leaders demonstrating these qualities are more likely to emulate them in their own work and interactions, leading to a more cohesive, respectful, and high-performing organisation.

Furthermore, noble leadership enhances the organisation's reputation and builds strong, trusting relationships with external stakeholders. Clients, partners, and investors are drawn to organisations led by individuals who consistently demonstrate integrity, fairness, and a commitment to the greater good. This trust is invaluable in building long-term partnerships and achieving sustainable success. By leading with true nobility, leaders not only strengthen their own organisation but also contribute positively to the wider community and society.

CHAPTER 57 – EXCESSIVE CONTROL

Chapter 57 of the *Tao Te Ching* discusses the principles of ruling through non-action *Wú Wéi (*無為/无为*)*, the consequences of excessive control, and the transformative power of simplicity and stillness. Here's how these teachings can be applied to modern-day strategic management:

EMBRACING NON-ACTION & TRUST

> A state may be ruled by (measures of) correction; weapons of war may be used with crafty dexterity; (but) the kingdom is made one's own (only) by freedom from action and purpose.

Lao Tzu's Chapter 57 of the *Tao Te Ching* profoundly explores the concept of non-action, or *Wú Wéi (*無為/无为*)*, as a guiding principle for effective leadership and strategic management. The wisdom embedded in this teaching emphasises the importance of aligning with the natural flow of processes and allowing events to unfold organically. Non-action does not equate to passivity or inaction; rather, it signifies a deliberate choice to trust the intrinsic capabilities of individuals and systems, thus avoiding the pitfalls of micromanagement and excessive control.

In the context of strategic management, embracing non-action means that leaders must cultivate a deep sense of trust in their teams. This trust is fundamental to empowering employees, granting them the autonomy to take ownership of their work and make decisions within their areas of expertise. By relinquishing the need to control every detail, leaders create an environment where creativity and innovation can flourish. Employees who are trusted to take initiative are more likely to feel valued and motivated, which can lead to increased productivity and engagement. This empowerment fosters a sense of responsibility and accountability, as team members understand that their contributions have a direct impact on the organisation's success.

Implementing non-action in leadership involves a shift from traditional command-and-control approaches to a more facilitative and supportive style. Leaders must focus on providing the necessary resources, guidance, and support while allowing their teams the freedom to explore and experiment. This balance between direction and autonomy is crucial for fostering an innovative organisational culture. When employees are free to approach problems creatively, they can develop novel solutions that drive the organisation forward. Leaders who practise non-action understand that their role is not to dictate but to enable and support their teams in achieving their fullest potential.

Furthermore, non-action encourages leaders to embrace patience and trust in the natural progression of events. This involves recognising that not all outcomes can be controlled or predicted and that sometimes the best course of action is to allow processes to unfold in their own time. By adopting a mindset of patience and acceptance, leaders can reduce stress and create a more harmonious work environment. This approach also promotes a culture of resilience, where team members are better equipped to handle uncertainty and change. Embracing non-action helps leaders stay focused on long-term objectives, rather than becoming overly reactive to immediate challenges.

A critical aspect of non-action is also the understanding that true leadership is about creating conditions for others to succeed. Leaders who adopt this philosophy prioritise the development and well-being of their employees. They invest in training, mentorship, and professional growth opportunities, recognising that the success of the organisation is intrinsically linked to the success of its people. This investment in human capital not only enhances individual capabilities but also strengthens the overall organisational fabric. By fostering a supportive and empowering environment, leaders can build a cohesive and high-performing team that is capable of achieving extraordinary results.

The principles of non-action extend to organisational communication and decision-making processes as well. Leaders who embrace non-action prioritise transparency and inclusivity, ensuring that all voices are heard and considered. This inclusive approach to decision-making promotes a sense of ownership and buy-in among team members, leading to more effective and sustainable outcomes. By valuing input from diverse perspectives, leaders can make more informed and balanced decisions that reflect the collective wisdom of the organisation.

AVOIDING EXCESSIVE CONTROL & REGULATION

> *In the kingdom the multiplication of prohibitive enactments increases the poverty of the people; the more implements to add to their profit that the people have, the greater disorder is there in the state and clan; the more acts of crafty dexterity that men possess, the more do strange contrivances appear; the more display there is of legislation, the more thieves and robbers there are.*

The chapter provides a profound commentary on the pitfalls of excessive control and regulation within an organisation. The essence of this teaching is the recognition that over-regulation can lead to inefficiency, disorder, and stifled innovation. In a modern organisational context, leaders who impose too many rules and restrictive measures can inadvertently create an environment where creativity and initiative are suppressed. This micromanagement approach often results in employees feeling constrained, leading to decreased motivation and engagement.

Excessive control can manifest in various forms, such as stringent policies, cumbersome procedures, and an overemphasis on compliance. While some level of regulation is necessary to ensure order and consistency, an overabundance of rules can create a bureaucratic culture that hampers productivity. Employees may spend more time navigating administrative hurdles than focusing on their core tasks. This not only slows down processes but also generates frustration and disengagement among staff. In such an environment, the organisation's ability to innovate and respond to changing market demands is significantly diminished.

Leaders can counteract the negative effects of excessive control by establishing clear, simple guidelines that provide a framework for action while allowing flexibility. These guidelines should be designed to support, rather than restrict, the creative and operational capacities of the team. By focusing on principles rather than rigid rules, leaders can create a more dynamic and adaptive organisation. This approach encourages employees to exercise their judgment and take ownership of their work, fostering a sense of autonomy and responsibility.

Trust and accountability are fundamental to creating a productive and harmonious work environment. Leaders must demonstrate trust in their employees' abilities and intentions by giving them the freedom to make decisions and take risks. This trust is not blind; it is built on clear expectations and mutual respect. When employees feel trusted, they are more likely to be motivated and committed to their roles. They are also more willing to experiment and innovate, knowing that their leaders support their efforts and recognise their contributions.

Creating a culture of trust also involves transparent and open communication. Leaders should actively seek input from their teams and involve them in decision-making processes. This inclusivity ensures that diverse perspectives are considered, leading to more well-rounded and effective solutions. Moreover, when employees feel that their voices are heard and valued, they are more likely to take initiative and collaborate towards common goals. This collaborative spirit enhances teamwork and strengthens the overall organisational fabric.

Accountability is the counterpart to trust. While leaders should provide their teams with autonomy, they must also establish mechanisms for accountability. Clear performance metrics and regular feedback are essential for ensuring that employees stay on track and meet their objectives. However, accountability should not be punitive; it should be constructive and supportive. Leaders should focus on providing guidance and resources to help employees succeed, rather than merely enforcing compliance. This balanced approach fosters a culture of continuous improvement and mutual support.

CREATING A CULTURE OF SIMPLICITY & STILLNESS

> *I will do nothing (of purpose), and the people will be transformed of themselves; I will be fond of keeping still, and the people will of themselves become correct. I will take no trouble about it, and the people will of themselves become rich; I will manifest no ambition, and the people will of themselves attain to the primitive simplicity.*

The chapter also profoundly emphasises the creation of a culture that values simplicity and stillness, both of which are essential for fostering an environment where individuals and organisations can thrive. The wisdom contained in these teachings encourages leaders to strip away unnecessary complexities and allow space for reflection, mindfulness, and clarity. In the context of strategic management, embracing simplicity involves streamlining processes and focusing on the core elements that drive success, while fostering stillness allows for moments of contemplation that enhance overall well-being and decision-making.

Creating a culture of simplicity begins with the intentional effort to reduce unnecessary complexity within the organisation. Leaders must evaluate existing processes, policies, and structures to identify areas where simplification can be achieved. This might involve eliminating redundant procedures, clarifying roles and responsibilities, and ensuring that communication channels are straightforward and efficient. By simplifying the organisational framework, leaders can minimise confusion and free up resources that can be better utilised elsewhere. This not only enhances productivity but also creates a more focused and coherent work environment where employees can concentrate on what truly matters.

The concept of stillness, as articulated by Lao Tzu, underscores the importance of allowing space for reflection and mindfulness within the organisation. In a fast-paced and often hectic business world, it is easy for leaders and employees to become consumed by constant activity and noise. However, true clarity and insight often emerge during moments of stillness and quiet contemplation. Leaders who value stillness understand the power of taking a step back to reflect on their actions, decisions, and the broader context in which they operate. This practice fosters a deeper understanding of the organisation's goals and challenges, enabling more thoughtful and effective decision-making.

Encouraging periods of stillness and reflection among employees is also crucial for maintaining their well-being and enhancing their creativity. Leaders can promote mindfulness practices, such as meditation or quiet reflection periods, which allow employees to recharge and regain focus. These practices help to reduce stress and prevent burnout, creating a healthier and more sustainable work environment. Moreover, when employees have the opportunity to step back and reflect, they are more likely to come up with innovative ideas and solutions. This space for creativity can lead to breakthroughs that drive the organisation forward.

A culture of simplicity and stillness also aligns with the principle of focusing on the essential. Leaders should prioritise tasks and initiatives that have the most significant impact on the organisation's success, rather than spreading efforts too thinly across numerous projects. By concentrating on key priorities, leaders can ensure that resources are allocated effectively and that teams are working towards common goals. This focused approach not only enhances efficiency but also fosters a sense of purpose and direction among employees, as they understand how their contributions align with the organisation's mission.

Furthermore, simplicity and stillness are closely linked to the idea of creating a harmonious work environment. Leaders who embody these qualities set a tone of calm and measured deliberation, which can influence the entire organisational culture. When employees observe their leaders practising simplicity and stillness, they are more likely to adopt these behaviours themselves. This creates a ripple effect, fostering a work culture characterised by patience, thoughtfulness, and mutual respect. Such an environment encourages collaboration, reduces conflicts, and enhances overall morale.

CHAPTER 58 – HAPPINESS & MISERY

Chapter 58 of the *Tao Te Ching* highlights the benefits of minimal intervention, the interplay of happiness and misery, and the importance of non-harmful, straightforward leadership. Here's how these teachings can be applied to modern-day strategic management:

EMBRACING MINIMAL INTERVENTION

> *The government that seems the most unwise, Oft goodness to the people best supplies; That which is meddling, touching everything, Will work but ill, and disappointment bring.*

Lao Tzu's Chapter 58 of the *Tao Te Ching* presents a compelling argument for the principle of minimal intervention in leadership and governance. The wisdom in this teaching lies in the understanding that excessive control and micromanagement can lead to inefficiency, frustration, and a stifling of creativity. For leaders in strategic management, embracing minimal intervention involves creating an environment where employees are empowered to take initiative, make decisions, and execute their tasks independently, within a clear and supportive framework.

Leaders who adopt the principle of minimal intervention recognise that their role is not to dictate every action but to set the vision and provide the necessary resources and support. This approach begins with establishing a clear framework that outlines the organisation's goals, values, and expectations. Within this framework, employees are given the autonomy to determine the best ways to achieve their objectives. This empowers them to leverage their skills, creativity, and judgment, leading to more innovative solutions and a greater sense of ownership over their work.

By avoiding excessive meddling, leaders can foster a culture of trust and mutual respect. When employees feel trusted to manage their own tasks, they are more likely to be motivated and engaged. This trust encourages them to take risks and experiment with new ideas, knowing that they have the support of their leaders. Such an environment is conducive to innovation, as team members are not constrained by rigid protocols and can explore different approaches to problem-solving. The freedom to innovate not only enhances individual and team performance but also drives the organisation forward, enabling it to adapt to changing market conditions and stay competitive.

Minimal intervention also addresses the issue of employee frustration that often arises from micromanagement. When leaders are overly involved in the details of day-to-day operations, they can inadvertently create bottlenecks and slow down processes. This level of control can demoralise employees, who may feel that their expertise and judgment are not valued. By stepping back and allowing employees to take the lead, leaders can alleviate this frustration and create a more positive and empowering work environment. This shift not only improves morale but also boosts productivity, as employees are able to work more efficiently and effectively.

In practice, minimal intervention requires leaders to strike a balance between providing guidance and allowing autonomy. This involves clear communication of goals and expectations, as well as regular check-ins to offer support and feedback. However, these check-ins should not be intrusive; instead, they should serve as opportunities to reinforce trust and ensure alignment with the overall strategy. Leaders should focus on being available as mentors and coaches, rather than managers who control every aspect of their team's work. This supportive role helps to build confidence and competence within the team, fostering a culture of continuous learning and development.

Furthermore, embracing minimal intervention aligns with the broader philosophy of *Wú Wéi*, or effortless action, that Lao Tzu advocates. This philosophy emphasises the importance of aligning with the natural flow of events and allowing things to unfold organically. In a business context, this means trusting the processes and people within the organisation to operate effectively without constant oversight. By doing so, leaders can create a more harmonious and balanced work environment, where individuals feel empowered to contribute their best efforts.

RECOGNISING THE DUALITY OF HAPPINESS & MISERY

> *Misery!—happiness is to be found by its side! Happiness!—misery lurks beneath it! Who knows what either will come to in the end?*

The chapter delves into the inherent duality of happiness and misery, emphasising that these emotions are intertwined and often coexist. This profound observation is particularly relevant for leaders in the realm of strategic management, as it underscores the importance of maintaining perspective and balance throughout the organisational journey. Leaders must recognise that both success and challenges are integral to the growth and evolution of an organisation. By embracing this duality, leaders can better navigate the complexities of their roles and foster a resilient and adaptable team.

Understanding the duality of happiness and misery means acknowledging that periods of success and joy are often accompanied by challenges and setbacks. These fluctuations are natural and inevitable, and leaders must be prepared to handle both with equanimity. During times of success, it is crucial for leaders to remain grounded and avoid complacency. Celebrating achievements is important for morale and motivation, but it should be balanced with a forward-looking perspective that anticipates future challenges and opportunities for growth. By maintaining a balanced approach, leaders can ensure that their organisations continue to strive for excellence and are not derailed by unforeseen difficulties.

Conversely, during periods of difficulty or failure, leaders must remain hopeful and resilient. Misery and setbacks can provide valuable lessons and opportunities for improvement. By viewing challenges as a part of the learning process, leaders can help their teams develop a growth mindset that focuses on continuous improvement and innovation. This perspective not only enhances problem-solving capabilities but also builds a culture of resilience and perseverance. Leaders who can navigate through adversity with a calm and measured approach set a powerful example for their teams, demonstrating that challenges are temporary and can be overcome with effort and determination.

Fostering resilience within the team is essential for navigating the duality of happiness and misery. Resilience involves the ability to recover from setbacks and adapt to changing circumstances. Leaders can cultivate resilience by providing support and resources that enable employees to cope with stress and bounce back from difficulties. This may include offering professional development opportunities, promoting work-life balance, and creating a supportive work environment where team members feel safe to express their concerns and seek help. Encouraging open communication and providing constructive feedback can also help employees build resilience, as they learn to navigate challenges and grow from their experiences.

In addition to fostering resilience, leaders should encourage their teams to celebrate successes and recognise accomplishments. Positive reinforcement and acknowledgment of achievements can boost morale and motivation, reinforcing a sense of purpose and belonging within the organisation. However, these celebrations should be tempered with a realistic understanding of the ongoing journey and the need for continuous effort. By recognising both the highs and lows, leaders can create a culture that values perseverance and long-term commitment to the organisation's goals.

Leaders must also be mindful of their own emotional responses to the duality of happiness and misery. Maintaining emotional balance is crucial for effective leadership, as it allows leaders to remain focused and composed in the face of challenges. Practising mindfulness and self-reflection can help leaders manage their emotions and maintain a positive outlook, even during difficult times. By modelling emotional stability, leaders can inspire confidence and resilience in their teams, creating a supportive environment where employees feel empowered to tackle challenges and pursue success.

AVOIDING OVERCORRECTION

> *Shall we then dispense with correction? The (method of) correction shall by a turn become distortion, and the good in it shall by a turn become evil.*

The chapter thoughtfully discusses the dangers of overcorrection and the unintended negative consequences that can arise from excessive regulation and constant policy changes. In the context of strategic management, this wisdom serves as a vital reminder for leaders to exercise caution when implementing corrections and regulations within their organisations. The essence of this teaching lies in recognising that while some degree of regulation is necessary for maintaining order, an overabundance can distort the intended outcomes and create more harm than good.

Excessive correction often stems from a desire to maintain tight control over the organisation and its operations. However, when leaders impose too many rules or frequently change policies, it can lead to confusion, frustration, and a sense of instability among employees. This environment can stifle creativity and innovation, as team members become preoccupied with adhering to constantly shifting guidelines rather than focusing on their work. Furthermore, excessive correction can undermine trust within the organisation, as employees may feel that their judgment and abilities are not valued. This lack of trust can erode morale and engagement, ultimately reducing overall productivity and effectiveness.

Leaders should instead strive to create a balanced and fair environment where employees are trusted to make the right decisions. This involves establishing clear and simple guidelines that provide a framework for action while allowing flexibility for individual judgment. By empowering employees with the autonomy to navigate their roles, leaders can foster a culture of responsibility and ownership. This trust in employees' capabilities not only boosts their confidence and motivation but also encourages them to take initiative and innovate. When corrections are necessary, they should be implemented thoughtfully and with careful consideration of their long-term impact. This deliberate approach ensures that changes are meaningful and sustainable, rather than reactive and superficial.

A critical aspect of avoiding overcorrection is fostering open communication and collaboration within the organisation. Leaders should actively seek feedback from their teams and involve them in the decision-making process. This inclusive approach allows for a diversity of perspectives and ideas, leading to more well-rounded and effective solutions. By engaging employees in discussions about potential corrections and policy changes, leaders can ensure that these adjustments are informed by those who are directly affected by them. This collaborative process not only enhances the quality of decisions but also strengthens the sense of shared purpose and commitment within the team.

Moreover, leaders should focus on creating a supportive environment that prioritises learning and development. Instead of relying on punitive measures or strict regulations to drive behaviour, leaders can encourage growth and improvement through positive reinforcement and constructive feedback. This approach helps to build a culture of continuous improvement, where employees feel safe to take risks and learn from their mistakes. By emphasising development rather than correction, leaders can cultivate a resilient and adaptive workforce capable of navigating challenges and seizing opportunities.

In practice, leaders can implement this balanced approach by setting clear expectations and providing the necessary resources and support for employees to succeed. This includes offering training and development opportunities, creating channels for open dialogue, and recognising and rewarding achievements. By fostering an environment where employees feel valued and supported, leaders can mitigate the need for excessive correction and regulation. This supportive atmosphere encourages employees to take ownership of their work and contribute to the organisation's success.

LEADING WITH STRAIGHTFORWARDNESS & NON-HARM

Therefore the sage is (like) a square which cuts no one (with its angles); (like) a corner which injures no one (with its sharpness). He is straightforward, but allows himself no license; he is bright, but does not dazzle.

The chapter also provides profound insights into the virtues of straightforwardness and non-harm in leadership. This teaching emphasises the importance of being honest, transparent, and fair in interactions, ensuring that one's actions do not harm others. In the context of strategic management, leaders who embody these qualities can significantly enhance the organisational culture, fostering an environment of trust, respect, and mutual support.

Straightforwardness in leadership involves clear and direct communication. Leaders who are straightforward provide unambiguous guidance and feedback, which helps to eliminate misunderstandings and confusion. This clarity is crucial for ensuring that everyone in the organisation is aligned with its goals and expectations. By being open about intentions and decisions, leaders can build trust with their employees, as team members feel confident that they are being kept informed and that there are no hidden agendas. This transparency creates a foundation of trust that is essential for effective collaboration and teamwork.

Honesty is a fundamental aspect of straightforwardness. Leaders who value honesty are committed to truthfulness in all their dealings, even when it is challenging or uncomfortable. This commitment to truth fosters an environment where employees feel safe to express their ideas, concerns, and feedback. When leaders are honest, they set a standard for integrity that permeates the organisation. Employees are more likely to emulate this behaviour, leading to a culture of transparency and accountability. This honest communication also helps to build strong relationships, as employees trust that their leaders are reliable and sincere.

Non-harm in leadership, as described by Lao Tzu, means acting in ways that do not cause unnecessary harm or injury to others. This principle extends to both physical and emotional well-being. Leaders who prioritise non-harm are mindful of the impact their decisions and actions have on their team members. They avoid manipulative tactics that could undermine trust and morale, opting instead for approaches that foster empowerment and respect. By considering the well-being of their employees in their decision-making processes, leaders can create a supportive work environment that promotes overall health and satisfaction.

Fairness is a critical component of non-harm. Leaders who strive to be fair treat all employees with equity, ensuring that opportunities and resources are distributed justly. This fairness helps to build a sense of belonging and inclusion within the organisation, as employees feel that they are valued and respected. Fair treatment also contributes to a positive organisational culture, where individuals are motivated to perform at their best, knowing that their efforts will be recognised and rewarded appropriately.

Consistency in leadership is also vital for creating an open and respectful work environment. Leaders who are consistent in their actions and decisions provide stability and predictability, which are essential for building trust. When leaders act with integrity and adhere to the same standards they set for others, they demonstrate a commitment to fairness and transparency. This consistency helps to reinforce the values and principles of the organisation, creating a cohesive and unified team.

By leading with straightforwardness and non-harm, leaders can cultivate a positive organisational culture that enhances employee engagement and productivity. This approach not only fosters trust and respect but also encourages open communication and collaboration. Employees who feel valued and respected are more likely to contribute their best efforts, driving the organisation toward its goals. Through their commitment to these principles, leaders can create an environment where everyone feels empowered to succeed, ensuring long-term sustainability and success for the organisation.

CHAPTER 59 – MODERATION

Chapter 59 of the *Tao Te Ching* underscores the importance of moderation, accumulating virtuous attributes, and maintaining strong foundational principles. Here's how these teachings can be applied to modern-day strategic management:

PRACTISING MODERATION

> For regulating the human (in our constitution) and rendering the (proper) service to the heavenly, there is nothing like moderation.

Lao Tzu's Chapter 59 of the *Tao Te Ching* deeply emphasises the virtue of moderation, especially in the context of leadership and management practices. This teaching underscores the importance of avoiding extremes in decision-making and actions, advocating for a balanced approach that ensures sustainability and prevents burnout within teams. For contemporary leaders, embracing moderation means cultivating a management style that is thoughtful, measured, and consistently aligned with the long-term well-being of the organisation and its people.

Practising moderation involves a commitment to balanced decision-making, where leaders weigh various factors and potential outcomes before taking action. This approach avoids the pitfalls of impulsive or extreme measures that can lead to instability and inefficiency. Instead, leaders who value moderation consider the broader context, the immediate needs, and the long-term implications of their decisions. This careful deliberation helps to create a stable organisational environment where changes are implemented smoothly and thoughtfully, reducing the risk of disruptive consequences. By making balanced decisions, leaders can guide their teams through challenges with resilience and foresight.

One of the critical aspects of practising moderation is maintaining a sustainable pace for the organisation. Leaders must recognise the dangers of pushing their teams too hard or setting overly ambitious targets that lead to burnout. Moderation in goal-setting involves establishing realistic and achievable objectives that motivate employees without overwhelming them. This balanced approach ensures that team members can maintain a healthy work-life balance, which is crucial for their long-term productivity and well-being. By fostering a supportive and sustainable work environment, leaders can enhance employee satisfaction and retention, contributing to the overall stability and success of the organisation.

Furthermore, moderation in management practices includes being measured in responses to challenges and setbacks. Leaders who embrace moderation do not overreact to problems or crises but instead approach them with calm and rationality. This composed demeanour is essential for effective crisis management, as it enables leaders to assess situations objectively and develop thoughtful solutions. By avoiding extreme reactions, leaders can maintain morale and confidence within their teams, ensuring that everyone remains focused and committed to overcoming the challenges. This balanced approach to problem-solving helps to build a resilient organisational culture that can adapt and thrive in the face of adversity.

In addition to measured responses, practising moderation involves fostering a culture of continuous improvement rather than constant upheaval. Leaders should encourage incremental changes and gradual enhancements that align with the organisation's long-term vision. This approach allows for steady progress without the disruption that can come from frequent major changes. By focusing on sustainable growth and improvement, leaders can ensure that the organisation evolves in a stable and cohesive manner. This long-term perspective helps to build a strong foundation for future success, as employees are able to adapt to changes and continuously develop their skills and capabilities.

Another crucial aspect of moderation is the fair and equitable treatment of all team members. Leaders who practise moderation ensure that resources, opportunities, and recognition are distributed justly within the organisation. This fairness promotes a sense of inclusion and respect, fostering a positive and collaborative work environment. When employees feel that they are treated equitably, they are more likely to be engaged and motivated, contributing to the overall harmony and productivity of the team. By upholding principles of fairness and balance, leaders can build a cohesive and high-performing organisation that is aligned with its core values.

FOSTERING CONTINUOUS IMPROVEMENT

> *It is only by this moderation that there is effected an early return (to man's normal state). That early return is what I call the repeated accumulation of the attributes (of the Tao).*

The chapter emphasises the virtue of moderation and its role in fostering continuous improvement within an organisation. The principle of moderation is closely linked to the concept of returning to a natural state, which Lao Tzu describes as accumulating the attributes of the Tao. For leaders, this means creating an environment that encourages ongoing development and growth, ensuring the organisation remains dynamic and resilient in the face of change.

Fostering continuous improvement is crucial for achieving long-term success. Leaders must instil a culture of learning and self-improvement within their teams. This begins with setting an example by demonstrating a commitment to personal growth and development. Leaders who actively seek out opportunities to learn and improve inspire their team members to do the same. This culture of continuous improvement is built on the foundation of curiosity and openness to new ideas. By encouraging employees to pursue professional development, attend training sessions, and seek out feedback, leaders can create an environment where learning is valued and integrated into daily practices.

One of the key benefits of fostering continuous improvement is the ability to accumulate positive attributes and skills over time. This process of steady, incremental growth helps the organisation build a robust knowledge base and a highly skilled workforce. Employees who are encouraged to develop their skills and knowledge are better equipped to handle challenges and adapt to new situations. This adaptability is essential for maintaining a competitive edge in a rapidly changing business landscape. When employees are continually improving, the organisation as a whole becomes more agile and capable of responding to market shifts, technological advancements, and other external pressures.

Continuous improvement also involves creating systems and processes that support ongoing development. Leaders should implement regular performance reviews, provide constructive feedback, and set clear goals for individual and team growth. These systems help to ensure that progress is monitored and that employees have a clear understanding of their development paths. Additionally, leaders should provide access to resources such as training programmes, mentoring opportunities, and educational materials. By investing in these resources, leaders signal their commitment to employee development and create a supportive environment where continuous learning can thrive.

Furthermore, fostering continuous improvement requires leaders to cultivate a mindset of resilience and perseverance within their teams. Challenges and setbacks are inevitable, but they can be valuable learning experiences. Leaders should encourage their team members to view failures not as insurmountable obstacles but as opportunities for growth. By fostering a growth mindset, leaders can help their teams develop the resilience needed to bounce back from difficulties and continue progressing. This mindset is critical for maintaining momentum and ensuring that the organisation continues to evolve and improve over time.

In addition to individual development, continuous improvement should also focus on enhancing organisational processes and practices. Leaders should regularly review and assess the effectiveness of existing systems, seeking ways to streamline operations and eliminate inefficiencies. This iterative approach to improvement ensures that the organisation remains lean and effective, capable of delivering high-quality products and services. By continually refining processes, leaders can drive innovation and maintain a competitive advantage in the marketplace.

BUILDING RESILIENCE & ADAPTABILITY

> *With that repeated accumulation of those attributes, there comes the subjugation (of every obstacle to such return). Of this subjugation we know not what shall be the limit; and when one knows not what the limit shall be, he may be the ruler of a state.*

The chapter articulates the critical importance of building resilience and adaptability within organisations. This timeless wisdom emphasises that through the consistent development and reinforcement of core attributes, teams become more adept at navigating challenges and uncertainties. For leaders, fostering these qualities within their organisations is essential for achieving sustained success, even in the face of adversity.

Building resilience starts with cultivating a mindset that views challenges as opportunities for growth. Leaders who embrace this perspective can inspire their teams to approach difficulties with a proactive and solutions-oriented attitude. This involves fostering an environment where team members feel supported and encouraged to take risks, knowing that setbacks are part of the learning process. By promoting a culture of continuous learning and development, leaders can help their teams build the skills and confidence needed to overcome obstacles and adapt to changing circumstances. This resilience enables the organisation to maintain stability and progress, even during times of uncertainty.

Adaptability is another crucial component of long-term organisational success. In a rapidly evolving business landscape, the ability to pivot and respond to new opportunities and threats is invaluable. Leaders can enhance their teams' adaptability by encouraging flexibility in thinking and operations. This means being open to new ideas and approaches, and creating an organisational structure that allows for quick adjustments and innovations. By removing rigid hierarchies and fostering a collaborative environment, leaders can empower their teams to experiment and find creative solutions to emerging challenges. This adaptability not only improves the organisation's ability to respond to immediate issues but also positions it for long-term growth and success.

To build resilience and adaptability, leaders must also focus on developing strong, supportive relationships within their teams. Trust and collaboration are the foundation of a resilient organisation. Leaders should prioritise open communication and create a safe space for team members to share their thoughts and concerns. By actively listening and providing constructive feedback, leaders can help their teams build stronger connections and a sense of mutual support. This collective resilience ensures that the organisation can weather challenges as a united front, drawing strength from the diverse perspectives and skills of its members.

In addition to fostering a supportive culture, leaders should invest in the continuous development of their teams' skills and competencies. Providing regular training and professional development opportunities helps employees stay up-to-date with industry trends and best practices, enhancing their ability to adapt to changes. Leaders can also encourage cross-functional learning and collaboration, allowing team members to gain new insights and skills from different areas of the organisation. This holistic approach to development not only strengthens individual capabilities but also enhances the overall adaptability and resilience of the organisation.

Furthermore, resilience and adaptability are closely linked to the organisation's strategic vision and goals. Leaders should ensure that their strategies are flexible and can be adjusted in response to changing conditions. This involves setting long-term objectives that provide a clear direction, while also allowing for short-term adjustments based on new information and circumstances. By maintaining a balance between stability and flexibility, leaders can guide their organisations through uncertainty without losing sight of their overarching mission and vision.

MAINTAINING STRONG FOUNDATIONS

> *He who possesses the mother of the state may continue long. His case is like that (of the plant) of which we say that its roots are deep and its flower stalks firm:— this is the way to secure that its enduring life shall long be seen.*

The chapter also highlights the indispensable role of maintaining strong foundations for achieving enduring success. The metaphor of possessing the mother of the state, likened to a plant with deep roots and firm flower stalks, emphasises the importance of grounding an organisation in solid principles and values. For leaders, this means ensuring that their organisations are built on a foundation of ethical standards and core values that guide all actions and decisions. By doing so, leaders can create a resilient and stable organisation capable of weathering challenges and sustaining long-term growth.

Building deep roots involves a commitment to consistent adherence to ethical standards. Leaders must demonstrate unwavering integrity and transparency in their actions, setting a clear example for their teams. This commitment to ethics fosters a culture of trust and accountability, where employees feel confident that their leaders are acting in the organisation's best interests. When ethical standards are consistently upheld, it creates a stable foundation that supports all other aspects of the organisation's operations. This ethical grounding is essential for maintaining credibility and building strong relationships with stakeholders, including employees, customers, and partners.

Core values play a similarly crucial role in establishing a strong foundation. These values serve as the guiding principles that shape the organisation's culture, mission, and vision. Leaders must ensure that these core values are clearly defined, communicated, and integrated into every aspect of the organisation's activities. This involves not only articulating the values but also demonstrating them through everyday actions and decisions. By embodying the organisation's core values, leaders can inspire their teams to align their behaviours and attitudes with these principles, creating a cohesive and unified organisational culture.

Maintaining strong foundations also requires a commitment to continuous reflection and reinforcement of these principles and values. Leaders should regularly revisit and reaffirm the organisation's ethical standards and core values, ensuring that they remain relevant and aligned with the organisation's goals. This ongoing reflection helps to keep the organisation grounded and focused, even as it evolves and grows. Additionally, leaders should create mechanisms for feedback and dialogue, allowing employees to voice their perspectives and contribute to the continuous strengthening of the organisation's foundation. This inclusive approach fosters a sense of ownership and engagement among employees, reinforcing their commitment to the organisation's values and mission.

A strong foundation is not static; it must be nurtured and developed over time. Leaders should invest in the professional and personal development of their teams, providing opportunities for growth and learning that reinforce the organisation's core values. This investment in human capital ensures that employees have the skills and knowledge needed to uphold the organisation's standards and contribute to its success. By fostering a culture of continuous improvement and development, leaders can build a resilient and adaptable workforce capable of navigating challenges and driving innovation.

Moreover, maintaining strong foundations involves a holistic approach to organisational well-being. Leaders should prioritise the overall health and sustainability of the organisation, considering not only financial performance but also social and environmental impacts. This balanced perspective helps to ensure that the organisation is aligned with broader societal values and is contributing positively to the community. By integrating sustainability and corporate social responsibility into the organisation's foundation, leaders can enhance its long-term viability and reputation.

CHAPTER 60 – HARMONISING INFLUENCES

Chapter 60 of the *Tao Te Ching* uses the metaphor of cooking small fish to illustrate the delicate and subtle nature of effective governance. Here's how these teachings can be applied to modern-day strategic management:

PRACTISING SUBTLETY & CARE

Governing a great state is like cooking small fish.

Lao Tzu's Chapter 60 of the *Tao Te Ching* provides a nuanced metaphor for leadership and management, comparing the governance of a great state to the careful handling of small fish. This imagery powerfully illustrates the importance of subtlety and care in leadership, where a delicate touch is essential to maintain harmony and avoid unnecessary disruptions. In strategic management, this principle translates into a leadership style that is attentive to details and avoids heavy-handed interventions, fostering an environment where teams can thrive.

Practising subtlety in leadership begins with a recognition that not all problems require direct or forceful solutions. Leaders who employ a light touch understand the value of patience and the power of small, incremental adjustments. This approach is akin to gently turning a dial rather than flipping a switch, allowing for fine-tuning that addresses issues without causing upheaval. By making subtle, thoughtful changes, leaders can guide their organisations towards improvements in a way that feels organic and respectful to the existing structure and culture. This method preserves stability and allows for smoother transitions, minimising resistance and fostering acceptance among team members.

Attention to detail is another critical aspect of practising subtlety and care in leadership. Just as cooking small fish requires careful attention to avoid breaking them apart, managing an organisation effectively necessitates a keen awareness of the nuances and intricacies of the workplace. Leaders who are detail-oriented are better equipped to identify potential issues before they escalate and can address them in a timely and appropriate manner. This attention to detail extends to understanding the individual needs and strengths of team members, allowing leaders to tailor their support and guidance to maximise each person's contributions. By being attuned to these subtleties, leaders can create a more personalised and effective management approach.

Avoiding heavy-handed interventions is essential for maintaining harmony within the organisation. Leaders who rely on forceful measures often create an atmosphere of tension and fear, which can stifle creativity and open communication. In contrast, a more delicate and considerate approach fosters an environment where employees feel valued and respected. This involves listening to feedback, encouraging collaborative problem-solving, and giving team members the autonomy to take ownership of their work. By empowering employees and providing them with the tools and support they need, leaders can cultivate a culture of trust and mutual respect, which is crucial for long-term success.

A key component of this delicate approach is the ability to adapt and respond to the unique dynamics of each situation. Leaders must be flexible and willing to adjust their strategies based on the specific needs of their team and the context in which they operate. This adaptability requires a deep understanding of the organisation's goals, values, and challenges, as well as a willingness to experiment and learn from outcomes. By remaining open and responsive, leaders can navigate complexities with grace and ensure that their interventions are both effective and considerate.

Furthermore, practising subtlety and care in leadership involves fostering a culture of mindfulness and reflection. Leaders who prioritise these qualities encourage their teams to take the time to reflect on their actions, decisions, and their impact on others. This reflective practice helps to cultivate a deeper awareness of the interconnectedness of all aspects of the organisation, leading to more thoughtful and deliberate decision-making. By promoting a mindful approach, leaders can enhance the overall well-being and effectiveness of their teams, creating a more harmonious and productive work environment.

AVOIDING HARM & ENCOURAGING POSITIVE INFLUENCE

> *Let the kingdom be governed according to the Tao, and the manes of the departed will not manifest their spiritual energy. It is not that those manes have not that spiritual energy, but it will not be employed to hurt men. It is not that it could not hurt men, but neither does the ruling sage hurt them.*

The chapter offers profound insights into leadership, emphasising the importance of avoiding harm and encouraging positive influence within the organisation. This teaching suggests that governing according to the Tao, with principles that prevent causing harm, helps maintain harmony and minimises the potential for negative outcomes. For modern leaders, this means fostering a supportive and ethical work environment by making decisions that prioritise the well-being of employees and stakeholders, and by leading with integrity and fairness.

Leaders who aim to avoid harm in their governance must be deeply mindful of their actions' impact on others. This mindfulness involves a commitment to ethical decision-making, where leaders consider the broader implications of their choices and strive to act in ways that promote the common good. By prioritising the well-being of employees and stakeholders, leaders can create an environment of trust and respect. This ethical foundation is crucial for building a positive organisational culture where individuals feel valued and supported. When employees trust that their leaders have their best interests at heart, they are more likely to be engaged, motivated, and committed to their work.

Encouraging positive influence within the organisation means setting a tone of integrity and fairness. Leaders must model the behaviours they wish to see in their teams, demonstrating honesty, transparency, and accountability. By consistently acting with integrity, leaders build credibility and earn the respect of their employees. This respect fosters a culture of open communication, where team members feel comfortable voicing their ideas, concerns, and feedback. Transparent leadership also involves being open about decision-making processes and providing clear, honest explanations for actions taken. This openness helps to demystify leadership actions and builds a sense of shared understanding and purpose within the organisation.

Creating a supportive work environment is another key aspect of avoiding harm and fostering positive influence. Leaders should implement policies and practices that promote the physical, emotional, and psychological well-being of their employees. This includes ensuring fair treatment, providing opportunities for professional development, and offering resources for mental and physical health. A supportive environment also involves recognising and addressing the diverse needs of employees, from flexible work arrangements to creating inclusive spaces where everyone feels welcome and respected. By catering to these needs, leaders can help employees thrive both personally and professionally, which in turn enhances overall organisational performance.

Moreover, avoiding harm and encouraging positive influence means taking a proactive approach to conflict resolution. Leaders should be equipped to handle disagreements and disputes with fairness and empathy, aiming to resolve issues in a way that minimises harm and strengthens relationships. This involves active listening, validating the perspectives of all parties involved, and seeking mutually beneficial solutions. By addressing conflicts constructively, leaders can prevent minor issues from escalating and create a culture where problems are resolved in a healthy and respectful manner.

Leading by example is crucial for fostering an ethical and positive organisational culture. Leaders who demonstrate a commitment to ethical principles and positive influence set a powerful precedent for their teams. This involves not only adhering to high standards of conduct but also recognising and rewarding ethical behaviour among employees. By celebrating examples of integrity and fairness, leaders can reinforce the importance of these values and encourage others to follow suit. This positive reinforcement helps to embed ethical practices within the organisational fabric, ensuring that they are upheld consistently.

HARMONISING INFLUENCES FOR COLLECTIVE GOOD

When these two do not injuriously affect each other, their good influences converge in the virtue (of the Tao).

The chapter also imparts wisdom on the significance of harmonising influences within an organisation to foster a positive and virtuous culture. This teaching underscores the need for leaders to balance different perspectives, promote collaboration, and ensure alignment with the organisation's core values. By integrating these principles, leaders can cultivate a cohesive and unified team dedicated to common goals, enhancing the collective good and overall success of the organisation.

Harmonising influences within an organisation begins with recognising and valuing the diverse perspectives that each team member brings to the table. Leaders must create an inclusive environment where all voices are heard and respected. This involves actively seeking input from a variety of sources, encouraging open dialogue, and being receptive to different ideas and viewpoints. By doing so, leaders can tap into the collective wisdom of their teams, leading to more innovative and effective solutions. Embracing diversity in thought not only enhances decision-making but also fosters a sense of belonging and engagement among employees.

Fostering collaboration is another critical aspect of harmonising influences. Leaders should prioritise building strong, collaborative relationships within their teams. This requires creating opportunities for team members to work together on projects, share knowledge, and support one another. By promoting a culture of collaboration, leaders can break down silos and encourage cross-functional teamwork. Collaborative efforts often lead to the pooling of resources and expertise, resulting in more comprehensive and well-rounded outcomes. When team members feel supported and united in their efforts, they are more likely to be motivated and committed to achieving the organisation's goals.

Ensuring that all actions align with the organisation's core values is essential for creating a positive and virtuous culture. Leaders must consistently communicate and reinforce these values through their decisions and behaviours. This involves setting clear expectations for ethical conduct and leading by example. When leaders embody the organisation's values, they inspire their teams to do the same. This alignment creates a sense of shared purpose and integrity, guiding the organisation's actions and fostering a culture of trust and accountability. By integrating core values into every aspect of the organisation's operations, leaders can ensure that these principles are deeply ingrained and consistently upheld.

In addition to promoting collaboration and aligning with core values, harmonising influences requires a delicate balance between guidance and autonomy. Leaders should provide clear direction and support while allowing team members the freedom to take initiative and make decisions. This balance enables employees to leverage their skills and creativity, fostering a sense of ownership and responsibility. When employees feel empowered to contribute their best efforts, they are more likely to be engaged and motivated. This empowerment also encourages innovation, as team members are not constrained by rigid protocols and can explore new approaches to problem-solving.

Furthermore, leaders must be adept at managing conflicts and navigating the complexities of different influences within the organisation. This involves being attuned to potential areas of friction and addressing them proactively. By facilitating open and constructive dialogue, leaders can help team members resolve conflicts in a way that strengthens relationships and promotes mutual understanding. Effective conflict resolution ensures that differing perspectives do not become sources of division but rather opportunities for growth and improvement.

CHAPTER 61 — SERVICE & SUPPORT

Chapter 61 of the *Tao Te Ching* uses the metaphor of a low-lying stream and the qualities of stillness to highlight the power of humility and receptiveness. Here's how these teachings can be applied to modern-day strategic management:

EMBRACING HUMILITY

> *What makes a great state is its being (like) a low-lying, down-flowing (stream);—it becomes the centre to which tend (all the small states) under heaven.*

Lao Tzu's Chapter 61 of the *Tao Te Ching* eloquently illustrates the virtue of humility in leadership through the metaphor of a low-lying, down-flowing stream that nurtures everything around it. This metaphor encapsulates the essence of humble leadership, where the leader's primary focus is on serving and supporting their team. Humility in leadership is not about diminishing one's own strengths but about recognising the value and contributions of others and creating an environment where everyone can thrive.

Embracing humility requires leaders to adopt a low-profile approach, much like the stream that remains unobtrusive yet vital in sustaining life. This means shifting the focus from personal achievements and accolades to the collective success and well-being of the team. Humble leaders prioritise the needs of their team members, offering support, guidance, and encouragement to help them reach their full potential. By doing so, they create a nurturing environment where individuals feel valued and empowered, leading to greater overall productivity and morale.

Humility also involves active listening and openness to feedback. Leaders who embrace humility understand that they do not have all the answers and are willing to learn from others. This openness fosters a culture of continuous improvement and innovation, as team members feel safe to share their ideas and insights. When leaders are receptive to feedback, they demonstrate respect for their team members' perspectives and acknowledge the importance of diverse viewpoints. This inclusive approach not only strengthens decision-making but also builds trust and loyalty within the team.

In addition, humility in leadership is characterised by a willingness to admit mistakes and take responsibility for them. Leaders who own their errors and learn from them set a powerful example for their teams. This transparency and accountability build credibility and reinforce the leader's commitment to integrity. By acknowledging their imperfections, humble leaders create an environment where it is safe for others to take risks and learn from failures. This fosters a culture of resilience and growth, where team members are encouraged to push boundaries and innovate without fear of retribution.

Furthermore, humble leaders recognise the interconnectedness of their success with the well-being of their team. They understand that their role is to facilitate and enable others' success, rather than to dominate or control. This servant-leader mindset involves providing the necessary resources, removing obstacles, and creating opportunities for development. By putting the needs of their team first, humble leaders inspire loyalty and dedication, as team members feel genuinely supported and appreciated.

Building strong, trusting relationships is another key aspect of humble leadership. Trust is the foundation of effective teamwork and collaboration, and it is cultivated through consistent, honest, and respectful interactions. Humble leaders are approachable and accessible, making time to connect with their team members on a personal level. They show genuine interest in their employees' well-being and professional growth, which fosters a sense of belonging and engagement. By prioritising relationships over hierarchy, humble leaders create a cohesive and supportive team dynamic.

UTILISING THE POWER OF STILLNESS

> *(To illustrate from) the case of all females:—the female always overcomes the male by her stillness. Stillness may be considered (a sort of) abasement.*

The chapter eloquently discusses the power of stillness and its profound impact on leadership. The analogy of stillness as a subtle yet potent force draws a parallel to how effective leadership can be exercised through thoughtful and reflective practices rather than constant activity. In the context of strategic management, this principle encourages leaders to cultivate stillness, allowing for reflection, careful observation, and deliberate action.

The concept of stillness in leadership involves creating moments of pause amidst the busyness of organisational life. This pause is not indicative of inaction but rather a mindful approach to decision-making. By taking time to listen, observe, and reflect, leaders can gain deeper insights into the dynamics of their team and the organisation as a whole. This practice helps in understanding the underlying currents that might not be immediately visible during the hustle and bustle of everyday operations. It allows leaders to gather information, understand different perspectives, and consider the broader implications of their decisions.

Practising stillness enables leaders to remain calm and composed in challenging situations. In the face of crises or conflicts, a leader who can maintain their composure sets a powerful example for their team. This calmness is contagious, helping to de-escalate tensions and foster a more constructive environment for resolving issues. By staying centred and not reacting impulsively, leaders can think more clearly and make better decisions that are informed by a comprehensive understanding of the situation. This approach not only enhances decision-making but also builds confidence and trust within the team, as employees feel assured by their leader's steadiness.

Moreover, the power of stillness lies in its ability to facilitate thoughtful action. Leaders who embrace stillness do not rush into decisions or actions without careful consideration. They take the time to weigh options, anticipate potential outcomes, and plan their steps deliberately. This thoughtful approach helps to avoid hasty decisions that could lead to unintended consequences. It ensures that actions are aligned with the organisation's values and long-term goals. By integrating stillness into their leadership style, leaders can make more strategic and effective choices that drive sustainable success.

Stillness also fosters a deeper connection with the present moment, enabling leaders to be fully aware and attentive. This heightened awareness allows leaders to notice subtle changes and signals that might otherwise be overlooked. It enhances their ability to read the room, understand the needs and emotions of their team, and respond with empathy and insight. This attunement to the present moment strengthens relationships and builds a culture of trust and respect. When team members see that their leader is genuinely present and engaged, they feel more valued and supported.

Furthermore, practising stillness requires leaders to embrace humility and patience. It involves recognising that not every situation demands immediate intervention and that some issues may resolve themselves if given time. This humility allows leaders to step back and trust in the capabilities of their team, empowering employees to take initiative and ownership of their work. By creating space for others to lead and contribute, leaders can foster a collaborative and innovative environment where everyone's strengths are utilised.

BUILDING ALLIANCES THROUGH HUMILITY

> Thus it is that a great state, by condescending to small states, gains them for itself; and that small states, by abasing themselves to a great state, win it over to them. In the one case the abasement leads to gaining adherents, in the other case to procuring favour.

The chapter illuminates the profound impact of humility in leadership, particularly in building alliances and fostering unity. By comparing the dynamics between great and small states, Lao Tzu illustrates how humility can lead to powerful and mutually beneficial relationships. This principle is particularly relevant in modern organisational leadership, where the ability to build strong alliances through humility and respect can significantly enhance team cohesion and effectiveness.

In the context of leadership, humility involves recognising and valuing the contributions of all team members, regardless of their position or status. Leaders who practise humility understand that their success is intertwined with the efforts and talents of their team. By acknowledging this interconnectedness, they can foster an environment where everyone feels appreciated and valued. This sense of recognition and appreciation is crucial for building loyalty and cooperation within the team. When employees feel that their contributions are seen and valued, they are more likely to be engaged and committed to the organisation's goals.

Humility in leadership also means being open to learning from others. Leaders who adopt a humble approach are willing to admit that they do not have all the answers and that valuable insights can come from any level within the organisation. This openness to learning and growth helps to create a culture of continuous improvement and innovation. By seeking out and valuing diverse perspectives, humble leaders can make more informed decisions that benefit the entire organisation. This inclusive approach not only enhances the quality of decision-making but also strengthens the sense of unity and shared purpose among team members.

Building alliances through humility requires leaders to show respect for others, both within and outside the organisation. This respect is demonstrated through actions such as active listening, giving credit where it is due, and treating everyone with fairness and dignity. By consistently showing respect, leaders can build strong relationships based on trust and mutual regard. These relationships are the foundation of effective collaboration and teamwork. When team members trust and respect their leaders, they are more likely to work together harmoniously and support each other in achieving common goals.

Moreover, humility helps leaders connect with people on a deeper level. By being approachable and empathetic, humble leaders can create an environment where team members feel comfortable sharing their ideas and concerns. This emotional connection fosters a sense of belonging and inclusivity, which is essential for building a cohesive team. Leaders who can connect with their team members on a personal level are better able to understand their needs and motivations, allowing them to provide more effective support and guidance.

Humility also plays a crucial role in conflict resolution and problem-solving. Leaders who approach conflicts with humility are more likely to seek mutually beneficial solutions that consider the perspectives and needs of all parties involved. This collaborative approach to conflict resolution helps to prevent and mitigate disputes, maintaining harmony within the team. By addressing conflicts in a fair and respectful manner, humble leaders can build a culture of trust and cooperation, where team members feel confident that their concerns will be heard and addressed constructively.

FOCUSING ON SERVICE & SUPPORT

> *The great state only wishes to unite men together and nourish them; a small state only wishes to be received by, and to serve, the other. Each gets what it desires, but the great state must learn to abase itself.*

The chapter also profoundly illustrates the importance of leaders focusing on service and support within their organisations. This concept underscores the idea that effective leadership involves providing the necessary resources, guidance, and encouragement to help employees succeed. Just as a great state seeks to unite and nourish its people, leaders should prioritise the well-being and development of their teams to foster a positive and productive work environment.

Focusing on service in leadership means adopting a mindset that places the needs of the team at the forefront. Leaders who embrace this approach understand that their primary role is to serve and support their employees, enabling them to perform at their best. This involves actively listening to team members, understanding their challenges, and providing the tools and resources needed to overcome obstacles. By doing so, leaders can create an environment where employees feel valued and empowered, which in turn enhances their motivation and commitment to the organisation's goals.

Providing guidance is another critical aspect of service-oriented leadership. Leaders should act as mentors and coaches, offering advice and support to help team members develop their skills and achieve their professional goals. This involves setting clear expectations, providing constructive feedback, and recognising and rewarding achievements. By fostering a culture of continuous learning and development, leaders can help their teams build the capabilities needed to thrive in a rapidly changing business landscape. This investment in employee growth not only benefits individuals but also strengthens the organisation as a whole, creating a more resilient and adaptable workforce.

Encouragement plays a vital role in creating a supportive work environment. Leaders should strive to build a culture of positivity and recognition, where employees feel appreciated for their contributions. This can be achieved through regular expressions of gratitude, public acknowledgment of achievements, and opportunities for career advancement. Encouragement fosters a sense of belonging and pride among team members, motivating them to give their best effort and collaborate effectively with their colleagues. When employees feel supported and encouraged, they are more likely to be engaged and productive, driving the overall success of the organisation.

A service-oriented approach to leadership also involves creating an inclusive and collaborative work environment. Leaders should promote open communication and encourage the sharing of ideas and perspectives. This inclusivity helps to harness the collective intelligence of the team, leading to more innovative and effective solutions. By fostering a culture of collaboration, leaders can break down silos and create a sense of unity and shared purpose. This collective effort ensures that everyone is working towards common goals, enhancing the organisation's ability to achieve its mission and vision.

Furthermore, leaders who focus on service and support understand the importance of building trust and credibility. Trust is the foundation of effective leadership and is built through consistent, transparent, and ethical behaviour. Leaders who act with integrity and prioritise the well-being of their teams earn the trust and respect of their employees. This trust fosters a strong sense of loyalty and commitment, as employees feel confident that their leaders have their best interests at heart. By building trust, leaders can create a stable and supportive work environment where employees feel secure and motivated to perform at their best.

CHAPTER 62 - WORDS & DEEDS

Chapter 62 of the *Tao Te Ching* highlights the importance of the Tao as a guiding principle that offers value and protection to both good and bad individuals. It emphasises the power of words and deeds aligned with the Tao and the wisdom of seeking this path. Here's how these teachings can be applied to modern-day strategic management:

VALUING CORE PRINCIPLES & INTEGRITY

> Tao has of all things the most honoured place. No treasures give good men so rich a grace; Bad men it guards, and doth their ill efface.

Lao Tzu's Chapter 62 of the *Tao Te Ching* places significant emphasis on the importance of core principles and integrity in leadership. By valuing and adhering to these fundamental ethical principles, leaders can guide their organisations with a sense of purpose and righteousness, fostering a culture of trust and respect. The Tao, representing these core values, serves as a compass that ensures the organisation's actions are in harmony with its highest ideals. This adherence to integrity benefits not only those who naturally align with these principles but also provides guidance and rectification for those who may have deviated from the right path.

Leaders who prioritise core principles and integrity build a foundation of trust within their organisations. This trust is essential for creating an environment where employees feel secure, valued, and motivated to perform at their best. When leaders consistently demonstrate ethical behaviour, they set a standard for the entire organisation, making it clear that integrity is non-negotiable. This consistency helps to establish a culture where honesty, transparency, and accountability are deeply ingrained. Employees are more likely to emulate these behaviours when they see them modelled by their leaders, leading to a cohesive and principled organisational culture.

The adherence to core principles is not just about following rules but about embodying the values that define the organisation's identity. These values act as a guiding light, helping leaders navigate complex decisions and challenges. By staying true to these principles, leaders ensure that their actions are aligned with the organisation's mission and vision. This alignment creates a sense of coherence and direction, making it easier for employees to understand and commit to the organisation's goals. It also provides a framework for decision-making, ensuring that choices are made with integrity and consideration of their broader impact.

Integrity in leadership also involves being forthright and transparent. Leaders who are open about their intentions and actions build credibility and trust. This transparency fosters open communication and encourages employees to share their ideas and concerns without fear of retribution. When leaders communicate honestly, they create a culture of trust and mutual respect, where employees feel empowered to contribute their best efforts. This openness also helps to build strong relationships with external stakeholders, such as customers, partners, and investors, who appreciate the organisation's commitment to ethical conduct.

Moreover, valuing core principles and integrity means holding oneself and others accountable. Leaders must ensure that ethical standards are consistently upheld across the organisation. This involves implementing clear policies and procedures, providing training and resources, and taking corrective action when necessary. By holding everyone to the same standards, leaders reinforce the importance of integrity and demonstrate their commitment to ethical behaviour. This accountability helps to maintain a level playing field and ensures that the organisation's values are not compromised.

Leaders who prioritise integrity also play a crucial role in guiding and improving those who may have strayed from the path. By providing constructive feedback and support, leaders can help employees realign with the organisation's core values. This guidance is not about punishment but about fostering growth and development. Leaders can use their influence to mentor and coach employees, helping them understand the importance of ethical behaviour and how it contributes to the organisation's success. This supportive approach builds a culture of continuous improvement, where individuals are encouraged to learn from their mistakes and strive for excellence.

RECOGNISING THE POWER OF WORDS & DEEDS

> *(Its) admirable words can purchase honour; (its) admirable deeds can raise their performer above others. Even men who are not good are not abandoned by it.*

The chapter highlights the profound significance of recognising the power of words and deeds in leadership. The essence of this teaching is that the words a leader uses and the actions they take can significantly influence their standing and inspire those around them. Effective communication and integrity in actions can elevate a leader, garner respect, and foster a culture of excellence within the organisation. This understanding is crucial for leaders who wish to create a positive and productive work environment.

Communicating effectively means that leaders must be clear, authentic, and positive in their interactions. Clear communication ensures that messages are understood as intended, reducing the likelihood of misunderstandings and confusion. Authenticity in communication builds trust, as team members can see that their leader is genuine and sincere. Positive communication fosters a motivating atmosphere, encouraging employees to engage and contribute their best efforts. When leaders communicate in a way that is clear, authentic, and positive, they create an environment where team members feel valued and understood. This fosters a sense of belonging and encourages open dialogue, which is essential for innovation and problem-solving.

Acting with integrity means consistently aligning one's actions with ethical principles and core values. Leaders who act with integrity set a powerful example for their teams, demonstrating that ethical behaviour is non-negotiable. This consistency in actions builds credibility and trust, as team members can rely on their leader to do what is right, even when it is difficult. Integrity in actions also involves holding oneself accountable and being willing to admit mistakes. By acknowledging and learning from their errors, leaders model humility and a commitment to continuous improvement. This approach not only enhances the leader's credibility but also creates a culture where team members feel safe to take risks and learn from their own mistakes.

Recognising the impact of words and deeds also involves understanding that even those who have made mistakes can be guided back to the right path through positive actions and support. Leaders should approach errors and setbacks with empathy and a focus on growth. Rather than punishing mistakes, they should use these moments as opportunities for learning and development. This supportive approach helps to build resilience and encourages team members to view challenges as opportunities for growth. By providing constructive feedback and guidance, leaders can help employees realign with the organisation's values and goals, fostering a culture of continuous improvement.

Leading by example is a fundamental aspect of recognising the power of words and deeds. Leaders must embody the principles and values they wish to see in their teams. This means demonstrating ethical behaviour, effective communication, and a commitment to excellence in all their actions. When leaders lead by example, they set a standard for their teams to follow. This not only reinforces the importance of these principles but also inspires team members to strive for the same level of integrity and excellence. By consistently modelling the desired behaviours, leaders can create a cohesive and high-performing team that is aligned with the organisation's mission and values.

In addition, leaders should be mindful of the long-term impact of their words and deeds. Every interaction, decision, and action contributes to the organisation's culture and reputation. Leaders who prioritise ethical behaviour, clear communication, and positive actions can build a strong foundation for sustained success. This long-term perspective helps to ensure that the organisation's values are deeply embedded and consistently upheld, creating a stable and trustworthy environment for employees, customers, and other stakeholders.

VALUING WISDOM OVER MATERIAL WEALTH

> Though (a prince) were to send in a round symbol-of-rank large enough to fill both the hands, and that as the precursor of the team of horses (in the court-yard), such an offering would not be equal to (a lesson of) this Tao, which one might present on his knees.

The chapter elegantly emphasises the paramount value of wisdom and ethical guidance over material wealth. This profound insight reveals that the true treasures of leadership lie not in tangible assets but in the intangible qualities of knowledge, wisdom, and moral integrity. For contemporary leaders, this principle underscores the importance of prioritising the cultivation of these virtues to create a sustainable and respected organisation.

The pursuit of material wealth often dominates the landscape of organisational goals, with success frequently measured by financial metrics and physical acquisitions. However, Lao Tzu's teachings invite leaders to shift their focus towards the more enduring and impactful benefits of wisdom and ethical behaviour. By valuing knowledge and ethical principles, leaders can guide their organisations toward a more meaningful and sustainable path. This shift in focus requires a deep commitment to personal and organisational development, where learning and growth are continuously fostered.

Wisdom in leadership involves the ability to make thoughtful and informed decisions that consider the long-term impact on the organisation and its stakeholders. Leaders who prioritise wisdom are not swayed by short-term gains or superficial successes but are guided by a deeper understanding of the interconnectedness of actions and consequences. This holistic approach to decision-making ensures that the choices made are sustainable and aligned with the organisation's core values. By emphasising wisdom, leaders can navigate complexities with clarity and insight, steering their organisations towards enduring success.

Ethical guidance is equally crucial in shaping a respected and trustworthy organisation. Leaders who adhere to ethical principles demonstrate a commitment to doing what is right, even when it is difficult or unpopular. This steadfastness in ethical behaviour builds a foundation of trust and credibility, both within the organisation and with external stakeholders. Employees are more likely to be loyal and engaged when they see their leaders acting with integrity and fairness. Similarly, customers, partners, and investors are more inclined to support an organisation known for its ethical conduct. This reputation for integrity becomes a valuable asset that enhances the organisation's standing and influence.

Prioritising wisdom and ethical behaviour also involves creating a culture that values continuous learning and growth. Leaders should foster an environment where employees are encouraged to seek knowledge, develop new skills, and engage in reflective practices. This culture of learning not only enhances individual capabilities but also strengthens the organisation as a whole. By investing in the development of their teams, leaders can build a resilient and adaptable workforce capable of thriving in an ever-changing business landscape. This emphasis on growth and development aligns with the principles of the Tao, where the journey towards self-improvement and enlightenment is continuous.

Moreover, leaders who value wisdom and ethical guidance recognise the importance of leading by example. Their actions and decisions serve as a model for their teams, demonstrating the principles that the organisation stands for. By embodying the values of wisdom and integrity, leaders inspire their teams to follow suit, creating a ripple effect that permeates the entire organisation. This alignment between leadership and organisational values fosters a cohesive and unified culture, where everyone is committed to the same high standards of conduct.

EMBRACING INCLUSIVITY & FORGIVENESS

> *Why was it that the ancients prized this Tao so much? Was it not because it could be got by seeking for it, and the guilty could escape (from the stain of their guilt) by it?*

The chapter also profoundly underscores the significance of inclusivity and forgiveness in effective leadership. These concepts are central to fostering a supportive and compassionate organisational culture where every individual feels accepted, valued, and given the opportunity for growth and redemption. In the realm of leadership, embracing inclusivity and forgiveness involves recognising that everyone, regardless of their past actions or mistakes, has the potential to contribute positively to the organisation.

Inclusivity in leadership is about creating an environment where diverse perspectives and experiences are welcomed and respected. This means actively working to remove barriers that might prevent individuals from fully participating in the organisation. Leaders must be mindful of the unique challenges faced by different team members and strive to create a level playing field where everyone has the opportunity to succeed. By promoting inclusivity, leaders ensure that all voices are heard, and diverse ideas can flourish. This diversity of thought leads to more innovative solutions and a richer organisational culture.

Forgiveness, as highlighted by Lao Tzu, plays a crucial role in this inclusive environment. Leaders who practise forgiveness understand that mistakes are an inevitable part of the human experience and that growth often comes from learning from these mistakes. Instead of holding past errors against team members, forgiving leaders focus on the future and the potential for improvement. This approach fosters a culture of trust and psychological safety, where employees feel comfortable taking risks and experimenting with new ideas without fear of harsh judgment. When team members know that their leaders are willing to forgive and support them, they are more likely to be open, honest, and engaged.

Providing opportunities for growth and redemption is essential in a compassionate organisation. Leaders should implement practices that allow individuals who have made mistakes to learn and recover. This could involve providing mentorship, additional training, or constructive feedback that helps individuals understand their errors and develop strategies to avoid them in the future. By supporting their development, leaders demonstrate their commitment to the well-being and potential of their team members. This support not only helps individuals to improve but also strengthens the overall capability and resilience of the organisation.

Inclusivity and forgiveness also contribute to a culture of continuous improvement and learning. In such a culture, every experience, including mistakes, is viewed as an opportunity for learning and growth. Leaders can encourage this mindset by celebrating not just successes but also the valuable lessons learned from failures. This shift in perspective helps to reduce the stigma associated with mistakes and encourages a more proactive and resilient approach to problem-solving. When employees see that their leaders value learning and improvement over perfection, they are more likely to adopt a growth mindset and continually strive for excellence.

Moreover, inclusivity and forgiveness reinforce the principles of empathy and compassion in leadership. Leaders who practise these qualities are better able to understand and address the needs and concerns of their team members. This empathy fosters deeper connections and stronger relationships within the team, promoting a sense of unity and collaboration. Compassionate leaders are also more likely to create a supportive and positive work environment, where employees feel motivated and empowered to do their best work.

CHAPTER 63 - CAUTION & FAITH

Chapter 63 of the *Tao Te Ching* provides insights into effortless action, small actions and kindness, anticipation of challenges, and the importance of maintaining faith and caution. Here's how these teachings can be applied to modern-day strategic management:

PRACTISING EFFORTLESS ACTION

> *(It is the way of the Tao) to act without (thinking of) acting; to conduct affairs without (feeling the) trouble of them; to taste without discerning any flavour; to consider what is small as great, and a few as many; and to recompense injury with kindness.*

Lao Tzu's Chapter 63 of the *Tao Te Ching* introduces the concept of effortless action, a principle that suggests performing tasks naturally and efficiently without overburdening oneself or others. In the realm of strategic management, this principle holds significant value, as it encourages leaders to create an environment where work is executed seamlessly and without unnecessary strain. Embracing effortless action involves developing processes that are streamlined and free of undue complexity, fostering a culture where productivity and job satisfaction are maximised.

Practising effortless action begins with simplifying organisational processes. Leaders should examine existing workflows and identify areas where tasks can be made more efficient. This might involve eliminating redundant steps, automating routine tasks, or reconfiguring teams to better align with the organisation's goals. By reducing complexity, leaders can minimise the mental and physical strain on employees, allowing them to focus on their core responsibilities with greater ease and effectiveness. This approach not only enhances productivity but also boosts morale, as employees feel less overwhelmed and more capable of managing their workloads.

A key aspect of effortless action is the ability to perform tasks with a sense of natural flow and ease. This means approaching work with a mindset that values simplicity and elegance in execution. Leaders can foster this mindset by encouraging a culture of continuous improvement, where employees are empowered to seek out and implement better ways of doing things. This involves fostering an environment that supports innovation and creativity, where new ideas are welcomed and tested. By valuing efficiency and simplicity, leaders can cultivate a workforce that approaches tasks with confidence and competence, leading to more effective and satisfying outcomes.

Effortless action also involves being present and mindful in each moment, focusing on the task at hand without being distracted by unnecessary concerns. Leaders can promote mindfulness in the workplace by encouraging practices such as regular breaks, mindfulness meditation, or reflective exercises. These practices help employees stay grounded and attentive, enhancing their ability to perform tasks with clarity and precision. Mindfulness also reduces stress and anxiety, contributing to a more positive and harmonious work environment. By integrating mindfulness into daily routines, leaders can help their teams achieve a state of effortless action, where work is performed with calm and focused energy.

Another important element of effortless action is the ability to respond to challenges with grace and adaptability. In strategic management, leaders often face unpredictable and complex situations that require quick and effective responses. Embracing effortless action means remaining flexible and open to change, without being rigid or resistant. Leaders can cultivate this adaptability by encouraging a growth mindset within their teams, where challenges are viewed as opportunities for learning and development. By fostering a culture of resilience and resourcefulness, leaders can ensure that their teams are prepared to navigate obstacles with ease and creativity.

VALUING SMALL ACTIONS & KINDNESS

The passage also imparts profound wisdom about the significance of small actions and the power of kindness. The exhortation to 'consider what is small as great, and a few as many; and to recompense injury with kindness' emphasises that even the most modest actions, when performed consistently, can lead to substantial results. This principle is especially pertinent to leadership, where the cumulative effect of small, thoughtful actions can significantly enhance the overall success and well-being of an organisation.

Leaders who value small actions understand that the path to greatness often begins with seemingly insignificant steps. By paying attention to the details and taking care of small tasks with diligence and care, leaders set a standard for their teams to follow. This approach not only ensures that the foundational aspects of the organisation are strong and reliable, but it also fosters a culture of excellence and accountability. When leaders demonstrate that they value and recognise the importance of every task, no matter how minor, they encourage their team members to take pride in their work and strive for perfection in all their endeavours.

Practising kindness, particularly in response to challenges and conflicts, is another critical aspect of this teaching. Leaders who approach difficult situations with kindness and understanding can transform potential sources of friction into opportunities for growth and learning. Kindness does not imply weakness; rather, it involves a compassionate and empathetic approach to problem-solving. By addressing conflicts with a calm and patient demeanour, leaders can de-escalate tensions and find mutually beneficial solutions. This fosters a positive and supportive work environment where employees feel valued and respected, enhancing overall morale and productivity.

Moreover, kindness can be a powerful tool for building strong and trusting relationships within the organisation. Leaders who consistently demonstrate kindness and consideration towards their team members create an atmosphere of mutual respect and loyalty. Employees are more likely to feel connected to and invested in an organisation where their well-being is prioritised. This sense of belonging and appreciation can lead to increased engagement, motivation, and retention, as team members are inspired to contribute their best efforts to a supportive and caring work environment.

The concept of recompensing injury with kindness is particularly relevant in today's diverse and dynamic work environments. Leaders who embody this principle understand the importance of empathy and forgiveness in fostering a cohesive and harmonious team. When misunderstandings or mistakes occur, responding with kindness and a willingness to forgive can help to heal rifts and rebuild trust. This approach encourages open communication and a willingness to admit and learn from errors, creating a culture of continuous improvement and resilience.

Furthermore, the emphasis on valuing small actions aligns with the principle of incremental progress. Leaders who recognise the power of small, consistent efforts understand that significant achievements are often the result of accumulated minor improvements. By focusing on making steady progress rather than seeking quick fixes or dramatic changes, leaders can ensure sustainable growth and development. This approach also reduces the pressure and stress associated with large, overwhelming goals, making it easier for teams to maintain motivation and momentum.

ANTICIPATING & ADDRESSING CHALLENGES EARLY

> *(The master of it) anticipates things that are difficult while they are easy, and does things that would become great while they are small. All difficult things in the world are sure to arise from a previous state in which they were easy, and all great things from one in which they were small.*

The chapter provides profound insights into the importance of anticipating and addressing challenges early in leadership. This principle underscores the value of foresight and proactive management in maintaining the smooth operation of an organisation. By recognising potential difficulties while they are still in their nascent stages, leaders can prevent them from escalating into significant issues that could disrupt the organisational flow and morale.

Anticipating challenges involves a keen awareness of the internal and external environment of the organisation. Leaders need to be vigilant and perceptive, constantly scanning for signs of potential problems. This requires a deep understanding of the organisation's processes, people, and market conditions. By staying attuned to these elements, leaders can identify small issues that may have the potential to grow if left unaddressed. Early detection is crucial because it allows for more options in terms of solutions and mitigates the impact of the challenges on the organisation.

Addressing challenges early is a proactive approach that ensures minor issues do not become major obstacles. This involves taking immediate action to resolve the problems before they have the chance to grow. Leaders must be decisive and ready to implement corrective measures swiftly. This might mean reallocating resources, adjusting strategies, or providing additional support to team members. By acting promptly, leaders can maintain control over the situation and prevent disruptions that could affect productivity and morale. This approach also builds confidence among team members, as they see their leaders taking decisive and effective actions to safeguard the organisation's well-being.

The foresight to anticipate and address challenges early allows for better planning and resource allocation. When leaders can foresee potential issues, they can prepare adequately, ensuring that the necessary resources are available to address these challenges. This might involve setting aside contingency funds, preparing backup plans, or training employees to handle unexpected situations. Effective planning reduces the element of surprise and enables the organisation to respond to challenges with agility and confidence. This preparedness not only mitigates the impact of challenges but also enhances the organisation's resilience and ability to thrive in the face of adversity.

Moreover, a proactive approach to managing challenges fosters a culture of continuous improvement. When leaders encourage early detection and resolution of issues, they create an environment where team members are constantly seeking ways to enhance processes and prevent problems. This culture of vigilance and improvement ensures that the organisation remains dynamic and adaptable. It also empowers employees to take ownership of their roles and contribute to the organisation's overall success. By fostering a proactive mindset, leaders can drive innovation and ensure that the organisation is always moving forward.

Effective communication is also a critical component of anticipating and addressing challenges early. Leaders must ensure that there are open channels of communication within the organisation, where employees feel comfortable reporting potential issues and suggesting solutions. This transparency allows for a more comprehensive understanding of the challenges and facilitates collaborative problem-solving. When team members are encouraged to share their insights, the organisation benefits from diverse perspectives and can develop more robust solutions. This inclusive approach to problem-solving strengthens the organisation's ability to navigate challenges effectively.

MAINTAINING CAUTION & FAITH

> He who lightly promises is sure to keep but little faith; he who is continually thinking things easy is sure to find them difficult. Therefore the sage sees difficulty even in what seems easy, and so never has any difficulties.

The chapter also highlights the importance of maintaining caution and faith in leadership, emphasising the need for realistic commitments and a prudent approach to potential challenges. In the realm of strategic management, this principle serves as a critical reminder that leaders must be careful with their promises and commitments, ensuring that they are both realistic and attainable. Overpromising can lead to a significant loss of trust and credibility, as failing to meet expectations can damage the leader's reputation and the team's morale. Therefore, it is essential for leaders to carefully evaluate tasks and acknowledge potential difficulties before making any commitments.

Maintaining caution in leadership begins with a thorough assessment of the situation at hand. Leaders should take the time to understand the complexity and scope of the tasks before them, considering all possible challenges and obstacles. This involves gathering relevant information, consulting with team members, and analysing potential risks. By doing so, leaders can develop a clear and realistic picture of what needs to be done and what resources are required. This careful evaluation helps to avoid the pitfalls of underestimating the effort or overestimating the ease of a task, ensuring that promises made are based on a solid understanding of reality.

Faith in this context refers to the confidence that comes from knowing that one has made well-considered commitments. When leaders make promises based on a realistic assessment of the situation, they can move forward with the assurance that they can deliver on their commitments. This confidence is crucial for maintaining the trust of the team. When team members see that their leader's promises are reliable, they are more likely to trust the leader and follow their guidance. This trust fosters a sense of security and stability within the team, enhancing overall morale and productivity.

Moreover, by acknowledging potential difficulties, leaders can plan more effectively. This proactive approach allows leaders to anticipate challenges and develop strategies to address them before they become significant problems. It involves creating contingency plans, allocating resources appropriately, and setting realistic timelines. This level of preparation helps to ensure that the team is ready to tackle any obstacles that may arise, reducing the likelihood of unexpected setbacks. Effective planning also involves clear communication with the team, ensuring that everyone understands the plan and their role within it. This transparency helps to align the team's efforts and fosters a sense of collective responsibility and collaboration.

In addition to careful planning, maintaining caution and faith requires leaders to be honest and transparent about the difficulties they foresee. This openness builds credibility and shows the team that the leader is realistic and grounded. It also encourages team members to share their own insights and concerns, fostering a culture of open communication and mutual support. By being upfront about potential challenges, leaders can engage the team in problem-solving and decision-making processes, leveraging the collective wisdom and creativity of the group.

Furthermore, maintaining faith involves a commitment to follow through on promises made. Leaders must ensure that they have the resources, support, and determination needed to deliver on their commitments. This follow-through builds trust and reinforces the leader's credibility. It also sets a standard for accountability within the team, demonstrating that commitments are taken seriously and must be honoured. This culture of accountability encourages team members to be equally diligent in meeting their own commitments, enhancing the overall reliability and performance of the organisation.

CHAPTER 64 – ULTERIOR MOTIVES

Chapter 64 of the *Tao Te Ching* emphasises the importance of foresight, starting small, avoiding ulterior motives, and maintaining consistency. Here's how these teachings can be applied to modern-day strategic management:

EXERCISING FORESIGHT & PREVENTIVE ACTION

> That which is at rest is easily kept hold of; before a thing has given indications of its presence, it is easy to take measures against it; that which is brittle is easily broken; that which is very small is easily dispersed. Action should be taken before a thing has made its appearance; order should be secured before disorder has begun.

Lao Tzu's Chapter 64 of the *Tao Te Ching* emphasises the importance of exercising foresight and taking preventive action in leadership. This principle underscores the value of addressing potential challenges and risks before they become significant issues. For contemporary leaders, this approach involves identifying potential risks early and implementing proactive measures to prevent disruptions and maintain stability. By anticipating challenges and taking action before they fully manifest, leaders can ensure that minor problems do not escalate into major crises, allowing the organisation to operate smoothly and efficiently.

Exercising foresight requires leaders to cultivate a keen sense of awareness and vigilance. This involves continuously monitoring the internal and external environment to identify emerging trends, potential threats, and opportunities. Leaders must stay informed about industry developments, competitive dynamics, and changes in the broader economic and social landscape. By maintaining a comprehensive understanding of these factors, leaders can anticipate potential challenges and prepare accordingly. This proactive stance enables leaders to stay ahead of the curve, making informed decisions that position the organisation for success.

Preventive action is a critical component of this foresight. Once potential risks are identified, leaders must take timely and decisive measures to mitigate these risks. This may involve implementing new policies, adjusting strategies, or reallocating resources to address vulnerabilities. Preventive action also includes building robust systems and processes that can withstand disruptions and maintain continuity. For example, leaders might invest in technology to enhance operational efficiency, develop contingency plans for various scenarios, or establish protocols for crisis management. By taking these steps, leaders can create a resilient organisation that is better equipped to handle unexpected challenges.

The principle of preventive action extends to the way leaders manage their teams and resources. Leaders should foster a culture of proactive problem-solving, where employees are encouraged to identify and address issues before they escalate. This involves creating an environment where team members feel empowered to take initiative and contribute their ideas for improvement. By promoting open communication and collaboration, leaders can harness the collective intelligence of the organisation to identify potential problems and develop effective solutions. This proactive approach not only prevents minor issues from becoming major problems but also enhances overall team performance and engagement.

Moreover, preventive action involves a commitment to continuous improvement. Leaders should regularly review and assess organisational processes to identify areas for enhancement. This iterative approach ensures that the organisation remains agile and adaptable, capable of evolving in response to changing conditions. Continuous improvement also involves learning from past experiences, both successes and failures, to refine strategies and practices. By fostering a culture of learning and innovation, leaders can ensure that the organisation is always moving forward and improving.

In addition to addressing potential challenges, foresight and preventive action also involve maintaining order and stability within the organisation. Leaders must ensure that systems and structures are in place to support smooth operations and prevent disorder. This includes establishing clear roles and responsibilities, setting realistic goals and expectations, and maintaining effective communication channels. By creating a stable and orderly environment, leaders can minimise disruptions and ensure that the organisation functions efficiently.

STARTING SMALL & BUILDING GRADUALLY

> *The tree which fills the arms grew from the tiniest sprout; the tower of nine storeys rose from a (small) heap of earth; the journey of a thousand li commenced with a single step.*

The chapter offers invaluable wisdom on the virtue of starting small and building gradually, an approach that is particularly relevant to leadership and strategic management. This principle underscores the importance of breaking down large projects or ambitious goals into manageable steps, making them more achievable and less daunting. By focusing on small, incremental progress, leaders can steadily work towards their larger vision, ensuring that each step taken is deliberate and well-considered.

Starting small involves recognising that even the most significant achievements begin with a modest initial effort. Leaders who embrace this principle understand that progress is often a series of small, cumulative steps rather than a single, monumental leap. This approach helps to demystify large projects and makes them more approachable. By setting small, attainable milestones, leaders can create a sense of momentum and accomplishment that motivates their teams. Each small victory builds confidence and demonstrates tangible progress towards the larger goal, fostering a positive and proactive organisational culture.

The process of building gradually allows for continuous learning and adaptation. As leaders and their teams work through the smaller steps, they have the opportunity to gather feedback, assess outcomes, and make necessary adjustments. This iterative process helps to refine strategies and improve methods, ensuring that each subsequent step is more informed and effective. By allowing room for adjustments along the way, leaders can respond to new information and changing circumstances, enhancing the overall resilience and agility of the organisation. This flexibility is crucial for navigating the complexities and uncertainties that often accompany large projects and ambitious goals.

Moreover, breaking down large projects into smaller tasks helps to distribute the workload more evenly and manageably. This approach prevents burnout and reduces the risk of overwhelm, as team members can focus on one step at a time without feeling daunted by the scale of the entire project. It also allows for better resource allocation, as leaders can assess the specific needs of each step and allocate resources accordingly. By managing tasks in smaller increments, leaders can ensure that resources are used efficiently and effectively, optimising overall productivity.

Starting small and building gradually also fosters a culture of patience and perseverance. Leaders who prioritise steady, incremental progress understand that meaningful change and significant achievements take time. This perspective encourages a long-term view, where short-term setbacks are seen as part of the journey rather than insurmountable obstacles. By cultivating patience and perseverance, leaders can inspire their teams to stay committed and motivated, even when progress seems slow. This resilience is essential for maintaining momentum and achieving sustained success.

In addition, this approach promotes a sense of collective ownership and collaboration. When large projects are broken down into smaller tasks, team members can take on specific responsibilities and contribute their unique skills and expertise. This distributed approach not only enhances individual accountability but also fosters a collaborative spirit, as team members work together towards common goals. By involving the entire team in the process, leaders can leverage diverse perspectives and create a more inclusive and dynamic organisational culture.

AVOIDING ULTERIOR MOTIVES & MAINTAINING INTEGRITY

> *He who acts (with an ulterior purpose) does harm; he who takes hold of a thing (in the same way) loses his hold. The sage does not act (so), and therefore does no harm; he does not lay hold (so), and therefore does not lose his hold.*

The chapter highlights the profound importance of acting with integrity and avoiding ulterior motives in leadership. This principle is crucial for creating and maintaining trust within an organisation. Leaders who prioritise transparency and the greater good over self-serving actions set the foundation for a positive and ethical work environment. Acting with integrity means that leaders' actions are guided by honesty, fairness, and a genuine commitment to the well-being of their teams and the organisation as a whole.

When leaders act with ulterior motives, their decisions and actions are often driven by personal gain or hidden agendas. Such behaviour can lead to negative consequences, including a breakdown of trust and a toxic work environment. Team members are quick to sense insincerity and self-interest, which can result in disengagement, low morale, and a lack of respect for leadership. The erosion of trust can make it difficult for leaders to effectively guide and motivate their teams, ultimately hindering organisational performance.

On the other hand, leaders who act with integrity and transparency foster an atmosphere of trust and mutual respect. By being open and honest about their intentions and decisions, leaders demonstrate that they have nothing to hide and are genuinely committed to the best interests of the organisation and its members. This transparency builds credibility and encourages open communication, allowing team members to feel safe in sharing their thoughts, concerns, and ideas. When employees trust that their leaders are acting in good faith, they are more likely to be engaged, motivated, and collaborative.

Maintaining integrity also involves being consistent in actions and decisions. Leaders who are reliable and stick to their principles, even in challenging situations, reinforce the organisation's core values and set a strong example for their teams. This consistency helps to establish a stable and predictable work environment, where employees understand what is expected of them and feel secure in their roles. Consistent integrity in leadership also means holding oneself and others accountable for their actions. Leaders must ensure that ethical standards are upheld at all levels of the organisation, and that any breaches of integrity are addressed promptly and fairly.

By focusing on the greater good, leaders can align their actions with the long-term success and well-being of the organisation. This approach involves considering the broader impact of decisions on employees, customers, stakeholders, and the community. Leaders who prioritise the greater good are committed to creating value and positive outcomes for all, rather than seeking short-term personal gains. This focus on collective well-being fosters a sense of purpose and shared responsibility within the organisation, motivating team members to contribute their best efforts.

Moreover, acting with integrity and avoiding ulterior motives also means being empathetic and considerate towards others. Leaders should strive to understand the needs and perspectives of their team members, and make decisions that reflect compassion and fairness. This empathetic approach helps to build strong relationships and a supportive work environment, where employees feel valued and appreciated. By leading with empathy and integrity, leaders can inspire loyalty and dedication, enhancing overall organisational cohesion and effectiveness.

CONSISTENCY & ATTENTION TO DETAIL

> *People in their conduct of affairs are constantly ruining them when they are on the eve of success. If they were careful at the end, as (they should be) at the beginning, they would not so ruin them.*

The chapter delivers a vital lesson on the importance of consistency and attention to detail in leadership, emphasising that many efforts falter just as they are on the brink of success due to a lapse in diligence. For leaders, maintaining unwavering focus and meticulous attention to detail throughout the entire journey of achieving their goals is paramount. This principle underscores the necessity of being just as careful and attentive at the end of a project as one is at the beginning to ensure its successful completion.

Consistency in leadership means maintaining a steady and reliable approach to managing tasks and guiding teams. It involves setting high standards from the outset and adhering to them throughout the entire process. Leaders must ensure that their commitment to excellence does not wane as a project progresses. Often, the initial stages of a project are met with enthusiasm and thorough planning, but as the project moves forward, this initial vigour can diminish. By consciously maintaining a high level of consistency, leaders can avoid the pitfalls of complacency and ensure that every phase of a project receives the necessary attention and effort.

Attention to detail is equally critical, especially as a project nears completion. The final stages of a project often involve complex tasks that require precision and care. It is at this point that small oversights can have significant consequences. Leaders must cultivate a mindset that values thoroughness and precision, recognising that even minor details can impact the overall success of a project. This involves regularly reviewing progress, checking for errors, and making necessary adjustments to stay on track. By paying close attention to details, leaders can identify potential issues early and address them before they escalate.

Maintaining high standards throughout the project lifecycle also involves effective delegation and accountability. Leaders should ensure that team members are aware of their responsibilities and the importance of maintaining consistency and attention to detail. This can be achieved through regular check-ins, clear communication of expectations, and providing the support and resources needed to meet these standards. By fostering a culture of accountability, leaders can encourage team members to take ownership of their tasks and commit to achieving high-quality outcomes.

Moreover, consistency and attention to detail require leaders to stay engaged and motivated, even when faced with challenges. The journey towards achieving goals is often fraught with obstacles and setbacks that can test one's perseverance. Leaders must remain resilient and maintain their focus, inspiring their teams to do the same. This involves maintaining a positive attitude, celebrating small victories, and keeping the team's vision and purpose at the forefront. By staying motivated and engaged, leaders can drive their teams forward, ensuring that the final stages of a project are executed with the same dedication as the beginning.

Effective leaders also recognise the importance of reflective practice in maintaining consistency and attention to detail. This involves regularly evaluating the progress of a project and reflecting on what is working well and what can be improved. By taking the time to reflect, leaders can gain valuable insights and make informed decisions that enhance the project's success. Reflective practice helps to identify gaps and areas for improvement, allowing for continuous learning and growth. Leaders who prioritise reflection are better equipped to maintain high standards and ensure that their projects are completed successfully.

EMBRACING A UNIQUE PERSPECTIVE

> *The sage desires what (other men) do not desire, and does not prize things difficult to get; he learns what (other men) do not learn, and turns back to what the multitude of men have passed by. Thus he helps the natural development of all things, and does not dare to act (with an ulterior purpose of his own).*

The chapter also provides profound insight into the importance of embracing unique perspectives and seeking out knowledge and opportunities that others may overlook. This principle is critical for contemporary leaders who aspire to drive innovation and foster a culture of continuous improvement within their organisations. By thinking creatively and remaining open to unconventional ideas, leaders can identify new opportunities and develop innovative solutions that contribute significantly to the organisation's growth and success.

Embracing unique perspectives begins with a willingness to challenge the status quo and explore paths less traveled. Leaders must cultivate a mindset that values diversity of thought and is open to new and sometimes radical ideas. This involves creating an environment where team members feel empowered to voice their unique perspectives and contribute their innovative ideas without fear of rejection or ridicule. By valuing and encouraging diverse viewpoints, leaders can harness the full potential of their teams' creativity and ingenuity. This openness to new ideas not only fosters a more inclusive and dynamic work culture but also leads to the discovery of novel solutions and opportunities that might otherwise be missed.

The ability to see what others do not see is a hallmark of visionary leadership. Leaders who can identify opportunities that others overlook are often those who can drive significant advancements and create competitive advantages for their organisations. This requires a keen sense of curiosity and a commitment to continuous learning. Leaders must be lifelong learners, constantly seeking out new knowledge and staying abreast of the latest trends, technologies, and developments in their field. By expanding their horizons and broadening their understanding, leaders can gain insights that enable them to spot emerging opportunities and anticipate future challenges.

Innovation often comes from the intersection of different disciplines and perspectives. Leaders who embrace a unique perspective understand the value of cross-functional collaboration and interdisciplinary approaches. By bringing together individuals with diverse backgrounds and expertise, leaders can create a fertile ground for innovation. This collaborative approach allows for the blending of different ideas and the development of creative solutions that address complex problems. Leaders who facilitate such interactions and encourage their teams to think beyond conventional boundaries can drive transformative change and innovation within their organisations.

Another critical aspect of embracing unique perspectives is the willingness to learn from failure. Innovative ideas often come with a degree of risk, and not all experiments will succeed. Leaders must create a safe environment where failure is viewed as a valuable learning experience rather than a setback. By encouraging a culture of experimentation and resilience, leaders can empower their teams to take calculated risks and explore new possibilities without fear of failure. This approach not only fosters innovation but also builds a more resilient and adaptable organisation capable of thriving in an ever-changing landscape.

Leaders who embrace unique perspectives also understand the importance of humility and the willingness to question their own assumptions. This involves recognising that no one has all the answers and being open to new information and different viewpoints. By practising humility, leaders can foster a culture of mutual respect and collaboration, where everyone feels valued and heard. This inclusive approach not only enhances team cohesion but also ensures that decisions are informed by a diverse range of perspectives, leading to more robust and effective outcomes.

CHAPTER 65 – OVERUSE OF KNOWLEDGE

Chapter 65 of the *Tao Te Ching* emphasises the importance of simplicity, the potential pitfalls of excessive knowledge, and the value of a humble and non-intrusive approach to leadership. Here's how these teachings can be applied to modern-day strategic management:

EMBRACING SIMPLICITY & CLARITY

The ancients who showed their skill in practising the Tao did so, not to enlighten the people, but rather to make them simple and ignorant.

Lao Tzu's Chapter 65 of the *Tao Te Ching* provides profound insights on the virtues of simplicity and clarity in leadership. The ancient sages, as Lao Tzu notes, did not aim to enlighten the people by adding layers of complexity, but rather by simplifying their understanding. This principle has significant implications for modern leaders, who often face the challenge of managing intricate processes and extensive communication networks. Simplifying these elements can significantly enhance organisational efficiency and effectiveness.

Embracing simplicity starts with the recognition that complexity can often lead to confusion, inefficiency, and misalignment. When processes are convoluted and communication is opaque, team members may struggle to understand their roles and responsibilities, leading to errors and delays. Leaders who prioritise simplicity aim to strip away unnecessary complications, creating streamlined processes that are easy to understand and follow. This involves examining existing workflows and identifying areas where steps can be eliminated or simplified. By reducing complexity, leaders can ensure that each team member has a clear understanding of their tasks and how they contribute to the organisation's goals.

Clarity in communication is equally crucial for effective leadership. Leaders must articulate their vision, goals, and expectations in a straightforward and comprehensible manner. This involves using plain language, avoiding jargon, and being concise. Clear communication ensures that messages are received and understood as intended, reducing the likelihood of misunderstandings. It also helps to build trust and transparency, as team members can rely on their leaders to provide accurate and honest information. By fostering open and clear lines of communication, leaders can create an environment where everyone feels informed and valued.

Simplifying processes and communication also facilitates better alignment within the team. When roles, responsibilities, and expectations are clearly defined, team members can coordinate their efforts more effectively. This alignment ensures that everyone is working towards the same objectives, enhancing overall productivity and cohesion. Leaders can achieve this by developing and communicating clear organisational structures, setting specific goals, and establishing straightforward procedures for collaboration and decision-making. By doing so, they can minimise confusion and ensure that all team members are moving in the same direction.

Moreover, simplicity and clarity in leadership allow for greater agility and responsiveness. In a rapidly changing business environment, organisations must be able to adapt quickly to new challenges and opportunities. Simple and clear processes enable faster decision-making and execution, as team members are not bogged down by unnecessary bureaucratic hurdles. This agility is essential for maintaining a competitive edge and achieving long-term success. Leaders who embrace simplicity can create a flexible and dynamic organisational culture that is better equipped to navigate uncertainty and change.

Embracing simplicity also involves creating an inclusive and supportive work environment. When processes and communication are clear and straightforward, all team members have equal access to information and resources. This inclusivity helps to ensure that everyone has the opportunity to contribute their ideas and talents. Leaders can foster this environment by promoting transparency, encouraging open dialogue, and providing regular feedback. By simplifying the ways in which team members interact and collaborate, leaders can create a more inclusive and cohesive team dynamic.

AVOIDING THE OVERUSE OF KNOWLEDGE

> *The difficulty in governing the people arises from their having much knowledge. He who (tries to) govern a state by his wisdom is a scourge to it; while he who does not (try to) do so is a blessing.*

The chapter offers a compelling perspective on the balance between knowledge and practical wisdom in leadership. While knowledge and intellectual understanding are indeed valuable, Lao Tzu warns against an overreliance on intellectualism, which can create barriers and alienate team members. This principle underscores the importance of leaders being mindful of how they convey information and the type of knowledge they prioritise. By focusing on practical, actionable insights that everyone can understand and apply, leaders can foster a more collaborative and approachable work environment.

The overuse of knowledge in leadership can lead to complexity and confusion. When leaders inundate their teams with excessive information or complex theories, it can become overwhelming and counterproductive. Team members may struggle to process the information, leading to misunderstandings and reduced effectiveness. This scenario can create a disconnect between leaders and their teams, as employees may feel alienated by the perceived elitism of excessive intellectualism. To avoid this, leaders must simplify their communication, distilling complex concepts into clear and concise messages that resonate with their audience.

Practical wisdom, as opposed to mere intellectual knowledge, is grounded in real-world applications and experiences. Leaders who prioritise practical wisdom focus on actionable insights that can be immediately implemented to improve processes and achieve goals. This approach involves translating theoretical knowledge into tangible actions that drive results. By doing so, leaders make knowledge accessible and relevant, enabling their teams to understand and apply it effectively. This practical focus not only enhances team performance but also empowers employees by giving them the tools they need to succeed.

Moreover, leaders should be cautious about the timing and delivery of knowledge. Effective leaders recognise when and how to introduce new information to their teams. They understand that the strategic dissemination of knowledge can prevent overload and ensure that information is absorbed and utilised. This involves breaking down information into manageable segments and presenting it in a context that makes it meaningful. By pacing the delivery of knowledge and aligning it with the team's current needs and capacities, leaders can facilitate better understanding and application.

Building a collaborative and approachable work environment requires leaders to foster open communication and mutual respect. Leaders should encourage their teams to ask questions, share their insights, and express their concerns without fear of judgment. This open dialogue helps to bridge the gap between intellectual knowledge and practical wisdom, as team members feel valued and heard. When leaders are approachable and willing to listen, they create a supportive atmosphere where knowledge is shared and built upon collectively. This collaborative culture enhances problem-solving and innovation, as diverse perspectives are brought together to develop effective solutions.

Furthermore, leaders must lead by example, demonstrating the application of practical wisdom in their own actions. By showing how theoretical knowledge can be translated into effective practices, leaders set a standard for their teams to follow. This not only builds credibility but also reinforces the importance of practical application over abstract theorising. When leaders model the behaviour they expect from their teams, they inspire confidence and trust, encouraging employees to embrace practical wisdom in their own work.

LEADING WITH HUMILITY & NON-INTRUSIVENESS

> *He who knows these two things finds in them also his model and rule. Ability to know this model and rule constitutes what we call the mysterious excellence (of a governor).*

The chapter also presents a profound insight into the virtues of humility and non-intrusiveness in leadership. This principle suggests that true excellence in leadership arises from guiding without imposing one's own intellect or ego, fostering an environment where team members feel valued and empowered. Leaders who adopt this approach create a harmonious and productive workplace by supporting the natural growth and development of their teams, rather than exerting overt control over every aspect of their work.

Leading with humility begins with the recognition that leadership is not about the leader's personal glory or intelligence but about enabling the success of others. Humble leaders understand that their primary role is to serve their team, providing the support and resources needed for team members to excel. This involves actively listening to team members, valuing their input, and recognising their contributions. By doing so, leaders build trust and respect, creating a strong foundation for collaboration and mutual support. Humility in leadership also means acknowledging one's limitations and being open to learning from others, fostering a culture of continuous improvement and shared knowledge.

Non-intrusiveness in leadership is about giving team members the autonomy to take ownership of their work and make decisions. This approach empowers individuals, encouraging them to use their creativity and expertise to solve problems and innovate. By stepping back and allowing team members to take the lead, leaders demonstrate their trust and confidence in their team's abilities. This empowerment leads to increased job satisfaction and motivation, as employees feel a greater sense of responsibility and pride in their work. Non-intrusive leaders provide guidance and support when needed but avoid micromanaging, allowing team members the space to grow and develop.

The concept of 'mysterious excellence' in Lao Tzu's teachings refers to the subtle yet powerful impact of leading with humility and non-intrusiveness. Leaders who embody these principles create an environment where natural growth and development are nurtured. This approach is characterised by a sense of ease and harmony, where the team's collective efforts are seamlessly integrated towards achieving common goals. By not seeking to control every detail, leaders allow the natural talents and strengths of their team members to flourish. This organic development leads to innovative solutions and sustainable success, as the team works together in a cohesive and supportive manner.

In practice, leading with humility and non-intrusiveness involves several key behaviours. Leaders should prioritise open and transparent communication, ensuring that team members are informed and involved in decision-making processes. This transparency helps to build trust and accountability, as everyone understands the rationale behind decisions and their role in implementing them. Leaders should also focus on providing constructive feedback and recognition, celebrating successes and offering guidance for improvement without being overly critical or controlling. This balanced approach helps to maintain morale and encourages a growth mindset within the team.

Additionally, leaders should create opportunities for professional development and growth, supporting team members in their career aspirations and personal development goals. This investment in individuals' growth demonstrates the leader's commitment to their team's success and fosters a culture of continuous learning and development. By providing mentorship, training, and opportunities for advancement, leaders can help their team members reach their full potential, contributing to the overall success of the organisation.

CHAPTER 66 – LEADING FROM BEHIND

Chapter 66 of the *Tao Te Ching* emphasises the power of humility and servant leadership, illustrating how true leadership is about positioning oneself in a way that uplifts and supports others. Here's how these teachings can be applied to modern-day strategic management:

PRACTISING HUMBLE LEADERSHIP

> That whereby the rivers and seas are able to receive the homage and tribute of all the valley streams, is their skill in being lower than they;—it is thus that they are the kings of them all.

Lao Tzu's Chapter 66 of the *Tao Te Ching* emphasises the profound impact of humble leadership and the inherent strength found in being lowly and supportive, much like how rivers and seas, by positioning themselves lower than the valley streams, are able to gather their waters and thus command respect and tribute. This metaphor is crucial for modern leaders, who can draw immense value from positioning themselves as servants to their teams. Humble leadership is about creating an environment where the needs of the team are prioritised, and where the leader's role is to support and uplift their members.

Practising humble leadership involves being approachable and accessible to team members. When leaders make themselves available and approachable, they encourage open communication and foster a sense of trust within the team. This openness makes it easier for employees to share their ideas, concerns, and feedback, knowing that their voices will be heard and valued. By being genuinely interested in the well-being and development of their team, leaders can build stronger, more cohesive relationships. This, in turn, leads to increased respect and loyalty, as team members feel supported and appreciated in their roles.

A key aspect of humble leadership is putting the needs of the team first. This means prioritising the collective success of the team over individual accolades. Leaders who practise humility understand that their success is intrinsically linked to the success of their team. They are willing to make personal sacrifices and put in the necessary effort to ensure that their team has the resources, guidance, and support needed to thrive. This selflessness fosters a culture of mutual support and collaboration, where team members are motivated to work together towards common goals. By focusing on the team's needs, leaders can create a sense of shared purpose and commitment, driving overall performance and satisfaction.

Humble leaders are also willing to step back and allow others to shine. They recognise and celebrate the achievements of their team members, giving credit where it is due. This not only boosts individual morale but also reinforces the importance of each team member's contributions. By highlighting the successes of others, humble leaders create an environment where everyone feels valued and motivated to contribute their best. This approach encourages a sense of ownership and pride in one's work, leading to greater engagement and productivity.

Furthermore, humble leadership involves recognising one's own limitations and being open to learning from others. Leaders who practise humility are not afraid to admit when they do not have all the answers. They seek out the expertise and perspectives of their team members, valuing their input and insights. This willingness to learn from others fosters a culture of continuous improvement and innovation, as team members feel empowered to share their ideas and contribute to the organisation's growth. By being open to new ideas and feedback, humble leaders can adapt and evolve, ensuring that their leadership remains effective and relevant.

The concept of 'mysterious excellence' in Lao Tzu's teachings refers to the subtle yet profound impact of humble leadership. Leaders who embody humility and non-intrusiveness create an environment where natural growth and development are nurtured. This approach is characterised by a sense of ease and harmony, where the team's collective efforts are seamlessly integrated towards achieving common goals. By not seeking to control every detail, leaders allow the natural talents and strengths of their team members to flourish. This organic development leads to innovative solutions and sustainable success, as the team works together in a cohesive and supportive manner.

LEADING FROM BEHIND

> *So it is that the sage (ruler), wishing to be above men, puts himself by his words below them, and, wishing to be before them, places his person behind them.*

The chapter illuminates the profound wisdom of leading from behind, a concept that emphasises the subtle yet powerful role of a leader in guiding and supporting their team. This principle suggests that effective leaders provide the necessary guidance and support without overshadowing their team members or imposing their will. By positioning themselves behind rather than in front, leaders can empower employees to take ownership of their work, develop their skills, and achieve their full potential. This approach fosters a culture of collaboration and innovation, where team members feel valued and motivated to contribute their best.

Leading from behind involves a delicate balance of providing direction while allowing team members the autonomy to make decisions and take initiative. Leaders who practise this approach understand that their role is not to dictate every action but to create an environment where employees can thrive. This means setting clear goals and expectations, providing the resources and support needed to achieve them, and then stepping back to let the team members take the lead. By doing so, leaders demonstrate trust in their team's abilities and encourage a sense of responsibility and accountability. This empowerment leads to higher levels of engagement and creativity, as team members feel confident and invested in their work.

A key aspect of leading from behind is the ability to provide guidance without micromanaging. Leaders must be available to offer support and advice when needed but avoid interfering unnecessarily in the team's processes. This requires a high level of emotional intelligence and a deep understanding of the team's dynamics and needs. By observing and listening, leaders can identify when to step in and when to let the team navigate challenges independently. This approach not only builds the team's problem-solving and decision-making skills but also fosters a sense of ownership and pride in their accomplishments.

Another critical component of leading from behind is recognising and celebrating the achievements of team members. Leaders who lead from behind give credit where it is due, highlighting the contributions of their team members and acknowledging their efforts. This recognition boosts morale and reinforces the importance of each individual's role in the team's success. By shifting the focus from themselves to their team, leaders create a positive and supportive work environment where everyone feels valued and motivated to excel. This approach also encourages a culture of collaboration, as team members are more likely to support and uplift one another when they see their contributions being recognised and appreciated.

Leading from behind also involves fostering a culture of continuous learning and growth. Leaders should create opportunities for professional development and encourage team members to pursue their career goals. This investment in the team's growth demonstrates the leader's commitment to their success and helps to build a more capable and resilient workforce. By providing mentorship, training, and opportunities for advancement, leaders can help their team members develop their skills and reach their full potential. This focus on growth and development aligns with the principles of the Tao, where the journey towards self-improvement and enlightenment is continuous.

Furthermore, leading from behind requires humility and self-awareness. Leaders must be willing to put their egos aside and prioritise the needs of their team. This means being open to feedback, admitting when they are wrong, and being willing to learn from their team members. By demonstrating humility, leaders set a powerful example for their team and create a culture of mutual respect and trust. This openness and vulnerability foster deeper connections and stronger relationships within the team, enhancing overall cohesion and performance.

ENSURING UNSEEN GUIDANCE

> *In this way though he has his place above them, men do not feel his weight, nor though he has his place before them, do they feel it an injury to them.*

The chapter delves into the art of providing guidance and influence in leadership without being burdensome. This principle underscores the importance of leaders being present and supportive while ensuring that their presence does not stifle or overwhelm their team members. Effective leaders understand that their role is to guide and support their team in a way that empowers rather than oppresses, fostering a work environment where employees feel encouraged and capable of performing at their best.

Unseen guidance starts with the ability to offer support and direction subtly and considerately. Leaders who master this art do so by being attentive to the needs of their team, offering help when needed without overshadowing or micromanaging. This approach involves understanding the strengths and weaknesses of team members, knowing when to step in and provide guidance, and when to step back and allow individuals to take initiative and ownership of their tasks. By doing so, leaders create a balance where their influence is felt in a positive and constructive manner, rather than as a domineering force.

An essential aspect of unseen guidance is the development of trust within the team. Leaders must demonstrate reliability and consistency in their actions, ensuring that team members feel confident in their leader's support and direction. Trust is built through open and transparent communication, where leaders share their vision and goals clearly and encourage team members to voice their opinions and concerns. This openness fosters a collaborative environment where everyone feels included and valued. When team members trust their leaders, they are more likely to be receptive to guidance and motivated to contribute their best efforts.

Furthermore, subtle guidance involves recognising and celebrating the achievements of team members. Leaders should highlight successes and provide positive reinforcement, showing appreciation for the hard work and dedication of their team. This recognition boosts morale and encourages a culture of mutual support and respect. By celebrating the contributions of individuals, leaders reinforce the idea that everyone plays a vital role in the team's success. This approach helps to create a positive and motivating work environment where team members feel empowered to excel.

Effective leaders also understand the importance of providing constructive feedback in a way that is supportive rather than critical. Feedback should be delivered with the intention of helping team members grow and improve, rather than pointing out faults. Leaders should focus on specific behaviours and outcomes, offering practical suggestions for improvement. This constructive approach helps to build confidence and competence within the team, as employees feel supported in their development journey. By providing feedback in a considerate and respectful manner, leaders ensure that their guidance is empowering and beneficial.

In addition, unseen guidance involves the ability to inspire and motivate without imposing one's will. Leaders should lead by example, demonstrating the values and behaviours they wish to see in their team. This includes showing commitment, integrity, and a strong work ethic. By embodying these qualities, leaders inspire their team to follow suit, creating a cohesive and dedicated workforce. Inspiration often comes from the leader's ability to connect with their team on a personal level, understanding their motivations and aspirations, and aligning them with the organisation's goals. This alignment fosters a sense of purpose and direction, driving collective success.

CULTIVATING RESPECT & LOYALTY

> Therefore all in the world delight to exalt him and do not weary of him. Because he does not strive, no one finds it possible to strive with him.

The chapter also delves into the profound concept of cultivating respect and loyalty through humility and servant leadership. This principle highlights the idea that leaders who eschew personal recognition and power in favour of serving their teams and fostering a collaborative environment are more likely to inspire genuine respect and loyalty from their employees. By focusing on the collective success of the team rather than individual accolades, leaders can create an atmosphere of harmony and cooperation that drives organisational success.

Practising humility in leadership means putting the needs and well-being of the team above one's own ego. Humble leaders understand that their primary role is to support and uplift their team members, recognising that their success is intertwined with the success of the team. This involves actively listening to team members, valuing their input, and giving credit where it is due. By doing so, leaders build trust and respect, as team members feel appreciated and recognised for their contributions. This mutual respect forms the foundation of a strong and cohesive team, where everyone is motivated to work towards common goals.

Servant leadership, a concept deeply rooted in humility, further emphasises the leader's role as a facilitator and supporter. Leaders who adopt this approach prioritise the development and well-being of their team members, providing the resources, guidance, and encouragement needed for them to excel. This involves creating opportunities for growth and professional development, fostering a culture of continuous learning, and being genuinely invested in the personal and professional success of each team member. By serving their team in this way, leaders create an environment where employees feel valued, supported, and empowered to reach their full potential.

A critical aspect of cultivating respect and loyalty is the leader's ability to foster a collaborative and inclusive work environment. This means encouraging open communication, promoting teamwork, and creating a space where diverse perspectives are welcomed and valued. Leaders should actively seek out and consider the ideas and feedback of their team members, fostering a sense of ownership and involvement in decision-making processes. This inclusivity not only enhances the quality of decisions but also strengthens the bonds within the team, as members feel that their contributions are meaningful and impactful.

Leaders who practise humility and servant leadership also understand the importance of leading by example. By demonstrating the values and behaviours they wish to see in their team, leaders set a standard for integrity, dedication, and collaboration. This modelling of desired behaviours reinforces the organisation's values and creates a culture of accountability and excellence. When team members see their leaders embodying these principles, they are more likely to adopt similar attitudes and approaches, creating a ripple effect that enhances the overall culture of the organisation.

Moreover, the concept of 'not striving' as highlighted by Lao Tzu, emphasises the importance of avoiding unnecessary competition and conflict. Leaders who do not seek to outshine others or engage in power struggles create a more harmonious and cooperative work environment. This approach fosters a sense of unity and collective purpose, as team members are encouraged to support and uplift each other rather than compete. By focusing on shared goals and mutual success, leaders can cultivate a culture of collaboration where everyone works together towards the greater good of the organisation.

CHAPTER 67 - ECONOMY

Chapter 67 of the *Tao Te Ching* focuses on the value of gentleness, economy, and humility, presenting them as essential attributes for greatness. Here's how these teachings can be applied to modern-day strategic management:

EMBRACING GENTLENESS

The first is gentleness; with that gentleness I can be bold.

Lao Tzu's Chapter 67 of the *Tao Te Ching* profoundly emphasises the power of embracing gentleness in leadership. Gentleness, as Lao Tzu articulates, is not synonymous with weakness. Instead, it is characterised by kindness, respect, and empathy, virtues that can significantly enhance strategic management and leadership effectiveness. In a world where leadership is often associated with assertiveness and dominance, Lao Tzu's counsel to embrace gentleness offers a refreshing and impactful perspective.

Embracing gentleness in leadership means prioritising the well-being of team members and fostering an environment of mutual respect. Gentle leaders approach their roles with a genuine concern for the welfare of their employees, understanding that treating others with kindness can inspire loyalty and trust. This compassionate approach creates a supportive and positive work environment where team members feel valued and respected. When leaders demonstrate empathy and understanding, they build stronger relationships with their team, encouraging open communication and collaboration. This sense of belonging and security can significantly enhance overall team cohesion and productivity.

A gentle leader recognises the importance of listening and being attentive to the needs and concerns of their team. This involves not only hearing what team members have to say but also understanding their perspectives and emotions. By being present and engaged, leaders can address issues more effectively and provide the necessary support to help their team succeed. This attentive approach fosters a culture of trust, as team members feel confident that their voices are heard and their contributions matter. Trust is a fundamental element of any successful team, and gentle leadership is a powerful means of cultivating it.

Moreover, gentleness in leadership allows for bold and decisive actions. Leaders who have the backing and goodwill of their team can make bold decisions with the confidence that their team will support and implement them. This support is rooted in the trust and respect that the leader has earned through their gentle and empathetic approach. When team members feel valued and appreciated, they are more likely to be motivated and committed to achieving the organisation's goals. This collective effort enables leaders to take risks and pursue innovative solutions, knowing that their team is aligned and ready to move forward together.

Gentleness also involves a commitment to fairness and integrity. Gentle leaders are consistent and transparent in their actions, ensuring that they treat everyone with the same level of respect and consideration. This fairness builds credibility and reinforces the leader's commitment to ethical behaviour. By leading with integrity, gentle leaders create a culture of honesty and accountability, where team members feel comfortable expressing their opinions and taking responsibility for their actions. This ethical foundation is crucial for maintaining a positive and productive work environment.

In addition, embracing gentleness helps to reduce conflict and tension within the team. Gentle leaders approach conflicts with a focus on resolution and understanding, rather than aggression or blame. This involves being patient and open-minded, seeking to understand the root causes of disagreements and working collaboratively to find solutions. By addressing conflicts in a gentle and respectful manner, leaders can prevent issues from escalating and maintain a harmonious work environment. This proactive approach to conflict resolution enhances overall team dynamics and ensures that challenges are addressed constructively.

PRACTISING ECONOMY

The second is economy; with that economy I can be liberal.

The chapter presents a profound reflection on the principle of economy in leadership, emphasising the wise and efficient use of resources as a pathway to greater generosity and sustainability. In the context of strategic management, economy refers to the careful and judicious allocation of resources to achieve organisational goals while avoiding wastefulness. This principle underscores the importance of frugality not for its own sake, but as a means to create a more sustainable and effective organisation that can invest generously in its people and future.

Practising economy in leadership begins with a thorough understanding of the organisation's resources and how they are being utilised. Leaders must be vigilant in assessing expenditures, identifying areas where resources can be conserved or reallocated more effectively. This involves a detailed analysis of budgets, operations, and processes to pinpoint inefficiencies and eliminate waste. By streamlining operations and reducing unnecessary costs, leaders can ensure that resources are directed towards the most critical areas that drive organisational success. This disciplined approach to resource management not only enhances financial stability but also positions the organisation for long-term growth and resilience.

The concept of economy also extends to how leaders invest in their team's development. By being frugal and efficient with resources, leaders can free up funds to invest in the growth and advancement of their employees. This might include providing opportunities for professional development, offering training programmes, and creating pathways for career progression. Investing in the team's development is a strategic move that pays dividends in the form of enhanced skills, increased productivity, and higher employee engagement. When team members feel supported and valued, they are more likely to be motivated and committed to the organisation's goals, leading to a more dynamic and innovative workplace.

Moreover, practising economy allows leaders to be more generous in rewarding performance. Recognising and rewarding employees for their contributions is an essential aspect of building a motivated and high-performing team. By managing resources wisely, leaders can ensure that there are sufficient funds available to offer competitive salaries, bonuses, and other forms of recognition. This generosity, rooted in prudent resource management, reinforces a culture of excellence and appreciation, where employees feel their hard work and dedication are acknowledged and valued.

Another critical aspect of economy in leadership is the ability to balance short-term needs with long-term goals. Leaders must navigate the delicate equilibrium between addressing immediate operational requirements and making strategic investments for the future. This involves making thoughtful and informed decisions that consider the long-term impact on the organisation. By practising economy, leaders can build a sustainable foundation that supports continuous growth and adaptation. This forward-thinking approach ensures that the organisation remains agile and prepared to meet future challenges and opportunities.

Furthermore, the principle of economy encourages leaders to adopt a mindset of continuous improvement. Leaders should constantly seek ways to enhance efficiency and effectiveness, exploring new technologies, processes, and methodologies that can drive better outcomes. This commitment to improvement fosters a culture of innovation, where team members are encouraged to think creatively and contribute ideas for optimising resource use. By embedding the value of economy into the organisational culture, leaders can inspire a collective effort towards achieving greater efficiency and sustainability.

CULTIVATING HUMILITY

> *The third is shrinking from taking precedence of others; with that, I can become a vessel of the highest honour.*

The chapter presents a timeless lesson on the importance of cultivating humility in leadership. This principle suggests that true honour and effective leadership come not from seeking personal glory but from prioritising the needs and successes of others. In a world where leadership is often associated with assertiveness and self-promotion, Lao Tzu's call for humility offers a powerful counterbalance, emphasising the value of selflessness and service in guiding and inspiring teams.

Cultivating humility in leadership begins with the recognition that the leader's role is to serve their team, not to dominate it. Leaders who embrace humility understand that their primary responsibility is to elevate and support their team members. This involves acknowledging the contributions of others and giving credit where it is due. By doing so, leaders build a culture of mutual respect and collaboration, where everyone feels valued and appreciated for their efforts. This culture fosters strong relationships and trust, as team members see that their leader is genuinely invested in their success and well-being.

A humble leader is also open to learning from others. They recognise that they do not have all the answers and are willing to seek out and consider the perspectives and expertise of their team members. This openness to learning not only enhances the leader's own knowledge and skills but also creates a more dynamic and innovative organisation. By valuing the input of others and being willing to adapt to new ideas, humble leaders can drive continuous improvement and foster a culture of curiosity and creativity. This inclusive approach encourages team members to share their insights and contribute to the organisation's growth and success.

Humility in leadership also means being willing to step back and allow others to take the spotlight. Leaders who prioritise the achievements of their team over their own personal recognition create an environment where everyone has the opportunity to shine. This not only boosts individual morale and motivation but also strengthens the overall performance of the team. By placing the needs of others first, leaders demonstrate their commitment to the collective success of the organisation. This selflessness inspires loyalty and dedication, as team members feel supported and empowered to reach their full potential.

Furthermore, humility involves recognising and embracing one's own limitations. Humble leaders are not afraid to admit when they are wrong or when they need help. This honesty and vulnerability build trust and credibility, as team members see that their leader is authentic and trustworthy. By modelling humility, leaders encourage their team members to do the same, creating a culture of transparency and continuous learning. This environment of openness and honesty fosters deeper connections and stronger relationships within the team, enhancing overall cohesion and collaboration.

Lao Tzu's teachings on cultivating humility also emphasise the importance of leading by example. Leaders who embody humility in their actions set a powerful standard for their team to follow. This involves demonstrating respect, kindness, and empathy in all interactions, treating everyone with dignity and consideration. By leading with humility, leaders create a positive and supportive work environment where team members feel safe and valued. This approach not only enhances individual and team performance but also contributes to a more inclusive and collaborative organisational culture.

RECOGNISING THE STRENGTH IN GENTLENESS

Gentleness is sure to be victorious even in battle, and firmly to maintain its ground.

The chapter beautifully underscores the paradoxical strength found in gentleness, particularly in leadership and conflict resolution. This principle suggests that gentleness, often perceived as a form of weakness, can be a formidable force when applied wisely. Leaders who approach challenges with calmness and composure are more likely to find effective solutions and maintain stability within their organisations. By embodying gentleness, leaders can navigate difficult situations and emerge victorious without resorting to aggression or force, thus fostering a more harmonious and cooperative work environment.

Recognising the strength in gentleness begins with understanding that true power does not always lie in force or dominance. Leaders who embrace gentleness approach conflicts and challenges with a mindset of understanding and empathy. They are able to remain calm and composed, even in the face of adversity, which allows them to think more clearly and make rational decisions. This calm demeanour helps to de-escalate tensions and fosters a more constructive atmosphere for problem-solving. By maintaining their composure, gentle leaders set an example for their team, encouraging them to respond to challenges with similar grace and poise.

Gentleness in leadership also involves active listening and seeking to understand the perspectives of others. Leaders who practise gentleness are skilled at empathising with their team members, acknowledging their concerns, and validating their feelings. This empathetic approach helps to build trust and rapport, as team members feel heard and respected. When conflicts arise, gentle leaders are able to navigate them with sensitivity and care, focusing on finding mutually beneficial solutions rather than imposing their will. This approach not only resolves conflicts more effectively but also strengthens the bonds within the team, fostering a sense of unity and collaboration.

Moreover, gentleness allows leaders to maintain stability within the organisation during times of change or uncertainty. By approaching transitions and challenges with a steady hand, leaders can provide reassurance and support to their team. This stability helps to reduce anxiety and maintain morale, as team members feel confident that their leader is capable of guiding them through difficult times. Gentle leadership also promotes resilience, as team members are encouraged to approach challenges with a positive and proactive mindset. This resilience is essential for navigating the complexities of the business world and achieving long-term success.

The strength of gentleness is also evident in decision-making processes. Gentle leaders are able to weigh options carefully, considering the impact of their decisions on all stakeholders. This thoughtful approach ensures that decisions are made with integrity and fairness, taking into account the well-being of the team and the organisation as a whole. By avoiding rash or impulsive actions, gentle leaders are able to make more informed and effective decisions that align with the organisation's values and goals. This deliberate decision-making process helps to build credibility and trust, as team members see that their leader is thoughtful and considerate in their actions.

Furthermore, gentleness fosters a culture of mutual respect and cooperation. Leaders who prioritise gentleness create an environment where team members feel valued and empowered to contribute their ideas and talents. This inclusive culture encourages innovation and collaboration, as team members are more likely to share their insights and work together towards common goals. By cultivating an atmosphere of gentleness and respect, leaders can enhance overall team performance and drive organisational success.

AVOIDING EXCESSIVE PURSUIT OF POWER

> *Now-a-days they give up gentleness and are all for being bold; economy, and are all for being liberal; the hindmost place, and seek only to be foremost;—(of all which the end is) death.*

The chapter also provides a critical commentary on the dangers of the excessive pursuit of power, recognition, and material success in leadership. This principle highlights the negative consequences that can arise from prioritising personal ambition and external achievements over more meaningful and sustainable values. Leaders who focus solely on gaining power and recognition may find themselves and their organisations facing burnout, unethical behaviour, and a toxic work environment. These adverse outcomes can erode the foundation of trust, respect, and well-being within the organisation, ultimately leading to its downfall.

The pursuit of power often entails a relentless drive for control and dominance, which can strain relationships and create an atmosphere of fear and competition. Leaders who are overly focused on their own advancement may neglect the needs and development of their team, resulting in disengagement and dissatisfaction among employees. This singular focus on personal gain can lead to unethical behaviour, as leaders may resort to manipulation, deceit, or exploitation to achieve their goals. Such actions not only compromise the leader's integrity but also set a negative example for the team, fostering a culture of mistrust and unethical conduct.

Recognition, while important for motivation and morale, can become detrimental when it is sought excessively. Leaders who crave constant validation and accolades may prioritise their public image over the genuine well-being of their team and organisation. This need for recognition can lead to performative actions that are more about gaining approval than achieving meaningful results. Additionally, the pressure to maintain a facade of perfection can lead to stress and burnout, as leaders strive to meet unrealistic expectations and avoid vulnerability. This relentless pursuit of external validation can create a superficial and unsustainable work culture, where true progress and growth are hindered.

Material success, often measured in terms of financial gain and tangible assets, can also become a pitfall for leaders. While financial stability is essential for any organisation, an excessive focus on material wealth can overshadow more critical aspects of leadership, such as ethical conduct, employee well-being, and long-term sustainability. Leaders who prioritise profit above all else may implement cost-cutting measures that harm employee morale and productivity or make short-sighted decisions that jeopardise the organisation's future. This narrow focus on material success can lead to a culture of greed and exploitation, where the well-being of employees and the broader community is disregarded.

In contrast, Lao Tzu advocates for a leadership approach grounded in gentleness, economy, and humility. By embracing these principles, leaders can create a more balanced and healthy organisational culture. Gentleness involves treating others with kindness, respect, and empathy, fostering a supportive and positive work environment. Leaders who approach challenges with calmness and composure are more likely to find effective solutions and maintain stability within the organisation. This gentle approach helps leaders navigate difficult situations and build strong, trusting relationships with their team.

Economy, or the wise and efficient use of resources, is essential for sustainable leadership. Leaders who practise economy avoid wastefulness and ensure that resources are allocated effectively to achieve organisational goals. This frugal approach allows leaders to be more generous in investing in their team's development, providing opportunities for growth, and rewarding performance. By focusing on economy, leaders can create a more resilient and adaptable organisation that is better equipped to navigate challenges and seize opportunities.

Humility, the third principle emphasised by Lao Tzu, involves recognising the value of placing others before oneself. Leaders who cultivate humility avoid seeking personal glory and instead focus on elevating their team members. This approach fosters a culture of mutual respect and collaboration, where everyone's contributions are valued and appreciated. Humble leaders are open to learning from others, adapting to new ideas, and creating a more inclusive and innovative organisation. By prioritising the collective success of the team over individual accolades, leaders can inspire loyalty and dedication, driving overall performance and satisfaction.

CHAPTER 68 – HIGHER GOALS

Chapter 68 of the *Tao Te Ching* explores the virtues of skillful conduct, humility, and non-contention in leadership. Here's how these teachings can be applied to modern-day strategic management:

LEADING WITH SKILL & HUMILITY

> *He who in (Tao's) wars has skill assumes no martial port; He who fights with most good will to rage makes no resort.*

Lao Tzu's Chapter 68 of the *Tao Te Ching* highlights the profound virtue of leading with skill and humility. This principle emphasises the importance of achieving goals through competence and expertise while maintaining a humble and composed demeanour. In the realm of strategic management, this approach is particularly impactful, as it enables leaders to inspire respect and foster cooperation without resorting to forceful or domineering tactics.

Leading with skill entails a deep understanding of one's field and the ability to navigate complex challenges with proficiency. Effective leaders continuously develop their expertise, staying informed about the latest trends, best practices, and innovations. This commitment to mastery allows them to make informed decisions and guide their teams effectively. However, skill alone is not enough. It must be coupled with humility to truly inspire and mobilise a team. Humble leaders do not boast about their capabilities or achievements; instead, they let their actions and results speak for themselves. This quiet confidence builds trust and respect among team members, as they see their leader as capable and reliable.

Humility in leadership also involves recognising and valuing the contributions of others. Leaders who practise humility understand that their success is intertwined with the efforts of their team. They acknowledge the strengths and expertise of their team members, creating an environment where everyone feels valued and appreciated. This recognition fosters a sense of ownership and responsibility, as team members are motivated to contribute their best efforts. By giving credit where it is due and celebrating the achievements of others, humble leaders build a culture of mutual respect and collaboration.

Furthermore, humility allows leaders to be approachable and open to feedback. Leaders who are not driven by ego are more likely to listen to their team members, consider different perspectives, and adapt their strategies based on constructive criticism. This openness to learning and improvement creates a dynamic and innovative work environment, where team members feel empowered to share their ideas and take risks. By being receptive to feedback, humble leaders demonstrate their commitment to growth and continuous improvement, both for themselves and the organisation.

Humility also plays a crucial role in conflict resolution. Leaders who approach conflicts with a calm and composed demeanour are better equipped to navigate tense situations and find amicable solutions. By avoiding aggression and maintaining a focus on understanding and empathy, they can de-escalate conflicts and foster a more cooperative atmosphere. This gentle approach to conflict resolution helps to build stronger relationships within the team, as members feel that their concerns are heard and addressed with respect.

In addition, leading with skill and humility involves setting an example for others to follow. Leaders who embody these qualities serve as role models, inspiring their team members to adopt similar attitudes and behaviours. This modelling of desired behaviours reinforces the organisation's values and creates a cohesive and aligned team. By demonstrating competence and humility in their actions, leaders encourage their team to strive for excellence while remaining grounded and respectful.

The combination of skill and humility in leadership ultimately leads to a more effective and harmonious organisation. Leaders who prioritise these qualities can achieve their goals while maintaining a positive and supportive work environment. This balanced approach not only enhances individual and team performance but also contributes to the long-term success and sustainability of the organisation. By leading with skill and humility, leaders can navigate the complexities of the business world with grace and effectiveness, ensuring that their leadership is both impactful and inspiring.

AVOIDING AGGRESSION & PROMOTING GOODWILL

> *He who vanquishes yet still keeps from his foes apart; He whose hests men most fulfil yet humbly plies his art.*

The chapter advocates for the avoidance of aggression and the promotion of goodwill in leadership. This principle is particularly significant in the realm of strategic management, where conflicts and challenges are inevitable. Lao Tzu suggests that leaders who can vanquish their challenges without resorting to aggression, and who maintain humility even when their directives are followed, can foster an environment of mutual respect and cooperation.

Leaders should approach conflicts and challenges with a calm and composed mindset. This means refraining from aggressive tactics and instead seeking solutions that are fair and beneficial to all parties involved. Aggression often leads to heightened tensions and prolonged disputes, which can be detrimental to the overall functioning and morale of an organisation. On the other hand, a calm and composed approach allows leaders to assess situations objectively, consider different perspectives, and develop well-rounded solutions. This method fosters a more positive and constructive atmosphere, where conflicts are resolved efficiently and amicably.

Promoting goodwill is essential for building strong and positive relationships within and outside the organisation. Leaders who prioritise goodwill demonstrate a genuine concern for the well-being of others, which helps to build trust and rapport. This involves showing empathy, being transparent in communication, and being willing to compromise when necessary. By fostering goodwill, leaders create an environment where team members feel valued and respected, which in turn motivates them to give their best effort. This positive atmosphere is conducive to collaboration and innovation, as employees are more likely to share their ideas and work together towards common goals.

Maintaining humility is a key aspect of promoting goodwill. Humble leaders recognise that their success is not solely a result of their efforts but is also due to the contributions of their team. They acknowledge and appreciate the hard work and talents of others, giving credit where it is due. This humility helps to build a culture of respect and mutual support, as team members see that their leader values their input and contributions. By remaining humble, even when in positions of power, leaders can avoid creating a hierarchical and authoritarian environment. Instead, they can foster a sense of equality and inclusion, where everyone's voice is heard and valued.

Moreover, humility allows leaders to be more adaptable and open to feedback. Leaders who are not driven by ego are more willing to listen to others, learn from their mistakes, and make necessary adjustments. This openness to improvement enhances the overall effectiveness of the organisation, as it ensures that strategies and practices are continuously refined and optimised. By being receptive to feedback, leaders can also build stronger relationships with their team, as employees feel that their opinions and insights are valued and taken into consideration.

The strength of promoting goodwill and avoiding aggression is also evident in external relationships. Leaders who approach negotiations and partnerships with a spirit of goodwill are more likely to build lasting and mutually beneficial alliances. This approach fosters trust and cooperation, as external partners see that the leader is fair and honourable. By avoiding aggressive tactics and instead focusing on creating win-win situations, leaders can enhance their organisation's reputation and establish a network of supportive and collaborative relationships.

EMBRACING NON-CONTENTION

> Thus we say, 'He ne'er contends, And therein is his might.' Thus we say, 'Men's wills he bends, That they with him unite.'

The chapter offers profound insight into the concept of non-contention as a powerful leadership principle. Non-contention involves avoiding unnecessary conflicts and focusing on fostering unity and cooperation within the team. Leaders who embrace this approach strive to create a harmonious and collaborative work environment, where the collective strength of the team can be harnessed to drive innovation and productivity. By steering clear of contentiousness, leaders can inspire their teams to work towards common goals with a sense of shared purpose and cooperation.

Non-contention begins with the recognition that conflicts, especially those that are unnecessary or avoidable, can be detrimental to the overall functioning and morale of an organisation. Leaders who are constantly engaged in disputes or power struggles create an atmosphere of tension and hostility, which can hinder productivity and damage relationships. On the other hand, leaders who prioritise harmony and collaboration can build a more positive and supportive work environment. This involves addressing issues constructively and finding common ground, rather than escalating conflicts or imposing their will.

A key aspect of non-contention is the ability to listen and understand different perspectives. Leaders who practise non-contention are skilled at empathising with their team members, considering their viewpoints, and validating their concerns. This empathetic approach helps to build trust and rapport, as team members feel heard and respected. By fostering open communication and encouraging dialogue, leaders can create an environment where conflicts are resolved amicably and collaboratively. This approach not only strengthens the bonds within the team but also enhances overall team cohesion and effectiveness.

Non-contention also involves leading by example and setting a tone of mutual respect and cooperation. Leaders who avoid aggressive or domineering behaviour demonstrate that success does not require conflict or competition. Instead, they show that collaboration and teamwork are more effective paths to achieving organisational goals. By modelling non-contentious behaviour, leaders inspire their team members to adopt similar attitudes and approaches. This creates a culture of unity and cooperation, where everyone works together towards shared objectives.

Moreover, non-contention allows leaders to focus on long-term success rather than short-term victories. Leaders who avoid unnecessary conflicts are better able to maintain a strategic perspective, making decisions that are in the best interest of the organisation as a whole. This involves considering the broader impact of actions and prioritising sustainable solutions over immediate gains. By fostering a culture of non-contention, leaders can ensure that their organisation is more resilient and adaptable, capable of navigating challenges and seizing opportunities without being bogged down by internal strife.

The strength of non-contention is also evident in external relationships. Leaders who approach negotiations and partnerships with a spirit of non-contention are more likely to build lasting and mutually beneficial alliances. This approach fosters trust and cooperation, as external partners see that the leader is fair and honourable. By avoiding aggressive tactics and instead focusing on creating win-win situations, leaders can enhance their organisation's reputation and establish a network of supportive and collaborative relationships.

ALIGNING WITH HIGHER GOALS

Thus we say, 'Like Heaven's his ends, No sage of old more bright.'

The chapter also eloquently emphasises the importance of aligning leadership actions with higher goals and values. This principle is particularly pertinent in the context of strategic management, where leaders are often tasked with making decisions that have far-reaching implications. Aligning with higher goals involves focusing on a long-term vision and adhering to ethical principles that serve as the guiding light for the organisation. This alignment not only inspires and motivates the team but also fosters a sense of purpose and direction that transcends short-term gains and individual interests.

In strategic management, aligning with higher goals begins with clearly defining the organisation's mission, vision, and values. Leaders must articulate a long-term vision that resonates with all members of the organisation, providing a shared sense of purpose. This vision serves as a roadmap, guiding the organisation's strategic decisions and actions. When leaders align their actions with this vision, they create a cohesive and unified organisation where everyone is working towards common objectives. This alignment helps to ensure that all efforts are directed towards achieving the overarching goals, rather than being fragmented or misaligned.

Ethical principles play a crucial role in aligning leadership with higher goals. Leaders must ensure that their decisions and actions are grounded in integrity and honesty. This involves considering the broader impact of their decisions on society and stakeholders, beyond just the immediate financial or operational outcomes. Ethical leadership fosters trust and credibility, as team members and stakeholders can see that the organisation is committed to doing what is right. This commitment to ethical behaviour not only enhances the organisation's reputation but also creates a positive and supportive work environment where employees feel proud to be a part of the organisation.

Aligning with higher goals also involves considering the long-term sustainability of the organisation. Leaders must make strategic decisions that ensure the organisation can thrive and grow over the long term. This may involve investing in innovation, developing talent, and building strong relationships with stakeholders. By focusing on sustainability, leaders can create an organisation that is resilient and adaptable, capable of navigating changes and challenges in the business environment. This forward-thinking approach helps to secure the organisation's future and ensures that it can continue to create value for all stakeholders.

Moreover, aligning with higher goals allows leaders to inspire and motivate their teams. When team members understand the larger purpose behind their work, they are more likely to be engaged and committed. This sense of purpose can drive higher levels of performance and satisfaction, as employees see that their efforts are contributing to something meaningful. Leaders can foster this sense of purpose by regularly communicating the organisation's vision and values, and by recognising and celebrating achievements that align with these goals. By reinforcing the connection between individual contributions and the organisation's higher goals, leaders can create a motivated and high-performing team.

Additionally, aligning with higher goals helps to build a culture of continuous improvement and innovation. When leaders prioritise long-term vision and ethical principles, they create an environment where everyone is encouraged to think creatively and contribute new ideas. This culture of innovation is essential for staying competitive and responding to changes in the market. By valuing and supporting innovative thinking, leaders can ensure that the organisation remains dynamic and forward-looking, always striving to improve and adapt.

CHAPTER 69 – RETREAT

Chapter 69 of the *Tao Te Ching* focuses on the principles of strategic retreat, defensive action, and the importance of avoiding unnecessary conflict. Here's how these teachings can be applied to modern-day strategic management:

EMBRACING STRATEGIC RETREAT & DEFENSIVE ACTION

> *A master of the art of war has said, 'I do not dare to be the host (to commence the war); I prefer to be the guest (to act on the defensive). I do not dare to advance an inch; I prefer to retire a foot.'*

Lao Tzu's Chapter 69 of the *Tao Te Ching* offers a compelling perspective on the importance of strategic retreat and defensive action in leadership. This principle underscores the value of caution and prudence in strategic management, suggesting that leaders should avoid initiating aggressive strategies and instead focus on protecting and fortifying their existing positions. By adopting a defensive stance, leaders can conserve valuable resources, mitigate risks, and ensure long-term stability, which in turn allows the organisation to respond more effectively to external challenges and opportunities.

Strategic retreat is not a sign of weakness; rather, it is a calculated decision that demonstrates foresight and wisdom. Leaders who understand the importance of retreat recognise that advancing recklessly can lead to unnecessary losses and vulnerabilities. By stepping back and reassessing the situation, leaders can gain a clearer understanding of the landscape and make more informed decisions. This approach is particularly relevant in times of uncertainty or when facing formidable adversaries. By retreating strategically, leaders can regroup, strengthen their defences, and prepare for future opportunities with greater resilience and readiness.

In practical terms, adopting a defensive stance involves several key actions. First, it requires a thorough assessment of the organisation's current strengths and weaknesses. Leaders must identify the areas that need reinforcement and allocate resources accordingly. This may involve investing in employee training, upgrading technology, or enhancing operational processes. By focusing on internal fortification, leaders can build a solid foundation that can withstand external pressures and adapt to changing circumstances.

Defensive actions also entail being vigilant and proactive in identifying potential threats. Leaders must constantly monitor the external environment, staying informed about market trends, competitor activities, and emerging risks. This proactive approach allows leaders to anticipate challenges and take preemptive measures to mitigate their impact. By being prepared, leaders can avoid being caught off guard and can respond swiftly and effectively to any threats that arise. This vigilance is crucial for maintaining stability and ensuring the organisation's long-term success.

Moreover, a defensive strategy emphasises the importance of resource conservation. Leaders must be judicious in their use of resources, avoiding wasteful expenditures and focusing on initiatives that offer the highest return on investment. This frugality allows the organisation to maintain financial stability and allocate resources to critical areas that drive growth and innovation. By conserving resources, leaders can ensure that the organisation is well-positioned to seize opportunities when they arise and to navigate periods of economic uncertainty with resilience.

Strategic retreat and defensive action also foster a culture of cautious optimism. Leaders who adopt this approach encourage their teams to be both vigilant and hopeful, recognising that setbacks and challenges are an inevitable part of the journey. This mindset fosters a sense of resilience and adaptability, as team members learn to view obstacles as opportunities for growth and improvement. By promoting cautious optimism, leaders can inspire their teams to remain focused and motivated, even in the face of adversity.

Additionally, embracing defensive strategies involves fostering strong relationships and alliances. Leaders should seek to build and maintain trust with stakeholders, including employees, customers, partners, and investors. These relationships are invaluable in times of crisis, as they provide support and resources that can help the organisation weather difficult periods. By nurturing these connections, leaders can create a network of allies who share a vested interest in the organisation's success and stability.

AVOIDING UNNECESSARY CONFLICT

There is no calamity greater than lightly engaging in war. To do that is near losing (the gentleness) which is so precious.

The chapter articulates a critical perspective on the importance of avoiding unnecessary conflicts in leadership. This principle emphasises the detrimental effects of engaging in aggressive actions without due consideration, highlighting the potential for resource depletion, damaged relationships, and disrupted organisational harmony. In strategic management, this approach is particularly relevant, as leaders are often faced with decisions that can either escalate or de-escalate tensions within and outside the organisation.

Avoiding unnecessary conflict requires a careful assessment of the potential consequences of aggressive actions. Leaders must weigh the immediate benefits of such actions against the long-term impacts on the organisation's stability and morale. Conflicts, if not managed properly, can lead to significant drains on resources, both in terms of time and finances. The costs of prolonged disputes can outweigh any short-term gains, leading to inefficiencies and diverted attention from core business objectives. By evaluating these risks, leaders can make more informed decisions that prioritise the well-being of the organisation and its members.

Preserving gentleness and cooperation is essential for maintaining a positive and productive work environment. Leaders who prioritise peaceful and constructive solutions demonstrate a commitment to the values of respect, empathy, and collaboration. This approach helps to build a culture of trust and mutual support, where team members feel safe to express their ideas and concerns. When conflicts arise, leaders should focus on facilitating open dialogue and seeking common ground. By encouraging constructive conversations, leaders can resolve issues amicably and strengthen the bonds within the team.

The principle of avoiding unnecessary conflict also involves being proactive in conflict prevention. Leaders should cultivate an environment where potential issues are identified and addressed early on, before they escalate into major disputes. This proactive approach includes setting clear expectations, providing regular feedback, and fostering open communication channels. By addressing concerns promptly and effectively, leaders can prevent misunderstandings and miscommunications from turning into significant conflicts. This not only enhances organisational harmony but also improves overall team performance and engagement.

Moreover, leaders who avoid unnecessary conflicts are better positioned to seize opportunities for growth and innovation. By maintaining a focus on collaboration and cooperation, leaders can create a more dynamic and adaptive organisation. This involves encouraging team members to work together towards shared goals, leveraging their diverse strengths and perspectives. When the team is united and motivated, they are more likely to generate creative solutions and drive continuous improvement. This collaborative spirit is essential for staying competitive in a rapidly changing business landscape.

Leaders should also consider the broader impact of their actions on stakeholders, including employees, customers, partners, and the community. Aggressive actions can damage these relationships, leading to a loss of trust and support. By prioritising peaceful and constructive solutions, leaders can build stronger and more resilient partnerships. This approach fosters goodwill and enhances the organisation's reputation, positioning it as a responsible and ethical leader in its industry. By maintaining positive relationships with stakeholders, leaders can ensure long-term success and sustainability.

DEMONSTRATING STRENGTH THROUGH RESTRAINT

> *This is called marshalling the ranks where there are no ranks; baring the arms (to fight) where there are no arms to bare; grasping the weapon where there is no weapon to grasp; advancing against the enemy where there is no enemy.*

The chapter emphasises the profound strength found in demonstrating restraint in leadership. This principle highlights the power of being prepared, vigilant, and strategically positioned without resorting to overt displays of force or aggression. In the context of strategic management, this approach underscores the importance of maintaining control and stability through careful deliberation and measured responses, rather than impulsive actions.

Demonstrating strength through restraint begins with the recognition that true power often lies in the ability to exercise self-control and patience. Leaders who master the art of restraint are able to navigate complex and challenging situations with composure, avoiding rash decisions that could escalate conflicts or create unnecessary risks. This approach requires a deep understanding of the strategic landscape and a commitment to thoughtful and deliberate action. By taking the time to assess the situation, consider all potential outcomes, and develop a well-considered plan, leaders can position themselves and their teams to respond effectively to any challenges that arise.

One of the key benefits of restraint is the ability to maintain a sense of control and stability within the organisation. When leaders act impulsively or aggressively, it can create uncertainty and anxiety among team members and stakeholders. In contrast, a leader who demonstrates restraint exudes confidence and calm, which helps to reassure and stabilise the organisation. This sense of stability is crucial for maintaining morale and productivity, as team members are more likely to feel secure and focused when they trust that their leader is in control.

Moreover, restraint allows leaders to build and maintain respect and trust from their teams and stakeholders. By avoiding unnecessary conflicts and acting with integrity and fairness, leaders can cultivate a reputation for wisdom and reliability. This trust is essential for fostering strong and positive relationships within the organisation and with external partners. When team members and stakeholders see that their leader is capable of exercising restraint and making sound decisions, they are more likely to support and follow their leadership. This respect and trust form the foundation for effective collaboration and collective success.

Restraint also involves being vigilant and prepared for potential challenges. Leaders must be proactive in identifying and addressing issues before they escalate. This includes staying informed about the external environment, monitoring internal dynamics, and being ready to take decisive action when necessary. By being prepared, leaders can respond to challenges with agility and confidence, minimising disruptions and maintaining stability. This proactive approach helps to ensure that the organisation remains resilient and adaptable, capable of navigating both expected and unforeseen challenges.

Furthermore, demonstrating strength through restraint fosters a culture of deliberate and thoughtful decision-making. Leaders who prioritise restraint encourage their team members to take a measured and reflective approach to their work. This involves promoting critical thinking, encouraging open dialogue, and valuing diverse perspectives. By creating an environment where decisions are made with careful consideration and input from all relevant stakeholders, leaders can enhance the quality and effectiveness of their strategic initiatives. This culture of thoughtful decision-making is essential for driving innovation and achieving sustainable success.

VALUING GENTLENESS & PATIENCE

> *Thus it is that when opposing weapons are (actually) crossed, he who deplores (the situation) conquers.*

The chapter also emphasises the significant impact of gentleness and patience in leadership. These qualities are particularly potent in conflict resolution, where the manner of approach can greatly influence the outcomes. Leaders who approach conflicts with empathy and a genuine willingness to find amicable resolutions can build stronger, more resilient relationships and cultivate a culture of mutual respect and understanding within their organisations. This approach is grounded in the belief that gentleness does not signify weakness but rather a deliberate and powerful choice to address challenges with compassion and foresight.

Valuing gentleness in leadership involves recognising the human element in every interaction and decision. Leaders who prioritise gentleness are attentive to the emotions, needs, and perspectives of their team members. This empathetic approach helps to create an environment where individuals feel valued and understood, reducing the likelihood of conflicts escalating into significant disputes. When team members see that their leader is genuinely concerned about their well-being and open to listening to their concerns, it fosters a sense of trust and loyalty. This trust is crucial for maintaining open lines of communication, which are essential for resolving conflicts constructively.

Patience is another vital attribute that complements gentleness in leadership. Patience allows leaders to take a step back and carefully consider their actions and responses rather than reacting impulsively. This thoughtful approach ensures that decisions are well-informed and considerate of the broader context. Patience enables leaders to gather all necessary information, consult with relevant stakeholders, and weigh the potential consequences of their actions. By exercising patience, leaders can avoid making hasty decisions that might exacerbate conflicts or create additional problems. Instead, they can develop more effective and sustainable solutions that address the root causes of issues.

In practice, leaders who value gentleness and patience demonstrate these qualities through their actions and interactions. They approach conflicts with a calm and composed demeanour, focusing on understanding the underlying issues rather than assigning blame. This approach involves active listening, where leaders pay close attention to what is being said and seek to understand the emotions and motivations behind the words. By showing empathy and validating the feelings of those involved, leaders can de-escalate tensions and create a space for open and honest dialogue. This collaborative approach encourages all parties to work together towards finding mutually acceptable resolutions.

The strength of gentleness and patience also lies in their ability to build a cohesive and supportive organisational culture. Leaders who embody these qualities set a positive example for their team, encouraging others to adopt similar behaviours. This creates a ripple effect, where the values of empathy, respect, and understanding become ingrained in the organisational culture. As a result, team members are more likely to approach conflicts with the same mindset, fostering a more harmonious and productive work environment. This culture of mutual respect and cooperation enhances overall team performance and drives innovation, as individuals feel safe to share their ideas and collaborate freely.

Furthermore, valuing gentleness and patience allows leaders to build stronger external relationships as well. Whether dealing with clients, partners, or the community, leaders who approach interactions with empathy and patience can establish trust and rapport more effectively. This strengthens the organisation's reputation and creates a network of supportive relationships that can be invaluable in times of need. By demonstrating these qualities consistently, leaders can position their organisation as a respected and ethical player in their industry.

CHAPTER 70 – CORE PRINCIPLES

Chapter 70 of the *Tao Te Ching* discusses the simplicity and profundity of the Tao's teachings, the rarity of true understanding, and the value of humility. Here's how these teachings can be applied to modern-day strategic management:

EMBRACING SIMPLICITY

> *My words are very easy to know, and very easy to practise; but there is no one in the world who is able to know and able to practise them.*

Lao Tzu's Chapter 70 of the *Tao Te Ching* emphasises the profound impact of simplicity in leadership. The principle of simplicity in leadership revolves around the idea that straightforward, clear messages and strategies can be more effective than complex and convoluted ones. Leaders who embrace simplicity strive to make their communication and actions easily understandable and implementable. However, Lao Tzu also acknowledges the inherent challenge in achieving true simplicity, as it requires a deep understanding and unwavering commitment.

In leadership, simplifying messages and strategies means distilling complex ideas into their essence, making them accessible and relatable for everyone in the organisation. This approach ensures that team members can easily grasp the leader's vision and objectives, fostering a sense of clarity and alignment. Clear communication helps to eliminate ambiguity and confusion, enabling employees to understand their roles and responsibilities within the broader organisational framework. When leaders articulate their goals and expectations in simple terms, they can effectively guide their teams towards achieving these objectives.

Simplicity in leadership also involves the implementation of straightforward principles that can be consistently applied across various situations. By focusing on fundamental values and priorities, leaders can create a cohesive and unified organisational culture. These principles serve as guiding lights, helping team members make decisions and take actions that are aligned with the organisation's mission and goals. Simplicity in principles ensures that everyone is on the same page, working towards a common purpose with a shared understanding of what is important.

However, achieving true simplicity is not an easy task. It requires leaders to possess a deep understanding of their organisation, its goals, and the external environment. Simplifying complex issues demands a keen insight into the underlying factors and the ability to identify the core elements that matter most. Leaders must be able to discern what is essential and what can be eliminated, a skill that comes from experience, reflection, and continuous learning. This depth of understanding allows leaders to craft messages and strategies that are not only simple but also impactful and relevant.

Commitment is another crucial aspect of embracing simplicity in leadership. Simplifying strategies and communication is not a one-time effort but an ongoing process that requires dedication and consistency. Leaders must be committed to maintaining clarity and avoiding the temptation to complicate matters. This commitment involves regularly reviewing and refining messages and strategies to ensure they remain clear and focused. By staying true to the principle of simplicity, leaders can build a culture of transparency and trust, where employees feel confident in their understanding of the organisation's direction.

Moreover, simplicity in leadership fosters a more agile and adaptable organisation. When strategies and communication are straightforward, the organisation can respond more quickly and effectively to changes in the external environment. Simplified processes and decision-making frameworks enable faster and more efficient execution, reducing the risk of delays and misunderstandings. This agility is essential for staying competitive and seizing opportunities in a rapidly evolving marketplace. By embracing simplicity, leaders can create an organisation that is both resilient and responsive, capable of thriving in any situation.

Simplicity also enhances collaboration and innovation within the organisation. When team members have a clear understanding of the organisation's goals and priorities, they are better equipped to work together and contribute their ideas. Simplified communication fosters open dialogue and the sharing of insights, leading to more creative and effective solutions. Leaders who prioritise simplicity create an environment where everyone feels empowered to participate and make meaningful contributions. This collaborative spirit drives continuous improvement and propels the organisation towards sustained success.

UNDERSTANDING THE CORE PRINCIPLES

> There is an originating and all-comprehending (principle) in my words, and an authoritative law for the things (which I enforce). It is because they do not know these, that men do not know me.

The chapter emphasises the importance of grounding leadership in core principles and values. These foundational elements serve as the bedrock for consistency and integrity in decision-making, ensuring that leaders remain true to their mission and vision even in the face of challenges. For contemporary leaders, this means that every strategy and action must align with the fundamental values that define the organisation. This alignment not only guides decision-making but also enhances credibility and trust among team members and stakeholders.

Understanding and adhering to core principles is essential for maintaining consistency in leadership. When leaders base their actions on a clear set of values, they create a predictable and stable environment. Team members know what to expect and can rely on their leader's decisions being fair, ethical, and aligned with the organisation's mission. This consistency fosters a sense of security and trust, as employees are confident that the leadership will uphold the same standards and principles in every situation. It also ensures that the organisation remains focused on its long-term goals, rather than being swayed by short-term pressures or external influences.

Integrity in decision-making is another crucial aspect of grounding leadership in core principles. Leaders who prioritise integrity make decisions that are not only effective but also ethical and responsible. This involves considering the broader impact of their actions on all stakeholders, including employees, customers, partners, and the community. By staying true to their core values, leaders can navigate complex situations with honesty and transparency, building trust and respect. This ethical approach also sets a powerful example for the rest of the organisation, encouraging all team members to act with integrity in their roles.

Clear communication of core principles is vital for fostering greater buy-in and commitment from the team. Leaders must articulate their values and the reasoning behind their actions in a way that is easily understood by everyone. This transparency helps team members grasp the underlying motivations and objectives, making it easier for them to align their efforts with the organisation's goals. When employees understand the 'why' behind decisions and policies, they are more likely to support and commit to them. This alignment not only enhances individual and team performance but also strengthens the overall cohesion and unity of the organisation.

Communicating core principles effectively also involves demonstrating them through actions. Leaders must 'walk the talk' by embodying the values they espouse in their daily interactions and decisions. This authenticity reinforces the importance of the core principles and shows team members that the leadership is genuinely committed to them. By leading by example, leaders inspire others to uphold the same standards, creating a culture of integrity and accountability. This culture is essential for sustaining long-term success, as it ensures that the entire organisation operates with a shared sense of purpose and commitment.

In addition, grounding leadership in core principles provides a framework for navigating uncertainty and change. In today's fast-paced and unpredictable business environment, leaders must be able to adapt quickly while staying true to their values. Core principles serve as a compass, guiding leaders through difficult decisions and ensuring that they remain focused on their long-term vision. This clarity of purpose helps to maintain stability and direction, even in the face of disruptions or challenges. By adhering to their core values, leaders can make strategic decisions that are both agile and aligned with the organisation's mission.

VALUING TRUE UNDERSTANDING

They who know me are few, and I am on that account (the more) to be prized.

The chapter emphasises the profound importance of recognising and valuing true understanding within an organisation. This principle highlights that those who truly grasp and embody the core principles and values of an organisation are rare and therefore highly valuable. Leaders who identify and cherish these individuals can significantly enhance the organisational culture and drive positive change.

Recognising true understanding starts with leaders being deeply aware of the organisation's core principles and values themselves. They must clearly define and consistently communicate these foundational elements to their team. When leaders are transparent about the organisation's mission, vision, and values, it sets the stage for team members to align with these principles. True understanding goes beyond mere comprehension; it involves internalising these values and reflecting them in everyday actions and decisions.

Leaders should look for team members who not only understand but also embody the organisation's principles. These individuals often exhibit behaviours and attitudes that align with the organisation's goals and values, serving as role models for their peers. By acknowledging and rewarding these team members, leaders reinforce the importance of living the organisation's values. This recognition can take various forms, such as public acknowledgment, career advancement opportunities, or other incentives that highlight the individual's contribution to the organisational culture.

Valuing true understanding helps build a strong and cohesive team. When team members see that their alignment with the organisation's values is appreciated and rewarded, it fosters a sense of belonging and purpose. This shared commitment to core principles enhances teamwork and collaboration, as everyone is working towards common goals with a unified understanding. It also creates a positive work environment where individuals feel motivated and engaged, knowing that their efforts to embody the organisation's values are recognised and valued.

Moreover, those who truly understand and embody the organisation's principles can act as key allies in promoting and sustaining the desired culture. These individuals often become informal leaders and influencers within the team, guiding their peers and reinforcing the organisation's values through their actions. Leaders should leverage these allies to drive initiatives that align with the organisation's mission and foster positive change. By empowering these individuals, leaders can amplify their impact and create a ripple effect that strengthens the entire organisation.

Rewarding true understanding and alignment is not just about individual recognition; it also sends a powerful message to the entire team. It signals that the organisation values integrity, commitment, and alignment with its core principles over short-term achievements or superficial success. This emphasis on values-driven performance helps to cultivate a culture of ethical behaviour and long-term thinking, which is crucial for sustainable success.

In addition, recognising and valuing true understanding supports the development of a more resilient and adaptable organisation. Individuals who are deeply aligned with the organisation's values are more likely to navigate challenges with integrity and a focus on the greater good. They are better equipped to make decisions that reflect the organisation's principles, even in difficult or uncertain situations. This alignment ensures that the organisation remains true to its mission and can weather external pressures without compromising its values.

PRACTISING HUMILITY

> It is thus that the sage wears (a poor garb of) hair cloth, while he carries his (signet of) jade in his bosom.

The chapter also highlights the essential quality of humility in effective leadership. This principle is encapsulated in the metaphor of the sage, who outwardly wears humble garments while carrying the precious signet of jade close to his heart. This imagery emphasises that true leaders do not seek to draw attention to themselves through ostentatious displays of power or success. Instead, they remain grounded, focusing on their internal values and the greater good of the organisation.

Practising humility in leadership means recognising that one's role is to serve the team and the organisation rather than to aggrandise oneself. Humble leaders understand that their success is intertwined with the success of their team members. Therefore, they prioritise the needs and development of their team over their personal ambition. This selfless approach fosters an environment where employees feel valued and supported, which in turn drives higher levels of engagement and performance.

Avoiding ostentatious displays of power is a key aspect of humble leadership. Leaders who are humble do not feel the need to constantly assert their authority or showcase their achievements. Instead, they lead through example and quiet confidence. This approach builds respect and trust among team members, as they see their leader as someone who is approachable and genuinely invested in their well-being. By focusing on actions rather than words, humble leaders can create a more inclusive and cohesive work environment.

Focusing on internal values is another critical component of practising humility. Leaders must be guided by a strong sense of purpose and ethical principles. These values act as a compass, directing their decisions and actions towards the greater good of the organisation. By staying true to their values, leaders can navigate complex situations with integrity and fairness. This consistency builds trust and credibility, as team members know that their leader will act in accordance with the organisation's core principles, even when faced with difficult choices.

Moreover, humility in leadership involves recognising and appreciating the contributions of others. Humble leaders give credit where it is due, acknowledging the hard work and achievements of their team members. This recognition boosts morale and motivates employees to continue striving for excellence. By celebrating the successes of others, leaders create a culture of mutual respect and collaboration, where everyone feels that their efforts are valued and appreciated. This positive reinforcement strengthens team cohesion and drives collective success.

Humility also allows leaders to remain open to learning and growth. Leaders who are humble do not assume that they have all the answers. Instead, they seek feedback, listen to diverse perspectives, and are willing to learn from their mistakes. This openness to improvement not only enhances the leader's own capabilities but also creates a culture of continuous learning within the organisation. By demonstrating that growth and development are ongoing processes, humble leaders inspire their team members to adopt the same mindset, driving innovation and progress.

Creating a positive and supportive work environment is a natural outcome of humble leadership. When leaders prioritise humility, they foster a sense of belonging and trust within the team. Employees feel comfortable sharing their ideas and concerns, knowing that their input will be heard and respected. This open and inclusive atmosphere encourages collaboration and creativity, as team members work together towards common goals. By building a supportive environment, humble leaders can enhance overall team performance and job satisfaction.

CHAPTER 71 – COMPLACENCY

Chapter 71 of the *Tao Te Ching* speaks to the wisdom of recognising one's own limitations and the dangers of false knowledge. Here's how these teachings can be applied to modern-day strategic management:

EMBRACING HUMILITY & CONTINUOUS LEARNING

> *To know and yet (think) we do not know is the highest (attainment); not to know (and yet think) we do know is a disease.*

Lao Tzu's Chapter 71 of the *Tao Te Ching* highlights the profound importance of humility and the pursuit of continuous learning in leadership. The essence of this teaching is that true wisdom lies in recognising the limits of one's knowledge and maintaining a mindset of perpetual curiosity and openness. Leaders who embody this principle create a culture of growth and innovation within their organisations by acknowledging their own limitations and fostering an environment where learning and exploration are valued.

Embracing humility in leadership means understanding that no one has all the answers, and there is always more to learn. This recognition is the foundation of a culture of continuous learning, where both leaders and their teams are encouraged to seek out new knowledge and stay curious about the world around them. By admitting that they do not know everything, leaders demonstrate a commitment to growth and improvement, setting an example for their teams to follow. This humility fosters an atmosphere of psychological safety, where team members feel comfortable asking questions, sharing ideas, and exploring new possibilities without fear of judgment or failure.

Continuous learning is essential for staying competitive and adaptable in today's fast-paced and ever-changing business environment. Leaders who prioritise learning and development are better equipped to navigate complexities and anticipate future challenges. This commitment to learning involves not only acquiring new skills and knowledge but also staying open to different perspectives and ways of thinking. By exposing themselves and their teams to diverse viewpoints, leaders can gain a more comprehensive understanding of issues and develop more innovative solutions. This openness to learning from others enriches the organisation's intellectual capital and drives creativity and innovation.

Recognising one's limitations is a crucial aspect of humility. Leaders who are aware of their own gaps in knowledge and expertise are more likely to seek out the insights and contributions of others. This collaborative approach enhances decision-making and problem-solving, as it leverages the collective intelligence and diverse experiences of the team. By valuing and incorporating the input of team members, leaders can make more informed and effective decisions that reflect a broader range of perspectives. This inclusivity not only improves outcomes but also strengthens the sense of ownership and commitment within the team.

Moreover, fostering a culture of continuous learning involves creating opportunities for professional development and growth. Leaders should invest in training programmes, workshops, and other learning initiatives that enable team members to expand their skills and knowledge. This investment demonstrates the organisation's commitment to its employees' growth and development, boosting morale and motivation. By providing avenues for learning, leaders empower their teams to take charge of their own development and pursue their career aspirations. This proactive approach to learning and development ensures that the organisation remains agile and prepared to meet future challenges.

Preventing complacency is another key benefit of embracing humility and continuous learning. Leaders who are aware of their own limitations and actively seek out new knowledge are less likely to become complacent or resistant to change. This mindset encourages a constant reassessment of strategies and processes, driving continuous improvement and innovation. By challenging the status quo and remaining curious, leaders can identify new opportunities for growth and improvement, keeping the organisation dynamic and forward-thinking. This commitment to ongoing learning ensures that the organisation remains competitive and able to adapt to evolving market conditions.

AVOIDING THE PITFALLS OF OVERCONFIDENCE

Not to know (and yet think) we do know is a disease.

The chapter underscores the significant dangers of overconfidence in leadership. This principle highlights the critical insight that believing we know everything, when in fact we do not, is a harmful mindset that can lead to poor decision-making and missed opportunities. Leaders who fall into the trap of overconfidence may make hasty or uninformed decisions, as they fail to consider alternative perspectives or new information. This closed-minded approach can prevent the organisation from adapting to changes, seizing opportunities, and addressing potential risks effectively.

To avoid the pitfalls of overconfidence, leaders must remain vigilant about their own limitations and embrace intellectual humility. This mindset involves recognising that no one has all the answers and that continuous learning and questioning are essential for sound decision-making. Leaders who promote intellectual humility create a culture where team members feel encouraged to ask questions, challenge assumptions, and seek out diverse viewpoints. This open and inquisitive environment fosters critical thinking and helps to ensure that decisions are well-rounded and based on a thorough understanding of the facts.

Encouraging questioning and critical thinking within the organisation requires leaders to model these behaviours themselves. Leaders should demonstrate a willingness to question their own assumptions and be open to feedback and new ideas. By showing that they value input from others, leaders can build a culture of collaboration and continuous improvement. Team members are more likely to engage in thoughtful analysis and contribute their insights when they see that their contributions are valued and taken seriously. This collaborative approach not only enhances decision-making but also strengthens team cohesion and trust.

Moreover, promoting intellectual humility involves creating structures and processes that facilitate critical thinking and diverse perspectives. Leaders can implement regular brainstorming sessions, cross-functional teams, and feedback loops to encourage the exchange of ideas and viewpoints. These practices help to ensure that different angles are considered and that potential blind spots are addressed. By leveraging the collective intelligence of the team, leaders can make more informed and effective decisions that are responsive to the complex and dynamic business environment.

Leaders must also be mindful of the potential consequences of overconfidence. When leaders assume they have all the answers, they may overlook important details, dismiss valuable input, and fail to recognise emerging threats or opportunities. This can lead to strategic missteps, operational inefficiencies, and missed opportunities for innovation. By fostering a culture of intellectual humility, leaders can mitigate these risks and create a more adaptable and resilient organisation. Encouraging ongoing learning and critical thinking helps to ensure that the organisation remains agile and capable of navigating change effectively.

In addition, intellectual humility supports ethical decision-making and integrity. Leaders who are aware of their limitations are more likely to seek out accurate and reliable information, consider the ethical implications of their actions, and make decisions that align with the organisation's values. This thoughtful and principled approach builds trust and credibility, both within the organisation and with external stakeholders. By prioritising intellectual humility, leaders can create a culture of transparency and accountability, where decisions are made with integrity and a focus on the greater good.

BEING VIGILANT AGAINST COMPLACENCY

It is simply by being pained at (the thought of) having this disease that we are preserved from it.

The chapter underscores the critical necessity for leaders to remain vigilant against the dangers of complacency. This principle emphasises that the awareness and discomfort associated with the thought of becoming complacent are crucial for maintaining an active and engaged approach to leadership. Complacency, often born from overconfidence, can lull leaders into a false sense of security, leading them to overlook potential risks and miss opportunities for growth and improvement. Recognising this threat can serve as a powerful motivator for leaders to stay proactive and committed to their ongoing development.

Vigilance against complacency begins with self-awareness. Leaders must be attuned to their own attitudes and behaviours, regularly reflecting on their actions and decisions to identify any signs of complacency. This reflective practice involves questioning assumptions, reassessing strategies, and seeking feedback from others. By maintaining a mindset of continuous self-examination, leaders can ensure that they remain responsive to changes and challenges in their environment. This self-awareness helps to prevent the stagnation that often accompanies complacency, keeping leaders dynamic and adaptable.

Understanding the potential negative impact of overconfidence is another key aspect of avoiding complacency. Overconfident leaders may believe that their past successes guarantee future outcomes, leading them to take undue risks or ignore critical feedback. This overreliance on past achievements can create blind spots, making leaders less receptive to new information or alternative perspectives. By acknowledging the dangers of overconfidence, leaders can adopt a more balanced and humble approach, remaining open to learning and growth. This humility enables them to make more informed and considered decisions, enhancing the overall effectiveness of their leadership.

Staying engaged and proactive in the pursuit of knowledge and improvement is essential for long-term success. Leaders who continuously seek out new learning opportunities are better equipped to navigate the complexities of their roles. This commitment to professional development involves staying informed about industry trends, acquiring new skills, and exploring innovative approaches. By actively pursuing knowledge, leaders can anticipate and respond to changes more effectively, positioning their organisations for sustained success. This proactive stance also sets a positive example for the rest of the team, fostering a culture of continuous improvement and learning.

Evaluating strategies and adapting to changing circumstances is a critical component of vigilance against complacency. The business environment is constantly evolving, and leaders must be prepared to adjust their strategies in response to new developments. This flexibility requires a willingness to let go of outdated practices and embrace new methods. By regularly reviewing and updating their strategies, leaders can ensure that their organisations remain relevant and competitive. This adaptive approach enables leaders to capitalise on emerging opportunities and mitigate potential threats, ensuring long-term viability and success.

Furthermore, fostering a culture that values continuous evaluation and adaptation helps to sustain vigilance against complacency. Leaders should encourage their teams to regularly assess their work, identify areas for improvement, and experiment with new ideas. This culture of innovation and critical thinking prevents complacency from taking root, as team members are constantly challenged to improve and evolve. By promoting an environment where questioning and exploration are encouraged, leaders can harness the collective intelligence and creativity of their teams, driving sustained growth and success.

LEADING BY EXAMPLE

> *The sage has not the disease. He knows the pain that would be inseparable from it, and therefore he does not have it.*

The chapter also emphasises the vital role of leading by example in fostering a culture of intellectual humility and continuous learning. This principle underscores the importance of leaders demonstrating a genuine commitment to their own learning journey and openly acknowledging when they do not have all the answers. By embodying these values, leaders can inspire their teams to adopt the same mindset, creating an environment of trust, collaboration, and mutual respect.

Leading by example involves more than just words; it requires actions that reflect the principles of intellectual humility and a dedication to learning. Leaders who openly share their learning experiences and admit their limitations demonstrate that growth and improvement are ongoing processes. This transparency helps to normalise the idea that not knowing something is not a weakness, but rather an opportunity for growth. When leaders model this behaviour, they create a safe space for team members to ask questions, seek feedback, and engage in their own learning journeys without fear of judgment.

Intellectual humility is a key component of effective leadership. Leaders who are humble recognise that their knowledge is limited and that there is always more to learn. By admitting when they do not know something and seeking out information or expertise, leaders show that they value truth and improvement over ego. This humility fosters a culture of continuous learning, where team members feel encouraged to expand their knowledge and skills. It also promotes a more collaborative environment, as team members see that their leader values diverse perspectives and is open to learning from others.

Demonstrating a commitment to continuous learning involves actively seeking out opportunities for growth and development. Leaders should participate in training programmes, attend workshops, and stay informed about the latest trends and best practices in their field. This proactive approach to learning not only enhances the leader's own capabilities but also sets a positive example for the team. By showing that they prioritise their own development, leaders encourage their team members to do the same. This commitment to learning helps to keep the organisation innovative and adaptable, as everyone is continuously striving to improve.

Building trust is another crucial outcome of leading by example. When leaders demonstrate intellectual humility and a commitment to learning, they build credibility and earn the trust of their team members. Trust is the foundation of effective teamwork and collaboration, as it ensures that team members feel safe to share their ideas and take risks. By fostering an environment of trust, leaders enable their teams to work more effectively together and achieve better outcomes. This trust also extends to the leader's decision-making, as team members are more likely to support and follow a leader they trust.

A collaborative and respectful work environment is essential for the success of any organisation. Leaders who model intellectual humility and a commitment to learning create a culture where everyone feels valued and respected. This inclusive environment encourages team members to share their unique perspectives and contribute to the collective knowledge of the team. By valuing and incorporating diverse viewpoints, leaders can make more informed and effective decisions. This collaboration drives innovation and problem-solving, as team members work together to find creative solutions to challenges.

CHAPTER 72 – BALANCE

Chapter 72 of the *Tao Te Ching* provides insights into managing fear, avoiding complacency, and practising humility. Here's how these teachings can be applied to modern-day strategic management:

ACKNOWLEDGING & ADDRESSING RISKS

> *When the people do not fear what they ought to fear, that which is their great dread will come on them.*

Lao Tzu's Chapter 72 of the *Tao Te Ching* profoundly emphasises the necessity for leaders to acknowledge and address potential risks and challenges within their organisations. This principle underlines the critical understanding that ignoring or underestimating risks can precipitate greater problems in the future. Leaders must, therefore, foster a culture of proactive risk management, ensuring their teams are well-prepared to handle uncertainties effectively. This involves a continuous and vigilant process of assessing potential risks and developing robust strategies to mitigate them.

A fundamental aspect of risk management is the recognition and acknowledgment of potential threats. Leaders must create an environment where team members feel comfortable discussing and identifying risks. This openness helps to uncover potential issues that may not be immediately apparent but could have significant impacts if left unaddressed. By encouraging a culture of transparency and honesty, leaders can gather comprehensive insights into the various risks the organisation may face. This collective awareness is crucial for developing effective risk management strategies, as it ensures that all possible angles and scenarios are considered.

Proactive risk management involves regularly assessing the organisation's external and internal environments. Leaders must stay informed about industry trends, regulatory changes, and economic conditions that could affect their operations. Additionally, they need to continuously evaluate internal processes, resources, and capabilities to identify potential vulnerabilities. This ongoing assessment helps to anticipate and prepare for potential challenges, rather than reacting to them after they occur. By maintaining a vigilant watch over the organisation's landscape, leaders can swiftly adapt to changes and mitigate risks before they escalate.

Developing strategies to mitigate risks is another critical component of proactive risk management. Leaders should work with their teams to devise comprehensive plans that address identified risks. These plans should include specific actions and contingencies for various scenarios, ensuring that the organisation is equipped to respond effectively. Regular training and simulations can help to prepare team members for potential crises, enhancing their ability to act decisively and efficiently under pressure. By having well-defined risk management strategies in place, leaders can provide their teams with a clear roadmap for navigating uncertainties, reducing anxiety and improving overall resilience.

Effective communication plays a vital role in addressing and managing risks. Leaders must ensure that risk management strategies are clearly communicated to all team members, so everyone understands their roles and responsibilities in mitigating risks. This clarity helps to ensure that the entire organisation is aligned and working cohesively towards minimising potential threats. Regular updates and feedback sessions can help to keep everyone informed about new risks and changes to existing strategies. This ongoing dialogue fosters a sense of shared responsibility and collaboration, as team members are actively engaged in the risk management process.

Moreover, leaders should cultivate a mindset of continuous improvement and learning within their organisations. By regularly reviewing and refining risk management strategies, leaders can adapt to new challenges and incorporate lessons learned from past experiences. This iterative approach ensures that the organisation remains agile and resilient, capable of evolving with the changing landscape. Encouraging a culture of innovation and flexibility allows teams to explore new solutions and strategies for mitigating risks, driving continuous improvement in the organisation's risk management capabilities.

AVOIDING COMPLACENCY

> *Let them not thoughtlessly indulge themselves in their ordinary life; let them not act as if weary of what that life depends on.*

The chapter offers a profound lesson on the dangers of complacency in leadership and the importance of maintaining engagement and motivation within a team. This principle highlights the need for leaders to ensure their teams do not become overly comfortable with their routines and to avoid the pitfalls of stagnation. Complacency can lead to a decline in performance, innovation, and overall effectiveness, as individuals lose sight of the broader goals and the vital importance of their contributions.

Leaders have a crucial role in creating an environment that promotes continuous improvement and a sense of purpose. This involves setting challenging goals that push team members out of their comfort zones and encourage them to strive for excellence. By establishing clear, ambitious targets, leaders can inspire their teams to reach new heights and achieve more than they previously thought possible. This approach not only drives performance but also keeps individuals engaged and motivated, as they see the tangible impact of their efforts and progress.

Providing opportunities for development is another essential strategy for avoiding complacency. Leaders should invest in the growth and advancement of their team members by offering training programmes, mentorship, and pathways for career progression. These opportunities help individuals to expand their skills, gain new knowledge, and stay current with industry trends and best practices. By prioritising development, leaders signal to their teams that continuous learning and improvement are valued and expected. This investment in personal and professional growth fosters a culture of resilience and adaptability, as team members are better equipped to navigate changes and challenges.

Recognising and celebrating achievements is a powerful way to combat complacency and reinforce a sense of purpose. Leaders should make it a priority to acknowledge the hard work and successes of their team members, both individually and collectively. This recognition can take various forms, such as public praise, awards, or other incentives that highlight the significance of their contributions. Celebrating achievements not only boosts morale but also reinforces the connection between individual efforts and the organisation's overall success. This positive reinforcement motivates team members to continue striving for excellence and maintaining high levels of engagement.

In addition to these strategies, leaders should encourage a mindset of curiosity and innovation within their teams. By fostering an environment where questioning the status quo and exploring new ideas are encouraged, leaders can prevent stagnation and promote a culture of creativity. This involves creating spaces for brainstorming and experimentation, where team members feel safe to take risks and learn from failures. Encouraging innovation helps to keep the organisation dynamic and forward-thinking, as new solutions and approaches are constantly being explored and developed.

Regularly assessing and refining strategies is also crucial for avoiding complacency. Leaders must be vigilant in evaluating the effectiveness of their approaches and making necessary adjustments based on feedback and changing circumstances. This iterative process ensures that the organisation remains agile and responsive, capable of adapting to new opportunities and threats. By continually reassessing and optimising strategies, leaders can maintain momentum and drive sustained success.

PREVENTING WEARINESS THROUGH BALANCE

It is by avoiding such indulgence that such weariness does not arise.

The chapter emphasises the critical importance of maintaining a healthy work-life balance to prevent weariness and burnout. This principle underlines the idea that indulgence in excessive work without adequate rest and personal time can lead to fatigue, decreased productivity, and ultimately, burnout. Leaders have a pivotal role in promoting a balanced approach to work and life, ensuring their teams have the necessary time and resources to recharge and maintain their well-being.

Maintaining a healthy work-life balance is essential for sustained productivity and overall health. Leaders should recognise that employees are most effective when they have time to rest, recover, and engage in activities outside of work that rejuvenate them. Encouraging a balanced lifestyle involves creating a work environment that values personal well-being as much as professional achievement. By fostering a culture that prioritises balance, leaders can help their teams avoid the weariness that comes from overworking and underestimating the importance of rest and leisure.

Promoting flexible working arrangements is one of the key strategies to achieve this balance. Flexibility allows employees to manage their work schedules in a way that aligns with their personal needs and responsibilities. This might include options for remote work, flexible hours, or compressed workweeks. By providing flexibility, leaders demonstrate trust in their team's ability to manage their time effectively, which can lead to higher job satisfaction and increased productivity. Flexibility also helps employees balance their work commitments with personal obligations, reducing stress and allowing them to be more focused and engaged during working hours.

Encouraging regular breaks is another vital component of preventing weariness. Leaders should advocate for short, frequent breaks throughout the workday, as well as longer periods of time off, such as vacation days. These breaks are crucial for maintaining mental and physical health, as they provide opportunities for relaxation and recharging. By normalising and encouraging breaks, leaders send a clear message that taking time to rest is not only acceptable but essential for optimal performance. This practice helps to prevent burnout and ensures that employees return to their tasks with renewed energy and focus.

Fostering a supportive work environment is equally important for maintaining a healthy work-life balance. Leaders should create a culture where employees feel comfortable discussing their needs and concerns related to work-life balance. This involves being approachable, empathetic, and responsive to individual circumstances. Providing support might include access to wellness programmes, mental health resources, and other initiatives that promote overall well-being. A supportive environment also means recognising and respecting boundaries, ensuring that employees do not feel pressured to be constantly available or to take on excessive workloads.

Additionally, leaders can set an example by practising what they preach. Demonstrating their own commitment to work-life balance by taking breaks, setting boundaries, and prioritising self-care can inspire employees to do the same. When leaders visibly uphold these principles, it reinforces the importance of balance and encourages the entire team to adopt healthier work habits. This modelling behaviour is crucial for creating a culture where work-life balance is genuinely valued and practised.

PRACTISING HUMILITY & LEADING BY EXAMPLE

> *Therefore the sage knows (these things) of himself, but does not parade (his knowledge); loves, but does not (appear to set a) value on, himself.*

The chapter also underscores the profound virtues of practising humility and leading by example in the realm of leadership. This principle highlights that true wisdom and effective leadership stem from understanding and applying knowledge without the need to flaunt it. Leaders who embrace humility and choose to lead by example create a foundation of trust and respect within their organisations, fostering an environment where team members feel valued and supported.

Practising humility in leadership involves a conscious effort to avoid ostentation and self-aggrandisement. Leaders who understand this principle recognise that their role is not to dominate or overshadow their team but to serve as a guide and facilitator. By focusing on the collective success of the team rather than seeking individual accolades, humble leaders create an atmosphere of collaboration and mutual respect. This approach enables leaders to connect with their team on a deeper level, understanding their needs, concerns, and aspirations, and providing the necessary support to help them succeed.

Leading by example is a powerful method for instilling core values and principles within an organisation. When leaders embody the behaviours and attitudes they wish to see in their team, they set a standard for others to follow. This alignment between words and actions builds credibility and trust, as team members observe that their leader is genuine and consistent in their approach. Leading by example also involves demonstrating a commitment to continuous learning and self-improvement. Leaders who openly acknowledge their own development journey and show a willingness to learn from others inspire their team to adopt a similar mindset of growth and humility.

Empathy is another crucial aspect of practising humility in leadership. Leaders who are empathetic actively listen to their team members, seeking to understand their perspectives and experiences. This empathetic approach fosters a sense of belonging and psychological safety, where team members feel comfortable expressing their ideas and concerns. By showing empathy, leaders demonstrate that they value their team members as individuals, not just as contributors to organisational goals. This genuine care and consideration strengthen the bonds within the team, promoting a culture of trust and collaboration.

Moreover, humility in leadership involves recognising and appreciating the contributions of others. Humble leaders do not feel threatened by the success of their team members; instead, they celebrate their achievements and give credit where it is due. This recognition boosts morale and motivates team members to continue striving for excellence. By acknowledging the efforts and accomplishments of their team, leaders reinforce the importance of collaboration and collective success. This positive reinforcement creates a virtuous cycle, where team members feel empowered and inspired to contribute their best.

Creating a culture of humility and leading by example also requires leaders to be transparent and authentic. Transparency involves being open and honest about challenges, uncertainties, and decision-making processes. When leaders communicate transparently, they build trust and foster a sense of shared responsibility. Authenticity means staying true to one's values and principles, even in the face of difficulties. Leaders who are authentic inspire their team to act with integrity and authenticity as well, creating a cohesive and values-driven organisational culture.

CHAPTER 73 - AWARENESS

Chapter 73 of the *Tao Te Ching* explores the themes of cautious boldness, the paradox of non-striving, and the subtle, effective influence of the Tao. Here's how these teachings can be applied to modern-day strategic management:

EMBRACING CAUTIOUS BOLDNESS

> He whose boldness appears in his daring (to do wrong, in defiance of the laws) is put to death; he whose boldness appears in his not daring (to do so) lives on.

Lao Tzu's Chapter 73 of the *Tao Te Ching* imparts essential wisdom on the concept of embracing cautious boldness in leadership. This principle underscores the importance of making bold decisions with a deep sense of caution and integrity. While boldness is a vital trait for leaders, driving innovation and progress, it must be exercised with careful consideration of ethical principles and the potential consequences. This balance ensures that bold actions do not devolve into recklessness, which can harm the organisation or its stakeholders.

Cautious boldness involves a thoughtful approach to decision-making. Leaders must thoroughly evaluate the risks and benefits associated with their bold initiatives. This process requires gathering comprehensive information, seeking input from diverse perspectives, and considering the long-term impact of their actions. By conducting a meticulous analysis, leaders can identify potential pitfalls and devise strategies to mitigate them. This careful planning not only enhances the likelihood of success but also demonstrates a commitment to due diligence and responsibility.

Integrity is a cornerstone of cautious boldness. Leaders who prioritise ethical principles ensure that their bold decisions align with the organisation's values and the broader societal good. This integrity-driven approach fosters trust and credibility, both within the organisation and among external stakeholders. When leaders act with honesty and transparency, they build a foundation of trust that supports their bold initiatives. This trust is crucial for gaining the buy-in and support necessary to implement significant changes effectively.

Cautious boldness also requires a willingness to take calculated risks. Leaders must recognise that bold actions often entail uncertainty and potential challenges. However, by approaching these risks with a strategic mindset, they can navigate complexities and turn challenges into opportunities. This involves being adaptable and prepared to adjust course as needed. Leaders who can pivot in response to changing circumstances while maintaining their core principles demonstrate resilience and agility, key traits for long-term success.

Moreover, cautious boldness empowers leaders to inspire and motivate their teams. When leaders make bold decisions thoughtfully and ethically, they set a powerful example for their team members. This modelling behaviour encourages a culture of innovation and calculated risk-taking within the organisation. Team members feel empowered to propose and pursue bold ideas, knowing that their leaders will support them with guidance and a strong ethical framework. This culture of cautious boldness drives continuous improvement and keeps the organisation dynamic and forward-thinking.

Effective communication is integral to embracing cautious boldness. Leaders must clearly articulate the rationale behind their bold decisions, including the anticipated benefits and the measures in place to address potential risks. This transparency helps to build understanding and alignment among team members and stakeholders. By fostering open dialogue, leaders can address concerns, gather valuable feedback, and strengthen their plans. This collaborative approach ensures that bold initiatives are well-supported and executed with confidence and clarity.

Additionally, balancing boldness with prudence enables leaders to make impactful decisions while maintaining ethical standards. Bold actions taken without caution can lead to unintended negative consequences, including legal and reputational risks. By integrating prudence into their decision-making process, leaders can avoid these pitfalls and ensure that their actions contribute positively to the organisation's mission and vision. This balanced approach fosters sustainable growth and positions the organisation for long-term success.

RECOGNISING THE PARADOX OF NON-STRIVING

> It is the way of Heaven not to strive, and yet it skilfully overcomes; not to speak, and yet it is skilful in obtaining a reply; does not call, and yet men come to it of themselves.

The chapter introduces the profound concept of the paradox of non-striving, which holds significant lessons for contemporary leadership. This principle teaches that true success can be achieved without forceful effort or excessive control, emphasising the importance of creating an environment where natural talents and processes can flourish organically. Leaders who understand and apply this paradox recognise that sometimes the most effective results are obtained by stepping back and allowing things to develop naturally. This approach not only reduces stress and resistance but also fosters a more sustainable and harmonious work environment.

Recognising the paradox of non-striving begins with the understanding that forceful effort and over-management can often hinder progress rather than promote it. Leaders who constantly push and control every aspect of their team's work may stifle creativity and initiative. Excessive interference can create an atmosphere of stress and tension, where team members feel pressured to conform to rigid expectations rather than explore their potential and innovate. By contrast, leaders who practise non-striving allow their teams the freedom to express their natural talents and abilities, encouraging a more organic and dynamic flow of ideas and solutions.

Creating an environment where natural talents can flourish involves trust and empowerment. Leaders must trust their team members to take ownership of their work and make decisions that align with the organisation's goals. This trust fosters a sense of autonomy and responsibility, empowering individuals to leverage their strengths and contribute meaningfully to the team's success. When team members feel trusted and valued, they are more likely to be motivated and engaged, leading to higher levels of productivity and innovation. Empowerment also encourages a culture of accountability, where individuals take pride in their work and strive to achieve excellence.

Allowing things to develop organically does not mean abandoning leadership or direction. Instead, it involves guiding the team with a light touch, providing the necessary support and resources while refraining from micromanaging. Leaders should set clear objectives and boundaries but allow team members the flexibility to determine the best paths to achieve these goals. This approach encourages creativity and problem-solving, as individuals have the space to experiment and learn from their experiences. By fostering an environment of exploration and discovery, leaders can tap into the collective intelligence of their team, driving continuous improvement and innovation.

The paradox of non-striving also highlights the importance of patience and timing in leadership. Effective leaders understand that not all progress happens on a strict timetable and that sometimes the best outcomes emerge gradually. By practising patience, leaders can avoid the pitfalls of rushing decisions or forcing results, allowing solutions to mature naturally. This patient approach ensures that decisions are well-considered and that actions are taken at the right moment for maximum impact. Patience also reduces stress and fosters a calm and focused work environment, where team members feel supported and unhurried in their pursuits.

Furthermore, the principle of non-striving promotes a harmonious and sustainable work environment. When leaders refrain from forceful effort and excessive control, they create a more relaxed and positive atmosphere. This harmony enhances collaboration and teamwork, as individuals feel more comfortable sharing ideas and working together towards common goals. A sustainable work environment also considers the well-being of team members, recognising that balanced workloads and healthy work-life integration are essential for long-term success. By prioritising harmony and sustainability, leaders can build a resilient and thriving organisation.

LEVERAGING SUBTLE INFLUENCE

> Its demonstrations are quiet, and yet its plans are skilful and effective.

The chapter emphasises the profound effectiveness of leveraging subtle influence in leadership. This principle teaches that quiet demonstrations and skillful planning can guide teams more effectively than overt control or forceful directives. Leaders who understand this approach focus on leading by example, creating a supportive environment, and providing gentle guidance. Subtle influence, when employed thoughtfully, can be a powerful tool for achieving long-term goals and building strong, trust-based relationships within the organisation.

Leading by example is a cornerstone of subtle influence. Leaders who embody the qualities and behaviours they wish to see in their team members set a powerful precedent. This approach involves demonstrating integrity, diligence, and dedication in everyday actions. When team members observe their leaders consistently upholding these values, they are naturally inspired to emulate them. This modelling behaviour fosters a culture of accountability and excellence, where everyone strives to contribute positively to the collective success of the organisation. Quiet competence, rather than loud proclamations, becomes the driving force behind the team's motivation and performance.

Creating a supportive environment is another critical aspect of leveraging subtle influence. Leaders should focus on cultivating a workplace where team members feel valued, respected, and empowered to contribute their best efforts. This supportive environment is characterised by open communication, mutual respect, and a collaborative spirit. By providing the necessary resources, encouragement, and recognition, leaders can create a foundation of trust and psychological safety. This trust enables team members to take initiative, share ideas, and pursue innovation without fear of judgment or failure. A supportive environment not only enhances individual well-being but also drives collective success.

Gentle guidance, as opposed to overt control, is a nuanced and effective way to lead. Leaders who practise gentle guidance offer direction and support without micromanaging or imposing their will. This approach involves asking insightful questions, providing constructive feedback, and encouraging self-reflection and growth. Gentle guidance allows team members to develop their problem-solving skills and confidence, fostering a sense of ownership and autonomy. By guiding rather than dictating, leaders empower their teams to find their paths to success, which often leads to more sustainable and innovative outcomes.

The effectiveness of subtle influence lies in its ability to inspire rather than coerce. Leaders who rely on subtle influence understand that true commitment and engagement come from within. Rather than using force or authority to compel action, they create conditions that naturally motivate team members to align with organisational goals. This intrinsic motivation is far more powerful and enduring than external pressure. When team members are inspired by their leaders' example and feel supported in their roles, they are more likely to be proactive, creative, and dedicated to their work.

Moreover, subtle influence helps to build strong, trust-based relationships within the organisation. Leaders who lead with subtlety and integrity cultivate a sense of loyalty and respect among their team members. This trust is foundational to effective collaboration and high-performance teams. Team members who trust their leaders are more willing to communicate openly, share their concerns, and work together towards common goals. This relational capital is invaluable, as it strengthens the organisation's resilience and adaptability in the face of challenges.

MAINTAINING COMPREHENSIVE AWARENESS

The meshes of the net of Heaven are large; far apart, but letting nothing escape.

The chapter also offers profound insight into the importance of maintaining comprehensive awareness in leadership. This principle suggests that leaders must keep a broad and detailed awareness of their organisations and the environments in which they operate. Effective leaders are not only focused on the overarching goals and vision but also pay close attention to the finer details that might influence outcomes. This dual focus allows them to navigate complexities, anticipate challenges, and seize opportunities with precision and foresight.

Maintaining comprehensive awareness involves a continuous process of gathering and analysing information from multiple sources. Leaders must stay informed about industry trends, economic conditions, technological advancements, and regulatory changes that could impact their organisation. This external awareness is crucial for identifying potential threats and opportunities that lie beyond the immediate organisational boundaries. By understanding the broader context in which they operate, leaders can make strategic decisions that position their organisation for long-term success and resilience.

Equally important is internal awareness. Leaders must have a deep understanding of their organisation's operations, culture, strengths, and weaknesses. This requires regular communication with team members at all levels, seeking feedback and insights that can inform decision-making. By staying attuned to the pulse of the organisation, leaders can identify emerging issues before they escalate and address them proactively. This internal vigilance also helps in recognising and nurturing talent, fostering a culture of continuous improvement, and ensuring that the organisation remains agile and adaptable.

The balance between big-picture thinking and attention to detail is a hallmark of effective leadership. While visionary leaders set ambitious goals and chart the course for the future, they also understand the importance of meticulous execution. Paying attention to details ensures that strategic plans are implemented effectively and that small issues do not become major obstacles. This attention to detail reflects a commitment to excellence and a thorough understanding of the intricacies that drive success. Leaders who excel in both areas can inspire confidence and trust, as their comprehensive awareness instils a sense of preparedness and competence.

Moreover, maintaining comprehensive awareness involves fostering a culture of vigilance and shared responsibility within the organisation. Leaders should encourage team members to stay informed, think critically, and contribute their observations and insights. This collaborative approach to awareness ensures that no critical information is overlooked and that diverse perspectives are considered in decision-making. By empowering team members to actively participate in maintaining awareness, leaders create a more resilient and responsive organisation.

Effective decision-making is a direct outcome of comprehensive awareness. Leaders who are well-informed and vigilant can evaluate options more thoroughly and anticipate the potential impacts of their decisions. This foresight allows them to choose paths that align with the organisation's values and goals while mitigating risks. In times of uncertainty or crisis, comprehensive awareness equips leaders to navigate challenges with confidence and agility, ensuring that the organisation remains on course and resilient.

CHAPTER 74 - ROLES

Chapter 74 of the *Tao Te Ching* emphasises the limits of using fear as a deterrent and the importance of understanding one's role and capabilities. Here's how these teachings can be applied to modern-day strategic management:

AVOIDING FEAR-BASED MANAGEMENT

> *The people do not fear death; to what purpose is it to (try to) frighten them with death?*

Lao Tzu's Chapter 74 of the *Tao Te Ching* conveys the profound lesson that leaders should avoid employing fear as a tool to manage or motivate their teams. This principle emphasises that fear-based management is not only ineffective but can also lead to a toxic work environment, where decreased morale and reduced productivity become the norm. Leaders who rely on fear to exert control may achieve compliance in the short term, but this approach ultimately undermines trust, creativity, and long-term engagement among team members.

Fear-based management creates a culture of anxiety and insecurity. When employees are driven by fear, they are less likely to take risks, innovate, or express their ideas. Instead, they may focus solely on avoiding negative consequences, which stifles creativity and limits potential growth. This atmosphere of fear can lead to high levels of stress and burnout, as team members constantly worry about making mistakes or facing reprimand. Over time, this can result in high turnover rates and a loss of valuable talent, as employees seek more positive and supportive work environments.

Furthermore, fear undermines the fundamental trust required for effective collaboration and teamwork. When leaders use fear to motivate, they erode the sense of psychological safety that is essential for open communication and mutual support. Team members may become hesitant to share their thoughts or ask for help, fearing criticism or punishment. This lack of trust and openness can lead to misunderstandings, decreased cooperation, and suboptimal performance. In contrast, a trust-based environment fosters transparency and encourages team members to work together towards common goals, enhancing overall productivity and success.

Creating a positive and supportive atmosphere involves cultivating a culture of respect, empathy, and encouragement. Leaders should focus on building strong relationships with their team members, understanding their individual strengths, needs, and aspirations. This approach requires active listening, genuine interest in employees' well-being, and providing constructive feedback. By showing appreciation and recognising achievements, leaders can boost morale and motivation, creating a more engaged and committed workforce. This positive reinforcement helps to build a culture where employees feel valued and supported, driving higher levels of performance and satisfaction.

Encouraging trust and collaboration is also essential for avoiding fear-based management. Leaders should promote a team-oriented mindset, where everyone feels responsible for contributing to the collective success. This involves fostering an inclusive environment where diverse perspectives are welcomed and respected. By creating opportunities for collaboration and encouraging open dialogue, leaders can harness the collective intelligence and creativity of the team. This collaborative spirit not only enhances problem-solving and innovation but also strengthens the bonds among team members, creating a cohesive and resilient organisation.

Moreover, leaders should lead with integrity and transparency, setting an example for their teams. By being honest and forthright in their communication, leaders can build credibility and trust. This transparency involves sharing information about organisational goals, challenges, and decision-making processes, helping employees understand the broader context of their work. When team members have a clear understanding of the organisation's direction and their role within it, they are more likely to feel empowered and motivated to contribute to its success. This clarity and alignment foster a sense of purpose and belonging, which are critical for long-term engagement and productivity.

UNDERSTANDING & RESPECTING ROLES

> *There is always One who presides over the infliction of death. He who would inflict death in the room of him who so presides over it may be described as hewing wood instead of a great carpenter.*

The chapter also emphasises the importance of understanding and respecting the roles and responsibilities within an organisation. This principle underscores the necessity for leaders to recognise the boundaries of their own authority and the expertise of others. Effective leadership is not about assuming all responsibilities but about delegating tasks to those who are best suited to handle them. By doing so, leaders can ensure that decisions are made with the appropriate knowledge and skill, thereby minimising the risk of errors and negative outcomes.

Respecting the roles within an organisation means acknowledging the specialised knowledge and experience that individuals bring to their positions. Leaders must trust in the expertise of their team members and allow them the autonomy to execute their tasks. This trust fosters a sense of ownership and accountability among employees, encouraging them to take pride in their work and strive for excellence. When leaders micromanage or overstep their boundaries, they not only undermine their team members' confidence but also disrupt the natural workflow, leading to inefficiencies and potential mistakes.

Delegation is a crucial aspect of respecting roles and responsibilities. Leaders should clearly define and communicate the scope of each role, ensuring that everyone understands their specific duties and how they contribute to the organisation's overall objectives. This clarity helps to prevent overlap and confusion, enabling team members to focus on their areas of expertise. Effective delegation also involves providing the necessary resources and support, allowing individuals to perform their roles to the best of their abilities. By empowering their team through delegation, leaders can leverage the full potential of their organisation's talent.

Moreover, respecting roles within an organisation promotes a culture of collaboration and mutual respect. When leaders demonstrate respect for their team members' expertise, it sets a positive example for the entire organisation. This respect is reciprocated, fostering an environment where collaboration thrives. Team members are more likely to seek input from their colleagues, share knowledge, and work together towards common goals. This collaborative spirit enhances problem-solving and innovation, as diverse perspectives and skills are brought to bear on complex challenges.

Understanding and respecting roles also involve being aware of one's limitations as a leader. No leader, regardless of their experience or qualifications, has all the answers. Recognising this fact is a sign of wisdom and humility. Leaders should be open to learning from others and seeking advice when needed. This openness not only improves decision-making but also strengthens relationships within the organisation. When leaders show that they value the contributions and insights of their team members, it builds trust and reinforces a sense of shared purpose.

Effective decision-making is another benefit of respecting roles and responsibilities. When decisions are made by those with the appropriate expertise, they are more likely to be informed and well-considered. This reduces the likelihood of errors and ensures that actions are aligned with the organisation's goals and values. Leaders who respect the decision-making authority of their team members can make more strategic and impactful choices, as they are based on a comprehensive understanding of the relevant information and context.

CHAPTER 75 – EXCESSIVE TAXATION

Chapter 75 of the *Tao Te Ching* explores the consequences of excessive taxation, overbearing governance, and the impacts of strenuous labour on people's lives. Here's how these teachings can be applied to modern-day strategic management:

AVOIDING OVERBURDENING EMPLOYEES

> *The people suffer from famine because of the multitude of taxes consumed by their superiors. It is through this that they suffer famine.*

Lao Tzu's Chapter 75 of the *Tao Te Ching* offers a crucial lesson on the dangers of overburdening employees. This principle highlights that, much like excessive taxation can lead to famine, imposing excessive demands and unrealistic expectations on employees can result in burnout and reduced productivity. Leaders must recognise the importance of creating a balanced work environment where employees feel supported and their well-being is a top priority. This balanced approach ensures that the workforce remains motivated, efficient, and capable of sustaining long-term performance.

Avoiding the overburdening of employees begins with setting realistic and achievable goals. Leaders should be mindful of the capacity and limitations of their team members, ensuring that the objectives set forth are both challenging and attainable. Unrealistic expectations can lead to frustration and disillusionment, as employees struggle to meet demands that are beyond their reach. By setting clear, manageable goals, leaders can help employees maintain a sense of accomplishment and progress, which is vital for sustaining motivation and engagement. This approach also involves regularly reviewing and adjusting goals based on feedback and changing circumstances, ensuring that they remain relevant and attainable.

Providing necessary resources is another critical aspect of avoiding employee overburdening. Leaders must ensure that their team members have access to the tools, training, and support needed to perform their tasks effectively. This might include investing in technology, offering professional development opportunities, and providing adequate staffing levels to distribute workloads evenly. When employees have the resources they need, they are better equipped to meet their goals and feel more confident in their abilities. This support also demonstrates that leaders value and respect their team's efforts, fostering a positive and collaborative work environment.

Ensuring a healthy work-life balance is paramount for preventing burnout and maintaining productivity. Leaders should encourage employees to take regular breaks, use their vacation days, and disconnect from work during off-hours. Promoting flexible working arrangements, such as remote work options or flexible scheduling, can also help employees manage their personal and professional responsibilities more effectively. By prioritising work-life balance, leaders can help employees recharge and return to their tasks with renewed energy and focus. This balance is essential for long-term well-being and productivity, as it prevents the negative impacts of chronic stress and overwork.

Creating a balanced work environment also involves fostering a culture of support and empathy. Leaders should actively listen to their employees' concerns and be responsive to their needs. This might include providing mental health resources, offering wellness programmes, and creating spaces for open dialogue about work-related challenges. By showing genuine care for their employees' well-being, leaders can build trust and loyalty within their teams. This supportive culture encourages employees to seek help when needed and to contribute to a positive and collaborative work atmosphere.

Additionally, leaders should recognise and celebrate the achievements of their team members. Acknowledging hard work and accomplishments can boost morale and reinforce a sense of purpose and belonging. This recognition can take many forms, such as verbal praise, awards, or opportunities for advancement. Celebrating success not only motivates employees but also reinforces the value of their contributions to the organisation's goals. This positive reinforcement helps to sustain high levels of performance and commitment.

SIMPLIFYING GOVERNANCE & PROCESSES

> *The people are difficult to govern because of the (excessive) agency of their superiors (in governing them). It is through this that they are difficult to govern.*

The chapter provides insightful commentary on the negative impact of excessive micromanagement and overly complex processes in leadership. This principle suggests that when leaders impose too much control and create cumbersome governance structures, it becomes difficult to manage and motivate people effectively. Leaders who focus on simplifying governance and streamlining processes can significantly enhance organisational efficiency and create a more empowering work environment.

Excessive micromanagement can stifle creativity and innovation. When leaders constantly oversee every detail, employees may feel constrained and unable to exercise their judgment or initiative. This control can lead to a lack of ownership and accountability, as team members become overly reliant on their superiors for direction. Simplifying governance involves delegating authority and trusting employees to make decisions within their areas of expertise. By empowering team members to take initiative, leaders can foster a culture of responsibility and encourage a proactive approach to problem-solving.

Streamlining processes is another essential aspect of effective leadership. Overly complex procedures can slow down operations, creating bottlenecks and inefficiencies. These cumbersome processes can frustrate employees, leading to disengagement and reduced productivity. Leaders should focus on identifying and eliminating unnecessary steps, making workflows more straightforward and efficient. This simplification can involve automating routine tasks, clarifying roles and responsibilities, and ensuring that communication channels are clear and direct. By streamlining processes, leaders can free up valuable time and resources, enabling employees to focus on more strategic and impactful activities.

Fostering a culture of trust is critical for successful governance and process simplification. Leaders must build trust with their teams by demonstrating transparency, consistency, and integrity in their actions. Trust is the foundation of a positive work environment where employees feel safe to express their ideas, take risks, and learn from their mistakes. Leaders can cultivate trust by involving employees in decision-making, seeking their input, and valuing their contributions. When employees trust their leaders, they are more likely to be engaged, motivated, and committed to the organisation's goals.

Empowering employees through simplified governance and processes also enhances overall engagement and effectiveness. When team members have the autonomy to make decisions and the clarity to understand their roles, they are more likely to be engaged and motivated. This empowerment encourages continuous improvement, as employees feel confident in their ability to contribute to the organisation's success. By reducing bureaucratic obstacles, leaders create an environment where innovation and creativity can thrive, driving the organisation forward.

Moreover, simplifying governance and processes supports agile and adaptable organisations. In today's rapidly changing business landscape, the ability to respond quickly to new opportunities and challenges is crucial. Simplified structures and processes enable faster decision-making and more effective implementation of changes. This agility allows organisations to stay competitive and resilient, capable of navigating uncertainties and seizing emerging opportunities. By fostering a culture of adaptability, leaders can ensure that their organisations remain dynamic and forward-thinking.

VALUING EMPLOYEE WELL-BEING

> *The people make light of dying because of the greatness of their labours in seeking for the means of living. It is this which makes them think light of dying.*

The chapter also presents a profound reflection on the importance of valuing employee well-being, highlighting the detrimental effects of neglecting the human element in the relentless pursuit of productivity. This principle underscores that when leaders focus solely on achieving targets without considering the well-being of their employees, it can lead to severe dissatisfaction, disengagement, and ultimately burnout. Leaders must recognise that their team's mental and physical health is paramount and that fostering a supportive environment is essential for sustainable success.

Valuing employee well-being begins with an understanding that productivity should not come at the cost of employees' health and happiness. When individuals are overworked and stressed, their ability to perform effectively diminishes, and their overall satisfaction with their work and life declines. This can lead to higher absenteeism, turnover, and a lack of engagement, all of which are detrimental to the organisation's long-term success. Leaders must prioritise creating a healthy work environment where employees feel supported and appreciated, which in turn enhances productivity and job satisfaction.

Creating a supportive environment involves several key practices. Firstly, leaders should promote open communication and encourage employees to voice their concerns and needs. This open dialogue helps to identify issues that may be impacting well-being and allows for timely interventions. Leaders can provide mental health resources, such as access to counselling services, wellness programmes, and stress management workshops. By offering these resources, leaders show that they care about their employees' well-being and are committed to supporting them through challenges.

Ensuring a healthy work-life balance is another critical aspect of valuing employee well-being. Leaders should encourage employees to take regular breaks, use their vacation days, and set boundaries between work and personal time. Flexible work arrangements, such as remote work options or flexible hours, can help employees manage their responsibilities more effectively. By respecting employees' need for time off and personal space, leaders foster a culture where rest and rejuvenation are seen as essential components of productivity.

Recognition and appreciation are powerful tools for enhancing employee well-being. Leaders should regularly acknowledge and celebrate the hard work and accomplishments of their team members. This recognition can take many forms, such as verbal praise, awards, or opportunities for professional development. Celebrating successes boosts morale and reinforces the value of employees' contributions, making them feel valued and motivated to continue performing at their best. This positive reinforcement helps to build a culture of appreciation and respect within the organisation.

Investing in employees' growth and development is also crucial for their well-being. Leaders should provide opportunities for continuous learning, skill development, and career advancement. By supporting employees' professional growth, leaders demonstrate that they are invested in their long-term success and fulfillment. This investment not only enhances employees' capabilities but also fosters a sense of purpose and belonging. When employees feel that their organisation is committed to their development, they are more likely to be engaged and motivated.

Furthermore, fostering a sense of community and belonging within the organisation can significantly impact employee well-being. Leaders should encourage team-building activities, social events, and collaborative projects that help employees build strong relationships with their colleagues. This sense of community creates a supportive network where employees can rely on each other for encouragement and assistance. A positive work culture, where employees feel connected and valued, enhances overall well-being and contributes to a more harmonious and productive workplace.

CHAPTER 76 – SOFTNESS

Chapter 76 of the *Tao Te Ching* underscores the importance of flexibility and adaptability over rigid strength and firmness. Here's how these teachings can be applied to modern-day strategic management:

EMBRACING FLEXIBILITY & ADAPTABILITY

> Man at his birth is supple and weak; at his death, firm and strong. (So it is with) all things. Trees and plants, in their early growth, are soft and brittle; at their death, dry and withered.

Lao Tzu's Chapter 76 of the *Tao Te Ching* highlights the essential qualities of flexibility and adaptability in leadership and organisational management. This principle draws a parallel between the natural world and the characteristics that organisations must embody to thrive in a dynamic environment. Just as living beings are soft and adaptable in their early stages, so too must organisations remain flexible to ensure their long-term success. Embracing flexibility and adaptability involves being open to change, continually adjusting to new circumstances, and fostering an innovative culture.

Flexibility in leadership is crucial for navigating the complexities and uncertainties of the modern business landscape. Leaders who are open to change can effectively respond to evolving market conditions, technological advancements, and shifting customer needs. This openness requires a willingness to let go of rigid plans and embrace new strategies that better align with the current environment. Flexible leaders are proactive rather than reactive, anticipating potential changes and preparing their organisations to pivot when necessary. This proactive stance enables organisations to stay ahead of the competition and capitalise on emerging opportunities.

Adaptability goes hand in hand with flexibility and is essential for sustaining organisational growth and resilience. Adaptable leaders are skilled at assessing situations and making adjustments to ensure continued progress. This involves being attuned to both external and internal factors that may impact the organisation. By regularly evaluating the effectiveness of their strategies and being willing to make necessary changes, leaders can foster a culture of continuous improvement. Adaptability also means being responsive to feedback and learning from both successes and failures. This iterative process of adaptation helps organisations remain robust and innovative in the face of challenges.

Encouraging innovation is a key component of fostering flexibility and adaptability within an organisation. Leaders should create an environment where creativity is valued and new ideas are welcomed. This involves providing the necessary resources and support for innovation, such as investing in research and development, offering training programmes, and creating spaces for experimentation. By empowering employees to think creatively and take calculated risks, leaders can drive innovation and ensure that the organisation stays relevant and competitive. This culture of innovation also promotes a sense of ownership and engagement among employees, as they feel their contributions are valued and impactful.

Moreover, flexibility and adaptability require a mindset shift at all levels of the organisation. Leaders should encourage their teams to embrace change as an opportunity for growth rather than a threat. This positive attitude towards change can help reduce resistance and foster a more agile organisation. Training programmes and workshops that focus on developing adaptive skills and resilience can also be beneficial. By equipping employees with the tools to navigate change effectively, leaders can build a more resilient workforce that is prepared to handle uncertainty and complexity.

Effective communication is vital for fostering flexibility and adaptability. Leaders must ensure that their vision and strategies are clearly communicated to all team members, providing a shared understanding of the organisation's direction. This transparency helps to align efforts and ensure that everyone is working towards common goals. Open communication channels also allow for the free flow of information and ideas, enabling leaders to make informed decisions and adapt quickly to changing circumstances. By fostering a culture of open dialogue, leaders can harness the collective intelligence of their teams and drive more effective and innovative solutions.

VALUING SOFTNESS & RESILIENCE

> *Thus it is that firmness and strength are the concomitants of death; softness and weakness, the concomitants of life.*

The chapter underscores the profound significance of valuing softness and resilience in both leadership and organisational culture. This principle highlights that true strength and vitality are found in traits often perceived as soft or weak, such as empathy, openness, and adaptability. For contemporary leaders, this means cultivating an environment where these qualities are not only encouraged but seen as fundamental to the organisation's success and sustainability. Embracing softness and resilience is about recognising that flexibility and compassion can lead to greater long-term stability and performance.

In leadership, softness manifests as empathy and understanding. Leaders who value empathy are attuned to the emotions and needs of their team members. They listen actively and respond with compassion, creating a work environment where employees feel heard and valued. This approach fosters trust and loyalty, as team members are more likely to engage and commit to their work when they feel understood and respected. Empathy also plays a crucial role in conflict resolution, allowing leaders to navigate disagreements and challenges with a focus on finding mutually beneficial solutions. By prioritising empathy, leaders can build strong, cohesive teams that work collaboratively towards common goals.

Openness is another critical aspect of valuing softness in leadership. Open leaders are transparent in their communication and willing to share information and insights with their teams. This transparency builds credibility and trust, as employees are kept informed about organisational developments and decisions. Open leaders also encourage feedback and diverse perspectives, creating an inclusive culture where everyone feels empowered to contribute. This openness fosters innovation, as team members are more likely to share their ideas and take risks when they know their input is valued. By maintaining an open and inclusive environment, leaders can drive creativity and continuous improvement within their organisations.

Resilience, often associated with adaptability, is a vital trait for navigating the complexities and uncertainties of the modern business world. Resilient leaders are not rigid in their approach but are flexible and adaptable, able to pivot in response to changing circumstances. This adaptability involves being open to new ideas and approaches, continuously learning, and being prepared to adjust strategies as needed. Resilient organisations are those that can withstand disruptions and emerge stronger, having learned and grown from their experiences. By fostering a culture of resilience, leaders can ensure that their teams are equipped to handle setbacks and challenges with a positive and proactive mindset.

Creating a supportive and inclusive environment is key to fostering softness and resilience in an organisation. Leaders should prioritise building a culture where employees feel safe to express themselves and take initiative. This involves providing support through resources such as training and development programmes, mental health services, and opportunities for professional growth. By investing in the well-being and development of their team members, leaders show that they value their contributions and care about their long-term success. This support helps to build a resilient workforce that is capable of navigating challenges and adapting to change effectively.

The notion of softness as a source of strength challenges traditional views of leadership that equate toughness with effectiveness. In reality, leaders who embrace softness demonstrate a profound understanding of the human element in organisational success. They recognise that creating a nurturing and compassionate work environment leads to higher levels of engagement, productivity, and innovation. This approach is not about being lenient or passive but about leading with emotional intelligence and recognising the power of human connection. Softness, in this context, is a strategic asset that enhances the organisation's ability to thrive in a dynamic and competitive landscape.

AVOIDING RIGID DEPENDENCE ON STRENGTH

> *Hence he who (relies on) the strength of his forces does not conquer; and a tree which is strong will fill the out-stretched arms, (and thereby invites the feller.)*

The chapter emphasises the dangers of relying solely on rigid strength and force. This principle cautions leaders against becoming too inflexible in their strategies and approaches. Rigidity can lead to downfall as it limits the ability to adapt to changing circumstances and stifles the potential for innovation. Instead, leaders should prioritise collaboration, communication, and adaptability, which are essential for navigating complex situations and achieving sustainable success.

In leadership, an over-reliance on sheer strength can manifest in various forms, such as authoritarian decision-making, inflexible policies, and a top-down management style. While these approaches may yield short-term compliance, they often result in long-term dissatisfaction and disengagement among team members. An authoritarian leader who imposes their will without considering the input of others may create an environment of fear and resentment, where employees feel undervalued and demotivated. This can lead to high turnover rates, decreased productivity, and a lack of innovation, as team members are not encouraged to contribute their ideas or take initiative.

To avoid the pitfalls of rigid dependence on strength, leaders should embrace a more collaborative approach. Collaboration involves actively seeking and valuing the input of team members, fostering a sense of shared ownership and accountability. By involving employees in decision-making processes, leaders can tap into the collective intelligence of the organisation, resulting in more well-rounded and effective solutions. This inclusive approach also enhances engagement and morale, as team members feel their contributions are recognised and valued. Collaboration promotes a culture of trust and respect, which is essential for building strong, cohesive teams.

Communication is another critical component of effective leadership. Clear, transparent, and open communication helps to build trust and ensures that everyone is aligned with the organisation's goals and strategies. Leaders should prioritise regular and meaningful communication with their teams, providing updates, seeking feedback, and addressing concerns. This two-way communication fosters a culture of openness and accountability, where team members feel comfortable sharing their ideas and perspectives. Effective communication also helps to prevent misunderstandings and conflicts, ensuring that everyone is on the same page and working towards common objectives.

Adaptability is essential for navigating the complexities and uncertainties of the modern business environment. Leaders who are flexible and open to change can respond more effectively to new challenges and opportunities. This adaptability involves being willing to reassess and adjust strategies as needed, rather than sticking rigidly to a predetermined plan. Leaders should encourage a culture of continuous learning and improvement, where team members are empowered to experiment, take risks, and learn from their experiences. By fostering an adaptive mindset, leaders can ensure that their organisations remain resilient and capable of thriving in a dynamic landscape.

Flexibility also involves being open to different perspectives and approaches. Leaders should actively seek out diverse viewpoints and consider alternative solutions to problems. This openness to diversity enhances creativity and innovation, as it brings together a wide range of ideas and experiences. By valuing and integrating these different perspectives, leaders can develop more comprehensive and effective strategies that address the needs and challenges of the organisation. Flexibility also helps to build an inclusive culture, where everyone feels their voice is heard and their contributions are valued.

LEADING WITH HUMILITY & OPENNESS

Therefore the place of what is firm and strong is below, and that of what is soft and weak is above.

The chapter also provides profound insight into the essence of true leadership, emphasising the virtues of humility and openness. The idea that what is firm and strong holds a position below, while what is soft and weak is elevated above, symbolises the importance of adopting a humble and open mindset in leadership. True strength in leadership does not come from rigidity and force, but from the capacity to embrace new ideas, learn from others, and remain adaptable. This perspective fosters a culture of continuous improvement and innovation, empowering every team member to contribute their best.

Leading with humility means recognising that, as a leader, one does not have all the answers. Humility allows leaders to seek out and value the insights and expertise of their team members. This approach involves actively listening to different perspectives, acknowledging one's own limitations, and being willing to change course based on new information. Humility in leadership creates an environment where team members feel respected and appreciated, knowing that their contributions are vital to the organisation's success. This sense of mutual respect builds trust and loyalty, as employees are more likely to engage and commit to their work when they feel their voices are heard and valued.

Openness in leadership is about fostering an environment where transparency and honesty are paramount. Open leaders communicate clearly and candidly with their teams, sharing both successes and challenges. This transparency helps to build a foundation of trust, as team members are kept informed about the organisation's direction and the rationale behind decisions. Open communication channels also encourage the free exchange of ideas and feedback, which is essential for continuous improvement. By being open to receiving feedback and willing to act on it, leaders demonstrate that they are committed to growth and learning, setting a positive example for their teams.

Adaptability is another crucial aspect of leading with humility and openness. The ability to adapt to changing circumstances is a hallmark of effective leadership. Adaptable leaders are flexible in their approach, able to pivot when necessary to respond to new opportunities or challenges. This adaptability is not a sign of weakness, but rather a reflection of strength and resilience. By being open to change and willing to experiment with new ideas, leaders can drive innovation and keep their organisations competitive in a constantly evolving landscape. This mindset encourages a culture of agility, where team members feel empowered to take risks and explore new possibilities.

Furthermore, fostering a culture of continuous improvement is central to the concept of leading with humility and openness. Leaders who embrace this approach understand that there is always room for growth and development. They encourage their teams to strive for excellence, providing opportunities for professional development and creating an environment where learning is valued. This focus on continuous improvement drives innovation, as team members are motivated to find new and better ways of doing things. It also ensures that the organisation remains dynamic and forward-thinking, always ready to adapt to the future's demands.

Empowerment is another key outcome of leading with humility and openness. When leaders value the contributions of their team members and create an inclusive environment, they empower individuals to take ownership of their work and make meaningful contributions. This empowerment leads to higher levels of engagement and motivation, as employees feel that they have a stake in the organisation's success. Empowered teams are more likely to collaborate effectively, share knowledge, and support each other, resulting in a more cohesive and productive work environment.

CHAPTER 77 - ARROGANCE

Chapter 77 of the *Tao Te Ching* draws a comparison between the Tao and the act of bending a bow, illustrating the principles of balance, humility, and the redistribution of resources. Here's how these teachings can be applied to modern-day strategic management:

PROMOTING BALANCE & EQUITY

> May not the Way (or Tao) of Heaven be compared to the (method of) bending a bow? The (part of the bow) which was high is brought low, and what was low is raised up.

Lao Tzu's Chapter 77 of the *Tao Te Ching* offers a powerful metaphor for promoting balance and equity within an organisation. The imagery of bending a bow, where the high part is brought low and the low part is raised up, symbolises the importance of levelling disparities and creating a harmonious environment. For leaders, this principle translates into the need to address inequities, ensuring that resources and opportunities are distributed fairly. By uplifting those who are in need and tempering the advantages of those who have excess, leaders can cultivate a more cohesive and inclusive workplace.

Promoting balance and equity begins with recognising the existing disparities within the organisation. Leaders must be attuned to the various ways in which inequalities manifest, whether through differences in pay, access to opportunities, or support systems. This awareness is the first step towards addressing these imbalances. Leaders can then take deliberate actions to identify and support those who may be disadvantaged or underserved. By providing additional resources, mentorship, and opportunities for development, leaders can help to level the playing field and ensure that everyone has the chance to succeed.

Creating equity also involves moderating the excesses of those who are more advantaged. This does not mean penalising success but rather ensuring that the benefits of success are shared and contribute to the overall well-being of the organisation. Leaders can implement policies that promote fair compensation, equitable distribution of workload, and equal access to professional development opportunities. This approach helps to prevent resentment and disengagement among team members, fostering a sense of fairness and inclusivity. When employees feel that their contributions are valued and that they have equal opportunities for advancement, they are more likely to be motivated and committed to their work.

Balance in leadership is also about creating a supportive environment where collaboration and mutual respect are paramount. Leaders should encourage open communication and create channels for feedback, ensuring that all voices are heard and considered. This inclusive approach helps to build trust and strengthens the bonds within the team. By involving team members in decision-making processes and recognising their input, leaders can create a sense of ownership and accountability. This collaborative spirit not only enhances the quality of decisions but also fosters a more engaged and cohesive workforce.

Moreover, promoting balance and equity requires a commitment to continuous improvement. Leaders should regularly assess the effectiveness of their policies and initiatives, seeking input from employees to identify areas for enhancement. This iterative process ensures that the organisation remains responsive to the evolving needs of its members and can adapt to new challenges. By being open to change and willing to adjust strategies, leaders demonstrate their dedication to creating a fair and inclusive environment.

The pursuit of equity also involves addressing systemic issues that may perpetuate disparities. Leaders must be willing to challenge and change organisational structures and practices that contribute to inequality. This might include revising recruitment and promotion processes to ensure diversity and inclusivity, implementing training programmes to address unconscious bias, and fostering a culture that values and respects differences. By tackling these systemic issues, leaders can create a more equitable organisation where everyone has the opportunity to thrive.

REDISTRIBUTING RESOURCES WISELY

> It is the Way of Heaven to diminish superabundance, and to supplement deficiency. It is not so with the way of man. He takes away from those who have not enough to add to his own superabundance.

The chapter presents a compelling perspective on the wise redistribution of resources, a principle that modern leaders can harness to cultivate equity and efficiency within their organisations. This principle challenges leaders to address imbalances in resource allocation, ensuring that all team members have the necessary tools and support to thrive. By redistributing resources to bridge gaps and address deficiencies, leaders can enhance overall productivity, morale, and cohesion, fostering a more equitable work environment where everyone benefits.

Mindfulness in resource allocation requires leaders to conduct thorough assessments of their teams' needs and existing disparities. This involves identifying areas where resources are lacking and recognising the potential impacts of these deficiencies on performance and morale. Leaders must take a proactive approach to ensure that resources—whether financial, technological, or human—are distributed in a manner that supports the success of the entire organisation. This redistribution is not about diminishing the achievements or resources of those who are well-equipped but about supplementing those who are underserved to create a more balanced and effective team.

Redistributing resources wisely has a direct impact on productivity. When team members have access to the necessary tools, training, and support, they can perform their tasks more efficiently and effectively. Addressing resource deficiencies enables employees to focus on their work without the hindrance of inadequate support. For example, providing access to updated technology or professional development opportunities can significantly enhance an employee's capabilities and contributions. This investment in resources translates into higher quality work, increased innovation, and overall better performance across the organisation.

Moreover, equitable resource allocation fosters a sense of fairness and inclusivity, which are critical for maintaining high morale and employee engagement. When leaders ensure that all team members have what they need to succeed, it demonstrates a commitment to valuing and supporting each individual. This approach helps to build trust and loyalty, as employees feel recognised and appreciated for their contributions. It also reduces feelings of resentment or disengagement that can arise when resources are perceived to be distributed unfairly. By promoting equity, leaders create a more positive and cohesive work culture where everyone feels motivated to give their best.

Preventing the concentration of resources in a few hands is essential for avoiding organisational stagnation and fostering innovation. When resources are hoarded by a select few, it can stifle creativity and limit the potential for diverse ideas and solutions. Leaders should encourage a more democratic distribution of resources, ensuring that all team members have the opportunity to innovate and contribute. This inclusive approach not only enhances individual performance but also drives collective progress and growth. By leveraging the diverse strengths and perspectives of the entire team, organisations can develop more robust and innovative strategies.

Effective resource redistribution also involves creating mechanisms for feedback and continuous improvement. Leaders should establish channels for employees to communicate their needs and concerns regarding resource allocation. Regular check-ins and surveys can provide valuable insights into areas where additional support may be needed. This ongoing dialogue ensures that resource distribution remains dynamic and responsive to changing circumstances. By staying attuned to the evolving needs of their team, leaders can make informed decisions that sustain balance and equity over time.

ACTING WITH HUMILITY & SERVICE

> *Who can take his own superabundance and therewith serve all under heaven?*
> *Only he who is in possession of the Tao!*

The chapter delivers a profound lesson on the essence of leadership, emphasising humility and a spirit of service. This principle suggests that true leaders are those who possess the wisdom and the moral compass to use their resources and influence for the benefit of the broader organisation and community. Such leaders do not seek personal gain or recognition but focus instead on the well-being and development of others. This approach builds trust and respect, fostering a positive and collaborative organisational culture that benefits everyone involved.

Acting with humility in leadership means recognising the value of every team member's contribution and understanding that leadership is not about exerting power but about serving the needs of others. Humble leaders do not see themselves as superior to their team members; instead, they view their role as one of support and facilitation. They are willing to listen, learn, and adapt, recognising that they do not have all the answers. This humility allows leaders to build strong, trusting relationships with their team members, as it demonstrates a genuine respect for their abilities and insights.

A spirit of service is central to effective leadership. Leaders who adopt a servant leadership approach prioritise the needs and well-being of their team members above their own ambitions. They focus on creating an environment where everyone can thrive, providing the necessary support, resources, and opportunities for growth. This might involve mentoring, offering professional development opportunities, or ensuring that employees have a healthy work-life balance. By investing in their team's success, servant leaders build a foundation of loyalty and commitment, as employees feel valued and appreciated.

Using resources and influence to benefit the broader organisation and community involves a strategic and thoughtful allocation of assets. Leaders should assess where their resources can have the most significant positive impact, whether it be through enhancing employee benefits, improving working conditions, or supporting community initiatives. This approach requires a deep understanding of the organisation's needs and a commitment to ethical decision-making. Leaders who prioritise the collective good over personal gain demonstrate integrity and inspire others to do the same. This ethical stance not only strengthens the organisation's internal culture but also enhances its reputation and standing in the wider community.

Focusing on the well-being of others rather than personal gain also cultivates a culture of trust and respect. When leaders demonstrate that their primary concern is the welfare of their team members, it builds a sense of psychological safety. Employees feel secure in the knowledge that their leaders have their best interests at heart, which encourages open communication, collaboration, and risk-taking. This trust is fundamental to a positive and productive work environment, where innovation and creativity can flourish without fear of retribution or failure.

A servant leadership approach also promotes collaboration and teamwork. By valuing each team member's contribution and creating a supportive environment, leaders encourage a sense of shared responsibility and collective effort. This collaborative spirit enhances problem-solving and decision-making, as diverse perspectives and skills are brought together to address challenges. It also fosters a sense of unity and purpose, as everyone works towards common goals with a shared understanding of the organisation's mission and values.

AVOIDING ARROGANCE & RECOGNISING COLLECTIVE ACHIEVEMENT

> *Therefore the (ruling) sage acts without claiming the results as his; he achieves his merit and does not rest (arrogantly) in it:—he does not wish to display his superiority.*

The chapter also imparts a crucial lesson for leaders on avoiding arrogance and recognising collective achievement. This principle underscores the importance of humility in leadership, emphasising that true leaders do not claim credit for successes solely as their own. Instead, they acknowledge the contributions of their team and celebrate collective accomplishments. By doing so, leaders foster a sense of camaraderie, motivation, and mutual respect, which are essential for sustaining a positive and productive organisational culture.

Arrogance in leadership can be detrimental to both the leader and the organisation. When leaders take sole credit for achievements, they alienate their team members, diminishing their sense of value and recognition. This can lead to disengagement, as employees feel that their efforts are overlooked and unappreciated. Moreover, arrogance can create a toxic work environment, where competition and resentment overshadow collaboration and teamwork. Leaders who focus on displaying their superiority may stifle innovation and creativity, as team members become hesitant to share ideas or take risks for fear of being overshadowed or dismissed.

Recognising collective achievement, on the other hand, cultivates a culture of inclusivity and respect. Leaders who share credit with their team members acknowledge that success is a result of collaborative effort. This recognition boosts morale and motivates employees to continue contributing their best. When leaders celebrate team accomplishments, they reinforce the idea that everyone plays a vital role in the organisation's success. This shared sense of purpose and achievement strengthens the bonds within the team, fostering a supportive and cohesive work environment.

Humility in leadership also involves being open to feedback and learning from others. Leaders who are humble understand that they do not have all the answers and are willing to seek advice and insights from their team members. This openness encourages a culture of continuous improvement, as team members feel empowered to provide constructive feedback and suggest new ideas. By valuing the input of others, humble leaders demonstrate their commitment to growth and development, both personally and organisationally. This approach fosters an environment where innovation and problem-solving thrive, as diverse perspectives are welcomed and considered.

Celebrating team accomplishments is a powerful way to reinforce the value of teamwork. Leaders should make it a priority to acknowledge and reward the collective efforts of their team. This can be done through public recognition, awards, or opportunities for professional development. By highlighting the achievements of the team as a whole, leaders emphasise the importance of collaboration and mutual support. This positive reinforcement encourages team members to continue working together towards common goals, enhancing overall productivity and performance.

Moreover, avoiding arrogance and recognising collective achievement builds trust and credibility within the organisation. Leaders who consistently demonstrate humility and appreciation for their team earn the respect and loyalty of their employees. This trust is crucial for effective leadership, as it ensures that team members feel confident in their leader's abilities and intentions. Trust also fosters open communication and transparency, which are essential for addressing challenges and navigating complexities. When employees trust their leaders, they are more likely to engage fully, take initiative, and contribute to the organisation's success.

CHAPTER 78 – EMPATHY

Chapter 78 of the *Tao Te Ching* provides profound insights into the power of softness and humility, as well as the paradoxical nature of true strength. Here's how these teachings can be applied to modern-day strategic management:

HARNESSING THE POWER OF SOFTNESS & FLEXIBILITY

> *There is nothing in the world more soft and weak than water, and yet for attacking things that are firm and strong there is nothing that can take precedence of it.*

Lao Tzu's Chapter 78 of the *Tao Te Ching* offers a profound metaphor on the power of softness and flexibility through the example of water. Though water is soft and yielding, it possesses the extraordinary ability to overcome the hardest and most rigid structures. This principle carries significant implications for strategic management and leadership, suggesting that adaptability and resilience are crucial for achieving success. Leaders who harness the power of softness and flexibility can navigate uncertainties and seize opportunities more effectively, driving their organisations towards sustained growth and innovation.

Softness in leadership is often misunderstood as a weakness, but in reality, it is a source of tremendous strength. Leaders who embrace softness are empathetic, understanding, and considerate of their team's needs and aspirations. This empathy fosters a supportive and inclusive work environment where team members feel valued and respected. Empathetic leaders listen actively, respond with compassion, and build strong relationships based on trust and mutual respect. This relational strength allows leaders to connect with their teams on a deeper level, fostering a sense of loyalty and commitment that drives collective success.

Flexibility, on the other hand, is about being open to change and willing to adapt to new circumstances. In the ever-evolving landscape of modern business, rigid adherence to established plans and strategies can be detrimental. Leaders must remain agile, ready to pivot in response to emerging challenges and opportunities. Flexibility involves a willingness to experiment, take calculated risks, and learn from both successes and failures. By fostering a culture of adaptability, leaders can encourage innovation and creativity, ensuring that their organisations remain competitive and resilient.

The combination of softness and flexibility enables leaders to respond to challenges with a composed and resourceful mindset. Just as water finds a way to flow around obstacles, adaptable leaders can navigate complexities with ease. This ability to remain calm and resourceful under pressure is crucial for effective problem-solving. Leaders who embrace flexibility are more likely to find creative solutions to problems, leveraging the diverse perspectives and skills of their team members. This collaborative approach not only enhances decision-making but also fosters a sense of shared responsibility and teamwork.

Moreover, the power of softness and flexibility extends to strategic planning and execution. Leaders should design strategies that are dynamic and responsive to change, rather than rigid and prescriptive. This involves setting clear goals and objectives while allowing for flexibility in the methods and approaches used to achieve them. By empowering team members to take ownership of their work and adapt their strategies as needed, leaders can drive innovation and continuous improvement. This approach ensures that the organisation can quickly respond to shifting market conditions and capitalise on new opportunities.

Creating an organisational culture that values softness and flexibility requires intentional effort from leaders. They must lead by example, demonstrating their commitment to these principles in their actions and decisions. This might involve regularly soliciting feedback, being open to new ideas, and fostering an environment where team members feel safe to take risks and experiment. Leaders should also invest in training and development programmes that enhance adaptability and resilience, equipping their teams with the skills needed to thrive in a dynamic environment.

EMBRACING THE STRENGTH OF HUMILITY

> *Every one in the world knows that the soft overcomes the hard, and the weak the strong, but no one is able to carry it out in practice.*

The chapter speaks to the profound strength found in humility, a trait often overlooked in the context of leadership. This principle highlights the wisdom in recognising that softness and weakness, exemplified through humility, can indeed overcome hardness and strength. Embracing humility in leadership involves acknowledging one's limitations, valuing the contributions of others, and maintaining an openness to learning and growth. This approach fosters a collaborative and supportive environment, ultimately strengthening the organisation from within and enhancing overall performance.

Humility in leadership starts with the recognition of one's own limitations. Leaders who are humble understand that they do not have all the answers and that they too can make mistakes. This self-awareness allows them to be more receptive to feedback and more willing to seek input from others. By acknowledging their fallibility, humble leaders create an environment where team members feel safe to share their ideas and concerns without fear of retribution. This openness leads to better decision-making, as it incorporates diverse perspectives and expertise, ensuring that the chosen course of action is well-rounded and thoroughly considered.

Valuing the contributions of others is another cornerstone of humble leadership. Leaders who practise humility are quick to give credit where it is due and to celebrate the achievements of their team members. They understand that success is rarely the result of a single individual's efforts but is instead a collective accomplishment. By recognising and valuing the hard work and talents of their team, humble leaders foster a sense of belonging and motivation. This acknowledgment not only boosts morale but also encourages team members to continue contributing their best efforts, knowing that their work is appreciated and makes a difference.

Humility also entails being open to learning and growth. Humble leaders are perpetual learners who are curious about new ideas and willing to adapt their approaches based on new information and experiences. This openness to change is crucial in a rapidly evolving business landscape, where flexibility and innovation are key to staying competitive. Leaders who are eager to learn are better equipped to navigate challenges and seize opportunities, as they are constantly enhancing their skills and knowledge. This commitment to personal and professional development sets a powerful example for the entire organisation, promoting a culture of continuous improvement and lifelong learning.

A humble approach to leadership creates a collaborative and supportive work environment. When leaders show humility, they model behaviours that encourage teamwork and mutual support. Team members are more likely to work together harmoniously, sharing knowledge and resources to achieve common goals. This collaborative spirit enhances the organisation's ability to innovate and solve problems, as it leverages the collective intelligence and creativity of the team. Furthermore, a supportive environment nurtures resilience, as team members feel confident that they can rely on each other and their leaders in times of difficulty.

ACCEPTING RESPONSIBILITY & LEADING WITH EMPATHY

> He who accepts his state's reproach, Is hailed therefore its altars' lord; To him who bears men's direful woes They all the name of King accord.

The chapter delves deeply into the virtues of accepting responsibility and leading with empathy, framing these traits as crucial for effective leadership. The notion that a leader who accepts reproach and bears the woes of others is honoured and respected captures the essence of servant leadership. Leaders who willingly accept responsibility for their actions, especially in times of failure or difficulty, demonstrate integrity and build trust within their organisation. This transparency fosters a culture of accountability, where team members feel secure in the knowledge that their leaders will stand by them and acknowledge their own shortcomings.

Accepting responsibility involves owning up to mistakes and taking corrective action. Leaders who demonstrate this quality show that they are willing to learn and grow from their experiences. This humility not only strengthens their credibility but also encourages team members to adopt a similar attitude towards personal and professional development. When leaders take responsibility, they set a powerful example for their team, promoting a culture of openness and continuous improvement. This willingness to address challenges head-on can transform obstacles into opportunities for growth, fostering resilience within the organisation.

Leading with empathy, on the other hand, means being attuned to the emotional and practical needs of team members. Empathetic leaders are skilled at understanding and addressing the concerns of their employees, creating an environment where individuals feel valued and supported. This approach requires active listening, genuine concern, and responsive action. By placing themselves in their team members' shoes, empathetic leaders can make informed decisions that reflect the best interests of both the individuals and the organisation. This empathy helps to build strong, trust-based relationships, as employees feel that their well-being is a priority.

Creating a culture of mutual respect and support is central to leading with empathy. Leaders who foster such a culture promote inclusivity and collaboration, where every team member feels empowered to contribute their ideas and perspectives. This inclusive environment encourages open communication and constructive feedback, enhancing problem-solving and innovation. When team members know that their leaders are approachable and empathetic, they are more likely to voice their concerns and seek guidance, leading to a more dynamic and engaged workforce.

Moreover, empathetic leadership strengthens the organisation's foundation by inspiring loyalty and commitment. Employees are more likely to remain dedicated to an organisation where they feel understood and appreciated. This loyalty translates into higher retention rates, as team members are less inclined to leave an environment that values their contributions and prioritises their well-being. Empathetic leaders also inspire a sense of purpose and alignment with the organisation's mission and values, motivating employees to strive for excellence and take pride in their work.

The combination of accepting responsibility and leading with empathy creates a powerful leadership model that fosters trust, accountability, and a positive organisational culture. Leaders who embrace these qualities can navigate the complexities of the business world with grace and wisdom, ensuring the long-term success and fulfillment of their organisations. By acknowledging their own limitations, valuing the contributions of others, and prioritising the needs and concerns of their team, these leaders build a resilient and supportive environment where everyone can thrive.

VALUING PARADOXICAL TRUTHS

Words that are strictly true seem to be paradoxical.

The chapter also presents a thought-provoking insight into the nature of paradoxical truths and their significance in leadership. The idea that strict truths often appear paradoxical encourages leaders to recognise that genuine strength frequently resides in qualities that may seem contradictory at first glance. By understanding and valuing these paradoxes, leaders can cultivate a more sophisticated and effective approach to management, enhancing their ability to navigate complex and dynamic environments.

One of the most profound paradoxes in leadership is the strength found in softness and yielding. In traditional views of leadership, firmness and rigidity are often seen as indicators of strength. However, Lao Tzu's teachings challenge this notion, suggesting that flexibility and adaptability are more potent forms of strength. Like water that shapes the hardest rocks through persistent softness, leaders who are adaptable can effectively address challenges and seize opportunities. This flexibility allows them to navigate uncertainties with grace, maintaining composure and resilience in the face of adversity. By being open to change and willing to adjust their strategies, these leaders inspire confidence and trust among their team members, fostering a culture of innovation and continuous improvement.

Humility is another paradoxical trait that can enhance leadership. While conventional wisdom may equate authority with dominance and control, true authority often arises from humility. Leaders who exhibit humility acknowledge their limitations and are open to learning from others. This openness creates an inclusive environment where team members feel valued and respected, knowing that their contributions are appreciated. Humble leaders are more approachable and build stronger relationships with their teams, as they demonstrate genuine concern for others' well-being. This approach fosters loyalty and commitment, as employees are more likely to engage fully and contribute their best efforts when they feel supported by their leaders.

The paradox of humility enhancing authority is also evident in the way such leaders handle success and failure. Humble leaders share credit for successes with their teams, recognising the collective effort involved. This sharing of credit boosts morale and reinforces the value of teamwork. Conversely, when faced with failure, humble leaders accept responsibility and use these experiences as opportunities for growth and learning. This attitude sets a powerful example for the organisation, promoting a culture of accountability and resilience. By embracing humility, leaders not only strengthen their own credibility but also empower their teams to strive for continuous improvement.

Another paradoxical truth in leadership is the strength derived from empathy and compassion. While these qualities may be perceived as signs of weakness, they are, in fact, foundational to effective leadership. Leaders who lead with empathy are attuned to the needs and emotions of their team members, creating a supportive and nurturing environment. This empathy fosters trust and collaboration, as employees feel understood and valued. Compassionate leaders can motivate and inspire their teams, as they demonstrate genuine care and concern for their well-being. This approach enhances overall performance, as team members are more likely to be engaged and committed when they feel supported by their leaders.

The concept of paradoxical truths also extends to decision-making. Leaders who appreciate the complexity of paradoxes are better equipped to make balanced and informed decisions. They recognise that effective solutions often require a blend of seemingly opposing qualities, such as being both strategic and empathetic or decisive and flexible. This nuanced understanding enables leaders to navigate the intricate dynamics of their organisations, making decisions that are both thoughtful and impactful. By embracing the richness of paradoxes, leaders can develop a holistic approach to management, one that leverages the full spectrum of human potential.

CHAPTER 79 – CONFLICT RESOLUTION

Chapter 79 of the *Tao Te Ching* delves into the nature of reconciliation, the importance of patience and fairness, and the ethical underpinnings of relationships. Here's how these teachings can be applied to modern-day strategic management:

PRACTISING PATIENCE & UNDERSTANDING IN CONFLICT RESOLUTION

When a reconciliation is effected (between two parties) after a great animosity, there is sure to be a grudge remaining (in the mind of the one who was wrong). And how can this be beneficial (to the other)?

Lao Tzu's Chapter 79 of the *Tao Te Ching* provides valuable insight into the delicate art of conflict resolution, particularly in the realm of strategic management. The principle that reconciliation can often leave lingering feelings of resentment highlights the necessity for leaders to approach conflict resolution with patience and understanding. Recognising that resolving disputes can be a complex process, leaders must ensure that all parties involved feel heard, respected, and valued. This approach not only addresses the immediate issues but also helps to prevent grudges from festering and impacting future interactions within the organisation.

Patience is a critical virtue in conflict resolution. Leaders must understand that reconciliation is not a quick fix but a process that requires time and effort. Rushing through conflict resolution can lead to superficial solutions that fail to address the root causes of the disagreement. Leaders should take the time to listen to all parties involved, understanding their perspectives and concerns. This patience allows for a deeper exploration of the underlying issues, enabling a more comprehensive and lasting resolution. By demonstrating patience, leaders show that they are committed to finding a solution that is fair and satisfactory for everyone involved.

Understanding, too, plays a crucial role in effective conflict resolution. Leaders must strive to empathise with the emotions and experiences of those involved in the conflict. This empathy involves recognising the pain and frustration that may have arisen from the disagreement and validating these feelings. When individuals feel that their emotions are acknowledged and respected, they are more likely to engage in the reconciliation process constructively. Understanding helps to create an environment of trust and safety, where parties feel comfortable expressing their true feelings and working towards a genuine resolution.

Fostering open communication is essential for addressing the underlying issues that contribute to conflicts. Leaders should create spaces where individuals can voice their concerns openly and honestly without fear of retribution. This open dialogue helps to uncover the deeper causes of the conflict, which may not be immediately apparent. By encouraging transparent and respectful communication, leaders can facilitate a mutual understanding that paves the way for reconciliation. This process involves active listening, where leaders pay close attention to what is being said and respond thoughtfully, showing that they value the perspectives of all parties involved.

Addressing underlying issues is crucial for achieving genuine reconciliation. Conflicts often stem from deeper, unresolved problems that need to be addressed to prevent future disagreements. Leaders should work collaboratively with the parties involved to identify these root causes and develop strategies to address them. This might involve revising policies, improving communication channels, or providing additional support and resources. By tackling these underlying issues, leaders can create a more harmonious and cohesive work environment, reducing the likelihood of future conflicts.

Preventing grudges from affecting future interactions requires ongoing effort and vigilance. Leaders must recognise that reconciliation is not a one-time event but an ongoing process. They should continue to monitor the situation, providing support and guidance as needed to ensure that the resolution is maintained. This might involve regular check-ins with the parties involved, offering mediation services, or creating opportunities for team-building and collaboration. By actively working to maintain harmony and address any lingering issues, leaders can foster a positive and productive organisational culture.

KEEPING COMMITMENTS & SHOWING EMPATHY

> *Therefore (to guard against this), the sage keeps the left-hand portion of the record of the engagement, and does not insist on the (speedy) fulfilment of it by the other party.*

The chapter provides a timeless perspective on the virtues of keeping commitments and showing empathy in leadership. This principle underscores the importance of understanding and patience in managing commitments and expectations. Leaders who practise empathy and flexibility demonstrate an appreciation for the complexities of each individual's circumstances, which is crucial for building trust and fostering goodwill within an organisation.

Keeping commitments with empathy means recognising that while agreements and deadlines are important, the human element cannot be overlooked. Leaders must be mindful that unexpected situations and challenges can affect the ability of team members to fulfil their commitments. By demonstrating patience and understanding when these situations arise, leaders show that they value their employees as individuals, not just as cogs in a machine. This empathetic approach helps to build a supportive and trusting environment, where team members feel appreciated and respected.

Flexibility is another key component of empathetic leadership. Flexibility involves being open to adjusting expectations and timelines to accommodate the needs and circumstances of others. When leaders show flexibility, they signal that they are willing to work with their team members to find solutions that work for everyone. This adaptability fosters a sense of collaboration and mutual respect, as employees feel that their leaders are partners in their success rather than taskmasters. By being flexible, leaders can help their teams navigate challenges more effectively and maintain morale and motivation.

Building trust through empathy and flexibility also involves transparent communication. Leaders should be open about their own expectations and the reasons behind them, while also being receptive to feedback and concerns from their team members. This two-way communication helps to establish a clear understanding of commitments and the potential obstacles that might arise. When team members feel that their leaders are listening to them and considering their input, it enhances their sense of belonging and engagement. Transparent communication also helps to prevent misunderstandings and conflicts, as everyone is on the same page regarding expectations and challenges.

Empathetic leadership also means being proactive in addressing the underlying issues that might impact the fulfillment of commitments. Leaders should take the time to understand the root causes of any delays or difficulties and work collaboratively with their team members to find solutions. This might involve providing additional resources, offering training or support, or adjusting workloads to ensure that everyone can meet their obligations without undue stress. By addressing these issues proactively, leaders demonstrate their commitment to their team's well-being and success.

Creating a culture of respect and support through empathy and flexibility ultimately leads to stronger relationships within the organisation. When employees feel that their leaders are empathetic and flexible, they are more likely to reciprocate these qualities in their interactions with others. This creates a positive ripple effect, where mutual respect and support become the norm. Strong relationships based on trust and empathy also enhance collaboration, as team members are more willing to work together and support each other in achieving common goals.

PRIORITISING FAIRNESS & INTEGRITY

> *He who has the attributes (of the Tao) regards (only) the conditions of the engagement, while he who has not those attributes regards only the conditions favourable to himself.*

The chapter highlights the fundamental importance of fairness and integrity in leadership. This principle teaches that true leaders consider the needs and perspectives of all parties involved, rather than focusing solely on their own advantage or that of their organisation. By prioritising fairness and integrity, leaders can build a reputation for reliability and ethical behaviour, fostering trust and respect both within their organisation and with external stakeholders.

Fairness in leadership means ensuring that decisions and actions are just and impartial. Leaders must strive to understand and balance the diverse interests and needs of their team members, customers, and other stakeholders. This involves actively seeking out and listening to different perspectives, recognising that each individual or group may have unique concerns and priorities. By incorporating these various viewpoints into their decision-making process, leaders can make more balanced and equitable choices that benefit the organisation as a whole. Fairness also entails being transparent about the reasoning behind decisions, providing clarity and building trust among those affected.

Integrity in leadership is about adhering to strong moral and ethical principles. Leaders who act with integrity are honest and consistent in their actions, even when faced with difficult choices or pressure to take shortcuts. This unwavering commitment to ethical behaviour sets a powerful example for the entire organisation, reinforcing the importance of acting with honesty and accountability. Integrity also involves being true to one's word and honouring commitments. When leaders consistently follow through on their promises, they build a foundation of trust and reliability that strengthens relationships both inside and outside the organisation.

Prioritising fairness and integrity fosters a positive organisational culture where trust and respect are paramount. When team members see that their leaders are committed to these values, they are more likely to feel valued and respected themselves. This sense of appreciation enhances motivation and engagement, as employees are more willing to invest their efforts in an organisation that they perceive as fair and ethical. Moreover, a culture of fairness and integrity encourages open communication and collaboration, as team members feel confident that their contributions will be recognised and their concerns addressed.

Fairness and integrity also play a crucial role in building and maintaining strong relationships with external stakeholders. Customers, partners, and investors are more likely to trust and support an organisation that demonstrates consistent ethical behaviour and fairness in its dealings. This trust is essential for long-term success, as it fosters loyalty and positive word-of-mouth, enhancing the organisation's reputation and competitive advantage. Acting with fairness and integrity can also mitigate risks and prevent conflicts, as stakeholders are more likely to cooperate and collaborate with a trusted and respected organisation.

Leaders who prioritise fairness and integrity must be vigilant in their efforts to uphold these values. This requires ongoing self-reflection and a willingness to address any biases or tendencies that may compromise their commitment to ethical behaviour. Leaders should also establish clear policies and practices that reinforce fairness and integrity throughout the organisation. This might include implementing transparent decision-making processes, providing training on ethical behaviour, and creating mechanisms for accountability and feedback. By embedding these values into the organisational fabric, leaders can ensure that fairness and integrity remain central to their leadership approach.

LEADING WITH ETHICAL PRINCIPLES

In the Way of Heaven, there is no partiality of love; it is always on the side of the good man.

The chapter also profoundly underscores the importance of leading with ethical principles. This principle emphasises that ethical leadership is rooted in the consistent application of fairness, respect, and integrity in all actions and decisions. Leaders guided by ethical principles ensure that their conduct aligns with the highest moral standards, treating all individuals with respect and fairness irrespective of their position or relationship to the organisation. Such an approach not only fosters a positive and inclusive organisational culture but also enhances the organisation's reputation and ability to attract and retain top talent.

Ethical leadership is fundamentally about fairness. Leaders who embody this principle ensure that their decisions are impartial and just, reflecting a deep commitment to equity. Fairness involves providing equal opportunities for all employees to succeed and advance within the organisation. It means evaluating performance and potential without bias, offering support and resources to those who need them, and making decisions that are transparent and based on merit. By prioritising fairness, leaders build trust and credibility, as team members feel confident that they will be treated with justice and respect.

Respect is another cornerstone of ethical leadership. Treating individuals with respect means recognising their inherent worth and dignity, regardless of their role or status within the organisation. Respectful leaders listen to their team members, value their contributions, and create an environment where everyone feels valued and included. This respect fosters a sense of belonging and engagement, as employees are more likely to be motivated and committed to their work when they feel appreciated and respected. Respectful interactions also enhance collaboration and teamwork, as individuals are more willing to share ideas and support one another in a respectful and inclusive environment.

Integrity is essential for ethical leadership. Leaders who act with integrity uphold their commitments and adhere to ethical standards even when it is difficult or inconvenient. This unwavering commitment to doing what is right builds a strong foundation of trust, as employees, customers, and stakeholders can rely on the leader's honesty and consistency. Integrity involves being truthful and transparent in communication, avoiding deceit or manipulation, and ensuring that one's actions align with one's words. Leaders who demonstrate integrity inspire others to act ethically, creating a culture of accountability and ethical behaviour throughout the organisation.

Creating a positive and inclusive organisational culture is one of the most significant benefits of leading with ethical principles. An ethical culture attracts and retains top talent, as individuals are drawn to organisations that prioritise fairness, respect, and integrity. Employees are more likely to stay with an organisation where they feel their values align with those of the leadership, leading to higher retention rates and lower turnover costs. Moreover, an inclusive culture that values diversity and promotes equity fosters innovation and creativity, as diverse perspectives and ideas are welcomed and integrated.

Ethical leadership also enhances the organisation's reputation and relationships with external stakeholders. Customers, partners, and investors are more likely to trust and support an organisation known for its ethical conduct and principled leadership. This trust is crucial for building long-term relationships and sustaining success in a competitive market. Ethical behaviour can also mitigate risks and prevent legal or reputational issues, as the organisation is less likely to engage in practices that could lead to scandals or disputes.

Implementing ethical principles in leadership requires ongoing reflection and commitment. Leaders must continuously evaluate their actions and decisions to ensure they align with ethical standards. This might involve seeking feedback from team members, participating in ethical training programmes, and establishing clear policies and procedures that promote ethical behaviour. By embedding ethics into the organisational framework, leaders can ensure that ethical principles guide every aspect of the organisation's operations.

CHAPTER 80 – SELF-SUFFICIENCY & EMPOWERMENT

Chapter 80 of the *Tao Te Ching* highlights themes of simplicity, self-sufficiency, and contentment with one's circumstances. Here's how these teachings can be applied to modern-day strategic management:

VALUING SIMPLICITY & CONTENTMENT

> They should think their (coarse) food sweet; their (plain) clothes beautiful; their (poor) dwellings places of rest; and their common (simple) ways sources of enjoyment.

Lao Tzu's Chapter 80 of the *Tao Te Ching* provides profound insights into the virtues of simplicity and contentment, especially within the context of leadership and organisational culture. The passage encourages leaders to foster an environment where simplicity and contentment are not only valued but also celebrated. By appreciating the basics and finding satisfaction in everyday work, leaders can help their teams find joy in their tasks and create a workplace that prioritises well-being and fulfillment over the relentless pursuit of more.

Fostering a culture of simplicity involves encouraging employees to recognise the value in the fundamentals of their work. This means highlighting the importance of their daily tasks and showing how these contribute to the overall goals of the organisation. Leaders can help team members see that every role, no matter how small, is integral to the collective success. By doing so, employees can find a deeper sense of purpose and satisfaction in their work. This appreciation for the basics fosters a mindset where the quality of work and the intrinsic rewards of a job well done are valued over external accolades or material gains.

Contentment in the workplace is closely tied to the idea of simplicity. When leaders model and promote contentment, they create an environment where employees feel secure and satisfied with their contributions. This does not mean complacency, but rather a balanced state where individuals are motivated to excel while also appreciating their current achievements. Leaders can cultivate contentment by acknowledging and celebrating the efforts and successes of their team members, no matter how modest. This recognition helps to build a positive and supportive culture where employees feel valued and motivated to continue performing at their best.

Encouraging simplicity and contentment also means reducing the pressure to constantly chase after more. In many organisations, there is an unspoken drive to always strive for higher goals, greater efficiency, and increased output. While ambition and growth are important, they should not come at the expense of well-being. Leaders can set the tone by emphasising the importance of work-life balance, providing opportunities for rest and relaxation, and ensuring that workloads are manageable. This approach helps to prevent burnout and fosters a sustainable work environment where employees can thrive.

Furthermore, simplicity and contentment can lead to greater job satisfaction and overall well-being. When employees are not constantly pressured to achieve more, they can focus on doing their work well and finding joy in their accomplishments. This satisfaction can improve mental health, reduce stress, and enhance the overall quality of life. Leaders play a crucial role in creating this positive atmosphere by setting realistic expectations, providing support, and recognising the value of each team member's contributions.

Valuing simplicity and contentment also has practical benefits for organisations. It can lead to increased productivity, as employees who are content and not overburdened are more likely to be engaged and focused. Additionally, a culture that prioritises well-being can attract and retain top talent, as potential employees are drawn to workplaces that value their overall health and happiness. This approach can also foster innovation, as employees feel more creative and empowered to think outside the box when they are not under constant pressure.

PROMOTING SELF-SUFFICIENCY & EMPOWERMENT

> *In a little state with a small population, I would so order it, that, though there were individuals with the abilities of ten or a hundred men, there should be no employment of them.*

The chapter offers a compelling vision for leadership that emphasises the importance of promoting self-sufficiency and empowerment within an organisation. This principle suggests that even in a small community, the goal should be to cultivate a sense of independence and resourcefulness among individuals rather than relying on the extraordinary abilities of a few. In the context of modern leadership, this means creating an environment where all team members are encouraged to take ownership of their work and develop their skills and confidence. By fostering self-sufficiency and empowerment, leaders can build a more innovative, resilient, and capable organisation.

Promoting self-sufficiency begins with empowering employees to take responsibility for their tasks and decisions. Leaders should provide their teams with the autonomy to manage their work and make decisions within their areas of expertise. This empowerment involves trusting employees to use their judgment and skills to solve problems and achieve goals without constant supervision. By giving team members the freedom to take initiative, leaders encourage a sense of ownership and accountability, which can lead to higher levels of motivation and engagement. When employees feel empowered to contribute meaningfully, they are more likely to invest in their work and strive for excellence.

Encouraging resourcefulness is another key aspect of fostering self-sufficiency. Leaders should create opportunities for employees to develop their problem-solving skills and creativity. This might involve providing training and development programmes that enhance technical and soft skills, as well as creating a culture that values innovation and experimentation. Resourcefulness also means equipping employees with the tools and resources they need to succeed while encouraging them to find new and effective ways to use these resources. By promoting a mindset of continuous learning and adaptability, leaders can help their teams become more resilient and capable of navigating challenges and changes.

A culture of empowerment and self-sufficiency also requires clear communication and support from leaders. While autonomy is important, employees must also know that they have access to guidance and support when needed. Leaders should foster open lines of communication where team members feel comfortable seeking advice or assistance without fear of judgment. This supportive environment helps employees build confidence in their abilities while knowing that they are not alone in their endeavours. Leaders should also provide regular feedback and recognition, reinforcing positive behaviours and achievements and helping employees understand areas for improvement.

Building a strong and capable organisation through self-sufficiency and empowerment has numerous benefits. It enhances overall productivity, as empowered and resourceful employees are more efficient and effective in their work. This approach also fosters innovation, as team members are encouraged to think creatively and take risks. Additionally, a culture of self-sufficiency can lead to higher job satisfaction and employee retention, as individuals feel valued and respected for their contributions. When employees are given the opportunity to grow and succeed, they are more likely to remain committed to the organisation and contribute to its long-term success.

Furthermore, promoting self-sufficiency aligns with the broader organisational goals of resilience and sustainability. In a dynamic and competitive business environment, organisations must be able to adapt quickly to changing conditions. By developing a workforce that is skilled, confident, and capable of independent action, leaders can ensure that the organisation is better prepared to handle disruptions and seize new opportunities. This resilience not only strengthens the organisation's position in the market but also fosters a culture of continuous improvement and growth.

REDUCING UNNECESSARY COMPLEXITY

> *Though they had boats and carriages, they should have no occasion to ride in them; though they had buff coats and sharp weapons, they should have no occasion to don or use them.*

The chapter underscores the wisdom in reducing unnecessary complexity within organisations. This principle can be applied to modern leadership by focusing on the importance of simplifying processes and systems. When leaders aim to reduce complexity, they can enhance efficiency and alleviate stress for employees. By eliminating redundant tasks and streamlining workflows, leaders enable their teams to concentrate on what truly matters, thus achieving better results with less effort.

The act of simplifying processes begins with a thorough evaluation of existing workflows. Leaders need to identify areas where unnecessary steps or redundant tasks hinder productivity. This analysis involves looking closely at the various processes within the organisation to determine which tasks add value and which do not. By removing steps that do not contribute meaningfully to the overall objectives, leaders can create more efficient pathways for their teams to follow. This simplification not only boosts productivity but also fosters a more organised and coherent approach to work.

Reducing complexity also requires the implementation of clear and straightforward communication channels. When communication is convoluted or overly hierarchical, it can lead to misunderstandings and delays. Leaders should establish clear lines of communication that allow for direct and effective exchanges of information. This might involve simplifying reporting structures or introducing collaborative tools that facilitate easier information sharing. By making communication more accessible and less complicated, leaders can ensure that everyone is on the same page and that projects move forward smoothly.

Eliminating unnecessary complexity has a direct impact on employee well-being. Complex and cumbersome processes can be a significant source of stress for employees, leading to frustration and burnout. When leaders simplify workflows, they reduce the cognitive load on their teams, allowing them to focus their energy on critical tasks. This reduction in stress can lead to higher job satisfaction, improved mental health, and greater overall well-being. Employees who are not bogged down by unnecessary complexities are more likely to feel motivated and engaged in their work.

Moreover, a streamlined approach encourages innovation and creativity. When teams are not burdened by redundant tasks, they have more time and mental bandwidth to think creatively and develop new ideas. Simplification frees up resources that can be redirected towards innovation and strategic initiatives. Leaders who prioritise reducing complexity create an environment where employees feel empowered to experiment and take risks, driving the organisation forward with fresh and innovative solutions.

Implementing simplification strategies also involves leveraging technology effectively. Many modern tools and systems are designed to automate routine tasks and improve efficiency. Leaders should identify and adopt technologies that can streamline operations and reduce manual workloads. For example, project management software can help organise tasks and deadlines, while automation tools can handle repetitive processes. By utilising technology thoughtfully, leaders can further reduce complexity and enhance the overall efficiency of their organisation.

Creating a culture that values simplicity and efficiency requires ongoing commitment from leaders. It is not enough to simplify processes once; leaders must continually assess and refine workflows to ensure they remain effective and relevant. This ongoing process of evaluation and adjustment helps to prevent the accumulation of new complexities over time. Leaders should encourage a mindset of continuous improvement, where employees are empowered to identify inefficiencies and suggest solutions. By fostering a culture that prioritises simplicity, leaders can sustain a streamlined and productive work environment.

FOSTERING A SENSE OF COMMUNITY

> *There should be a neighbouring state within sight, and the voices of the fowls and dogs should be heard all the way from it to us, but I would make the people to old age, even to death, not have any intercourse with it.*

The chapter eloquently underscores the significance of fostering a strong sense of community within an organisation. This principle can be applied to modern leadership by emphasising the importance of building a supportive and cohesive team environment where employees feel a profound sense of belonging and mutual support. While it is essential to maintain interaction with external stakeholders, the creation of a tight-knit internal community is crucial for enhancing collaboration, loyalty, and overall organisational success.

Building a sense of community within an organisation begins with cultivating relationships based on trust, respect, and shared values. Leaders play a pivotal role in setting the tone for these relationships by modelling behaviours that encourage openness, honesty, and inclusivity. When leaders prioritise authentic connections with their team members, it creates an atmosphere where employees feel safe to express themselves, share ideas, and collaborate effectively. This foundation of trust and respect is essential for fostering a sense of community that transcends mere professional interactions and builds genuine bonds among team members.

Creating a supportive team environment also involves recognising and celebrating the unique contributions of each individual. Leaders should take the time to understand the strengths, talents, and aspirations of their team members, providing opportunities for personal and professional growth. By valuing diversity and promoting a culture of inclusivity, leaders can ensure that everyone feels appreciated and empowered to contribute their best. This recognition and appreciation reinforce the sense of community, as employees see that their efforts are acknowledged and that they play a vital role in the organisation's success.

Encouraging mutual support among team members is another key aspect of fostering a strong sense of community. Leaders should create opportunities for collaboration and teamwork, where individuals can work together towards common goals. This might involve cross-functional projects, team-building activities, or peer mentoring programmes that facilitate knowledge sharing and support. By promoting a culture where helping one another is valued and encouraged, leaders can strengthen the bonds between team members and enhance overall team cohesion. This mutual support not only improves performance but also creates a more enjoyable and fulfilling work environment.

While fostering internal community is essential, it does not mean isolating the organisation from external interactions. On the contrary, leaders should strike a balance between maintaining strong internal bonds and engaging with external stakeholders. Interaction with clients, partners, and the broader community is crucial for the organisation's growth and development. However, by first building a robust internal community, leaders can ensure that their teams are more cohesive and better equipped to represent the organisation externally. This strong internal foundation enhances the organisation's reputation and effectiveness in external collaborations.

The benefits of fostering a sense of community within an organisation are manifold. A cohesive team environment leads to higher levels of employee engagement, satisfaction, and retention. When employees feel a sense of belonging and mutual support, they are more likely to be committed to their work and to the organisation as a whole. This loyalty translates into lower turnover rates and reduced recruitment costs, as employees are more likely to stay with an organisation where they feel valued and connected. Moreover, a strong sense of community enhances creativity and innovation, as team members are more willing to share ideas and collaborate on new solutions.

ENCOURAGING MINDFULNESS & PRESENCE

I would make the people return to the use of knotted cords (instead of the written characters).

The chapter also profoundly emphasises the importance of mindfulness and presence, which can be applied to modern leadership by fostering an environment that encourages employees to stay focused and present in their tasks. By promoting practices that enhance mindfulness, leaders can significantly improve productivity while also reducing stress and enhancing overall well-being. This principle aligns with the idea of returning to simpler methods, such as the use of knotted cords, which symbolises a shift towards simplicity and attentiveness in daily activities.

Encouraging mindfulness begins with recognising the importance of being fully present in the moment. Leaders can promote this by integrating mindfulness training into the workplace. Mindfulness training programmes can teach employees techniques such as meditation, deep breathing exercises, and mindful movement, which help cultivate a state of alertness and calm. These practices enable employees to focus more intently on their tasks, reducing the mental clutter that often leads to stress and inefficiency. By dedicating time and resources to mindfulness training, leaders signal their commitment to the mental health and well-being of their teams.

Regular breaks are another crucial aspect of fostering mindfulness and presence. Allowing employees to step away from their work periodically helps prevent burnout and maintains high levels of concentration and productivity. Leaders should encourage their teams to take short, frequent breaks throughout the day to relax and recharge. These breaks provide an opportunity for employees to reset their minds, making it easier to return to their tasks with renewed focus and energy. Encouraging outdoor walks, social interactions, or quiet reflection during breaks can further enhance the benefits of these intervals.

Creating a work environment that minimises distractions is essential for maintaining mindfulness and presence. Leaders should strive to design workspaces that support concentration and reduce interruptions. This might involve implementing policies that limit unnecessary meetings, providing quiet areas for focused work, and reducing digital distractions by setting guidelines for email and messaging usage. By creating an environment that prioritises focus, leaders help their teams stay engaged and productive. Additionally, providing ergonomic workstations and comfortable settings can contribute to a more mindful and attentive work experience.

Promoting a culture of mindfulness also involves setting an example as a leader. Leaders who practise mindfulness themselves and demonstrate its benefits through their actions can inspire their teams to adopt similar practices. This might include starting meetings with a brief mindfulness exercise, sharing personal experiences with mindfulness practices, or encouraging mindful communication in team interactions. By embodying mindfulness, leaders create a ripple effect, encouraging their teams to integrate these practices into their daily routines.

Mindfulness and presence are not just about individual practices but also about fostering a collective awareness and attentiveness within the team. Leaders can promote a culture of presence by encouraging open and mindful communication. This means actively listening to team members, being fully engaged in conversations, and fostering an environment where everyone feels heard and valued. Mindful communication helps build stronger relationships and enhances collaboration, as team members feel more connected and supported.

The benefits of encouraging mindfulness and presence extend beyond productivity. A mindful work environment can lead to greater job satisfaction, improved mental health, and a more positive organisational culture. Employees who feel supported in their mindfulness practices are likely to experience lower stress levels and higher overall well-being. This contributes to a more harmonious workplace where individuals are more resilient and better equipped to handle challenges.

CHAPTER 81 – GENEROSITY

The last chapter of the *Tao Te Ching*, Chapter 81, emphasises the value of sincerity, selflessness, and non-contention. Here's how these teachings can be applied to modern-day strategic management:

VALUING SINCERITY & AUTHENTICITY

> Sincere words are not fine; fine words are not sincere. Those who are skilled (in the Tao) do not dispute (about it); the disputatious are not skilled in it.

Lao Tzu's last chapter brings forth the essential leadership virtues of sincerity and authenticity in communication. This wisdom emphasises that honest and straightforward communication is fundamental to building trust and credibility within an organisation. Leaders must move beyond superficial, flowery language and avoid making empty promises. Instead, they should strive for clear, honest, and meaningful dialogue, fostering a culture of openness and respect that is vital for effective collaboration and sound decision-making.

Sincerity in communication involves being genuine and truthful in interactions with team members. Leaders who practise sincerity do not sugarcoat reality or manipulate facts to create a more favourable impression. Instead, they present information as it is, acknowledging both the positives and the challenges. This transparency helps to build trust, as employees can rely on their leaders to provide accurate and honest information. When team members feel that they are being told the truth, they are more likely to trust the leadership and remain engaged and motivated in their roles.

Authenticity goes hand in hand with sincerity and involves being true to oneself and one's values in all interactions. Authentic leaders are consistent in their words and actions, demonstrating integrity and alignment with their core principles. This consistency reinforces their credibility, as employees can see that their leaders are genuine in their intentions and commitments. Authentic leaders do not try to present a false image or conform to expectations that do not resonate with their true selves. Instead, they embrace their unique qualities and encourage others to do the same, creating an inclusive environment where diversity of thought and personality is celebrated.

Clear and honest communication is also crucial for effective decision-making. When leaders communicate openly about the reasoning behind their decisions, it helps team members understand the broader context and the factors that influenced the choice. This transparency not only builds trust but also fosters a sense of inclusion, as employees feel that they are part of the decision-making process. Clear communication reduces misunderstandings and ensures that everyone is aligned with the organisation's goals and strategies. By articulating their decisions thoughtfully and honestly, leaders can secure the support and cooperation of their teams, facilitating smoother implementation and execution.

Avoiding flowery language and empty promises is essential for maintaining credibility. Leaders who use elaborate language or make unrealistic commitments risk losing the trust of their employees. When promises are not kept, it undermines confidence in the leadership and can lead to disengagement and cynicism. Instead, leaders should focus on setting realistic expectations and delivering on their commitments. By being straightforward and reliable, leaders can build a reputation for dependability and integrity, which strengthens the overall trust within the organisation.

Fostering a culture of openness and respect involves encouraging honest and respectful dialogue at all levels of the organisation. Leaders should create an environment where team members feel comfortable expressing their thoughts, ideas, and concerns without fear of judgment or retaliation. This open communication fosters collaboration and innovation, as diverse perspectives are welcomed and valued. Leaders can facilitate this by actively listening, acknowledging contributions, and providing constructive feedback. When employees feel that their voices are heard and respected, they are more likely to be engaged and committed to the organisation's success.

Moreover, sincerity and authenticity in communication contribute to a positive organisational culture. When leaders model these qualities, it sets a standard for behaviour throughout the organisation. Employees are more likely to emulate sincere and authentic communication in their interactions, creating a ripple effect that enhances trust and collaboration across teams. This positive culture attracts and retains talent, as individuals are drawn to organisations where they feel valued and respected.

PRACTISING SELFLESSNESS & GENEROSITY

> *The sage does not accumulate (for himself). The more that he expends for others, the more does he possess of his own; the more that he gives to others, the more does he have himself.*

The chapter elucidates the profound virtues of practising selflessness and generosity in leadership. This principle underscores the idea that true leaders do not hoard resources or knowledge for personal gain; rather, they find fulfillment and strength through giving and supporting others. In a modern organisational context, this translates to leaders focusing on the well-being and development of their team members, thereby fostering a more supportive and engaged workforce. By practising selflessness and generosity, leaders can create a collaborative and empowered environment, which in turn enhances their own influence and effectiveness.

Practising selflessness in leadership involves prioritising the needs and growth of others over personal ambitions. Leaders who embody this principle seek to uplift their team members by providing the necessary support, guidance, and resources. This might mean taking the time to mentor and coach employees, helping them to develop their skills and achieve their professional goals. By investing in the personal and professional development of their team members, selfless leaders demonstrate their commitment to the collective success of the organisation. This approach not only builds trust and loyalty but also creates a more motivated and capable workforce.

Generosity in leadership goes beyond the mere allocation of resources; it encompasses the sharing of knowledge, opportunities, and recognition. Leaders who are generous with their knowledge ensure that information flows freely within the organisation, breaking down silos and fostering a culture of continuous learning. By sharing their expertise and insights, leaders empower employees to make informed decisions and contribute more effectively to the organisation's goals. Generosity in providing opportunities involves recognising and promoting the talents and potential of team members, giving them chances to take on new challenges and advance in their careers. This not only boosts individual morale but also enhances the overall capacity of the organisation.

The act of giving recognition is another vital aspect of generosity in leadership. Acknowledging and celebrating the achievements of team members reinforces positive behaviour and encourages continued effort and engagement. Generous leaders make it a point to publicly appreciate the contributions of their employees, ensuring that everyone feels valued and seen. This recognition fosters a culture of gratitude and respect, where team members are motivated to excel and support each other. By creating an environment where contributions are recognised and rewarded, leaders can sustain high levels of performance and job satisfaction.

Selflessness and generosity also contribute to a more collaborative and cohesive organisational culture. When leaders model these behaviours, they set a standard for others to follow, promoting a spirit of teamwork and mutual support. In such an environment, employees are more likely to collaborate and share resources, knowing that their leaders prioritise the collective well-being over individual gain. This collaborative culture enhances problem-solving and innovation, as diverse perspectives and talents are brought together to address challenges and seize opportunities. By fostering a sense of community and shared purpose, generous leaders build stronger, more resilient teams.

Moreover, the selfless approach to leadership has a reciprocal effect that enhances the leader's own influence and effectiveness. When leaders are perceived as genuinely caring and supportive, they earn the respect and trust of their team members. This trust translates into greater influence, as employees are more willing to follow and support a leader who consistently acts in their best interests. The generosity of spirit demonstrated by the leader creates a positive feedback loop, where the more they give, the more they receive in terms of loyalty, engagement, and cooperation. This virtuous cycle strengthens the leader's ability to guide and inspire their team, driving sustained organisational success.

EMBRACING NON-CONTENTION

> *With all the sharpness of the Way of Heaven, it injures not; with all the doing in the way of the sage he does not strive.*

The chapter invites leaders to embrace the principle of non-contention, a practice that involves avoiding unnecessary conflicts and striving for harmonious solutions. This approach emphasises the importance of fostering a culture where collaboration and mutual respect are valued over competition and strife. In a leadership context, embracing non-contention means addressing conflicts with empathy, seeking win-win outcomes, and creating an environment that supports positive and productive interactions among team members.

Non-contention in leadership begins with the recognition that not all conflicts are worth engaging in. Leaders should assess disputes with a discerning eye, understanding that some conflicts may cause more harm than good if pursued aggressively. By choosing to focus on harmonious solutions, leaders can defuse potential tensions before they escalate. This approach does not mean avoiding difficult conversations or necessary confrontations but rather approaching them with a mindset aimed at resolution and understanding. By prioritising harmony over contention, leaders can maintain a stable and peaceful work environment.

Fostering a culture of collaboration and mutual respect is essential for practising non-contention. Leaders should create opportunities for team members to work together towards common goals, promoting a sense of unity and shared purpose. This involves encouraging open dialogue, where individuals feel safe to express their ideas and concerns without fear of retribution. When team members see that their leaders value collaborative efforts and respect diverse viewpoints, they are more likely to engage in constructive discussions and seek cooperative solutions. This culture of collaboration fosters stronger relationships and a more cohesive team dynamic.

Empathy is a crucial component of non-contention in leadership. Addressing conflicts with empathy means understanding the emotions and perspectives of all parties involved. Leaders who demonstrate empathy actively listen to their team members, acknowledging their feelings and validating their experiences. This empathetic approach helps to build trust and rapport, making it easier to find common ground and mutually beneficial solutions. When individuals feel heard and understood, they are more likely to engage in the conflict resolution process positively and cooperatively. Empathy also allows leaders to identify underlying issues that may be contributing to the conflict, enabling them to address the root causes effectively.

Seeking win-win outcomes is another key aspect of non-contention. Leaders should aim to find solutions that satisfy the needs and interests of all parties involved, rather than pursuing a zero-sum approach where one side wins at the expense of the other. This involves creative problem-solving and a willingness to compromise. By focusing on win-win outcomes, leaders can create lasting resolutions that strengthen relationships and build a foundation of trust and collaboration. This approach also encourages a sense of fairness and equity, as team members see that their leaders are committed to finding solutions that benefit everyone.

Maintaining a positive and productive work environment is the ultimate goal of embracing non-contention. When leaders prioritise harmony and respect, they create a culture where individuals feel valued and supported. This positive atmosphere enhances job satisfaction and employee well-being, leading to higher levels of engagement and productivity. Team members are more likely to work together effectively and contribute their best efforts when they know that their leaders are committed to fostering a supportive and non-contentious environment. By reducing unnecessary conflicts and promoting harmonious interactions, leaders can ensure that their teams remain focused on achieving organisational goals and delivering high-quality results.

ENCOURAGING A CULTURE OF CONTINUOUS LEARNING

> *Those who know (the Tao) are not extensively learned; the extensively learned do not know it.*

The chapter also emphasises the significance of promoting a culture of continuous learning and humility within leadership and organisational contexts. This principle highlights the idea that true wisdom is derived from experience and self-reflection rather than merely from extensive formal education. For leaders, fostering such a culture involves encouraging curiosity, openness to new ideas, and a willingness to learn from mistakes. This approach not only enhances personal growth but also ensures that the organisation remains adaptable and innovative in a rapidly changing environment.

Promoting continuous learning begins with recognising the value of experiential knowledge. Leaders should understand that learning does not stop at the end of formal education; instead, it is an ongoing process that continues throughout one's career. This mindset encourages leaders to seek out new experiences, challenges, and opportunities for growth. By embracing the lessons learned from real-world situations, leaders can develop a deeper understanding of their work and the complexities of their industry. This experiential learning equips leaders with practical insights and skills that cannot be acquired solely through academic study.

Humility is a crucial component of fostering a culture of continuous learning. Leaders who exhibit humility acknowledge that they do not have all the answers and that there is always room for improvement. This humility opens the door to learning from others, regardless of their position or background. By valuing the contributions and perspectives of team members at all levels, leaders create an inclusive environment where everyone feels empowered to share their knowledge and ideas. This collaborative approach not only enhances the collective intelligence of the organisation but also promotes a sense of mutual respect and trust.

Encouraging curiosity is essential for sustaining a learning culture. Leaders should inspire their teams to ask questions, explore new possibilities, and challenge the status quo. This curiosity drives innovation, as employees are motivated to seek out novel solutions and approaches. Leaders can foster curiosity by providing opportunities for professional development, such as training programmes, workshops, and access to learning resources. Additionally, creating a safe space for experimentation and risk-taking allows employees to explore their ideas without fear of failure. This environment of curiosity and exploration leads to continuous improvement and a constant flow of new ideas.

Openness to new ideas is another key aspect of promoting continuous learning. Leaders should actively seek out diverse perspectives and be willing to consider alternative viewpoints. This openness involves being receptive to feedback and being willing to change course when necessary. By demonstrating a willingness to adapt and evolve, leaders set an example for their teams, encouraging them to remain flexible and open-minded. This adaptability is crucial for navigating the uncertainties of the modern business landscape, where staying ahead often requires the ability to pivot and innovate quickly.

A willingness to learn from mistakes is fundamental to a learning culture. Leaders should create an environment where mistakes are seen as valuable learning opportunities rather than as failures. This involves adopting a growth mindset, where challenges and setbacks are viewed as part of the learning process. By analysing and reflecting on mistakes, leaders and their teams can gain valuable insights and identify areas for improvement. This approach fosters resilience and a continuous cycle of learning and development. Leaders should also encourage transparency and openness about mistakes, promoting a culture where individuals feel safe to admit errors and share lessons learned.

CONCLUSION

As we come to the end of this exploration into the depths of Lao Tzu's *Tao Te Ching*, specifically focusing on Book 2 (The Book of Te), we find ourselves not at a conclusion but at a new beginning—a beginning of understanding, application, and transformation in our approach to leadership. This journey through *The Taoist MBA: Leading with Softness, Stillness & Silence* has aimed to bridge ancient wisdom with modern leadership challenges, offering a fresh perspective on how to lead with virtue and integrity.

The teachings of Book 2 emphasise the virtues of softness, stillness, and silence. These principles are not merely philosophical musings but practical guides that can profoundly impact how we lead our organisations. In a world that often celebrates the loud and the forceful, the Taoist approach reminds us of the strength found in gentleness, the clarity discovered in stillness, and the influence wielded through silence.

Softness, as Lao Tzu teaches, is not a sign of weakness but a testament to resilience and adaptability. Leaders who embrace softness are able to navigate the complexities of the business world with grace, bending without breaking, and responding to challenges with a calm and considered approach. This flexibility fosters a work environment where creativity can flourish, and where employees feel supported and valued.

Stillness, another core tenet of the Tao, invites leaders to cultivate a state of inner peace and reflection. In the midst of constant change and turmoil, stillness allows us to find clarity and purpose. It is in these moments of quiet introspection that the most innovative ideas can emerge, and the most thoughtful decisions can be made. By incorporating stillness into our leadership practices, we create space for wisdom and insight to guide our actions.

Silence, often underestimated, holds immense power in leadership. It is through listening—truly listening—that leaders can understand the needs and aspirations of their teams. Silence provides the opportunity to observe, to learn, and to connect on a deeper level. By practising silence, leaders can build stronger relationships and foster a culture of trust and respect.

The journey from *The Taoist CEO: Navigating Business with Ancient Wisdom* to *The Taoist MBA: Leading with Softness, Stillness & Silence* marks a progression from understanding the fundamental truths of the Tao to applying these truths in a practical, day-to-day context. While the first book laid the foundation by exploring the metaphysical aspects of the Tao, this sequel delves into the virtues of Te—how we embody the Tao through our actions and decisions.

The principles discussed in this book are not confined to the pages of ancient texts; they are living, breathing practices that can transform our approach to leadership. They encourage us to lead with authenticity, to value the small yet significant actions, and to approach challenges with kindness and understanding. By integrating these principles into our leadership styles, we can create organisations that are not only successful but also harmonious and sustainable.

As you reflect on the insights and lessons from this book, I invite you to consider how you can incorporate softness, stillness, and silence into your own leadership journey. Let these principles guide you in creating a work environment where every team member feels valued and empowered, where innovation thrives, and where integrity and kindness are the foundation of success.

Thank you for joining me on this journey. May the wisdom of Lao Tzu continue to inspire and guide you in your leadership endeavours, helping you to navigate the complexities of the business world with grace, wisdom, and a profound sense of purpose.

David Leung
Edinburgh, 28 November 2024

APPENDIX – TAO TE CHING BY LAO TZU

THE TAO TEH KING, OR THE TAO AND ITS CHARACTERISTICS

by Lao-Tse

Translated by James Legge

Release date: February 1, 1995
Most recently updated: May 11, 2015
The Project Gutenberg

BOOK 2: CHAPTERS 38–81

CHAPTER 38

1. (Those who) possessed in highest degree the attributes (of the Tao) did not (seek) to show them, and therefore they possessed them (in fullest measure). (Those who) possessed in a lower degree those attributes (sought how) not to lose them, and therefore they did not possess them (in fullest measure).

2. (Those who) possessed in the highest degree those attributes did nothing (with a purpose), and had no need to do anything. (Those who) possessed them in a lower degree were (always) doing, and had need to be so doing.

3. (Those who) possessed the highest benevolence were (always seeking) to carry it out, and had no need to be doing so. (Those who) possessed the highest righteousness were (always seeking) to carry it out, and had need to be so doing.

4. (Those who) possessed the highest (sense of) propriety were (always seeking) to show it, and when men did not respond to it, they bared the arm and marched up to them.

5. Thus it was that when the Tao was lost, its attributes appeared; when its attributes were lost, benevolence appeared; when benevolence was lost, righteousness appeared; and when righteousness was lost, the proprieties appeared.

6. Now propriety is the attenuated form of leal-heartedness and good faith, and is also the commencement of disorder; swift apprehension is (only) a flower of the Tao, and is the beginning of stupidity.

7. Thus it is that the Great man abides by what is solid, and eschews what is flimsy; dwells with the fruit and not with the flower. It is thus that he puts away the one and makes choice of the other.

CHAPTER 39

1. The things which from of old have got the One (the Tao) are—

Heaven which by it is bright and pure;
Earth rendered thereby firm and sure;
Spirits with powers by it supplied;
Valleys kept full throughout their void
All creatures which through it do live
Princes and kings who from it get
The model which to all they give.

All these are the results of the One (Tao).

2.

If heaven were not thus pure, it soon would rend;
If earth were not thus sure, 'twould break and bend;
Without these powers, the spirits soon would fail;
If not so filled, the drought would parch each vale;
Without that life, creatures would pass away;
Princes and kings, without that moral sway,
However grand and high, would all decay.

3. Thus it is that dignity finds its (firm) root in its (previous) meanness, and what is lofty finds its stability in the lowness (from which it rises). Hence princes and kings call themselves 'Orphans,' 'Men of small virtue,' and as 'Carriages without a nave.' Is not this an acknowledgment that in their considering themselves mean they see the foundation of their dignity? So it is that in the enumeration of the different parts of a carriage we do not come on what makes it answer the ends of a carriage. They do not wish to show themselves elegant-looking as jade, but (prefer) to be coarse-looking as an (ordinary) stone.

CHAPTER 40

1.

The movement of the Tao
By contraries proceeds;
And weakness marks the course
Of Tao's mighty deeds.

2. All things under heaven sprang from It as existing (and named); that existence sprang from It as non-existent (and not named).

CHAPTER 41

1. Scholars of the highest class, when they hear about the Tao, earnestly carry it into practice. Scholars of the middle class, when they have heard about it, seem now to keep it and now to lose it. Scholars of the lowest class, when they have heard about it, laugh greatly at it. If it were not (thus) laughed at, it would not be fit to be the Tao.

2. Therefore the sentence-makers have thus expressed themselves:—

'The Tao, when brightest seen, seems light to lack;
Who progress in it makes, seems drawing back;
Its even way is like a rugged track.
Its highest virtue from the vale doth rise;

> *Its greatest beauty seems to offend the eyes;*
> *And he has most whose lot the least supplies.*
> *Its firmest virtue seems but poor and low;*
> *Its solid truth seems change to undergo;*
> *Its largest square doth yet no corner show*
> *A vessel great, it is the slowest made;*
> *Loud is its sound, but never word it said;*
> *A semblance great, the shadow of a shade.'*

3. The Tao is hidden, and has no name; but it is the Tao which is skilful at imparting (to all things what they need) and making them complete.

CHAPTER 42

1. The Tao produced One; One produced Two; Two produced Three; Three produced All things. All things leave behind them the Obscurity (out of which they have come), and go forward to embrace the Brightness (into which they have emerged), while they are harmonised by the Breath of Vacancy.

2. What men dislike is to be orphans, to have little virtue, to be as carriages without naves; and yet these are the designations which kings and princes use for themselves. So it is that some things are increased by being diminished, and others are diminished by being increased.

3. What other men (thus) teach, I also teach. The violent and strong do not die their natural death. I will make this the basis of my teaching.

CHAPTER 43

1. The softest thing in the world dashes against and overcomes the hardest; that which has no (substantial) existence enters where there is no crevice. I know hereby what advantage belongs to doing nothing (with a purpose).
2. There are few in the world who attain to the teaching without words, and the advantage arising from non-action.

CHAPTER 44

1.
> *Or fame or life,*
> *Which do you hold more dear?*
> *Or life or wealth,*
> *To which would you adhere?*
> *Keep life and lose those other things;*
> *Keep them and lose your life:—which brings*
> *Sorrow and pain more near?*

2.
> *Thus we may see,*
> *Who cleaves to fame*
> *Rejects what is more great;*
> *Who loves large stores*

Gives up the richer state.

3.

Who is content
Needs fear no shame.
Who knows to stop
Incurs no blame.
From danger free
Long live shall he.

CHAPTER 45

1.

Who thinks his great achievements poor
Shall find his vigour long endure.
Of greatest fulness, deemed a void,
Exhaustion ne'er shall stem the tide.
Do thou what's straight still crooked deem;
Thy greatest art still stupid seem,
And eloquence a stammering scream.

2. Constant action overcomes cold; being still overcomes heat. Purity and stillness give the correct law to all under heaven.

CHAPTER 46

1. When the Tao prevails in the world, they send back their swift horses to (draw) the dung-carts. When the Tao is disregarded in the world, the war-horses breed in the border lands.

2. There is no guilt greater than to sanction ambition; no calamity greater than to be discontented with one's lot; no fault greater than the wish to be getting. Therefore the sufficiency of contentment is an enduring and unchanging sufficiency.

CHAPTER 47

1. Without going outside his door, one understands (all that takes place) under the sky; without looking out from his window, one sees the Tao of Heaven. The farther that one goes out (from himself), the less he knows.

2. Therefore the sages got their knowledge without travelling; gave their (right) names to things without seeing them; and accomplished their ends without any purpose of doing so.

CHAPTER 48

1. He who devotes himself to learning (seeks) from day to day to increase (his knowledge); he who devotes himself to the Tao (seeks) from day to day to diminish (his doing).

2. He diminishes it and again diminishes it, till he arrives at doing nothing (on purpose). Having arrived at this point of non-action, there is nothing which he does not do.

3. He who gets as his own all under heaven does so by giving himself no trouble (with that end). If one take trouble (with that end), he is not equal to getting as his own all under heaven.

CHAPTER 49

1. The sage has no invariable mind of his own; he makes the mind of the people his mind.

2. To those who are good (to me), I am good; and to those who are not good (to me), I am also good;—and thus (all) get to be good. To those who are sincere (with me), I am sincere; and to those who are not sincere (with me), I am also sincere;—and thus (all) get to be sincere.

3. The sage has in the world an appearance of indecision, and keeps his mind in a state of indifference to all. The people all keep their eyes and ears directed to him, and he deals with them all as his children.

CHAPTER 50

1. Men come forth and live; they enter (again) and die.

2. Of every ten three are ministers of life (to themselves); and three are ministers of death.

3. There are also three in every ten whose aim is to live, but whose movements tend to the land (or place) of death. And for what reason? Because of their excessive endeavours to perpetuate life.

4. But I have heard that he who is skilful in managing the life entrusted to him for a time travels on the land without having to shun rhinoceros or tiger, and enters a host without having to avoid buff coat or sharp weapon. The rhinoceros finds no place in him into which to thrust its horn, nor the tiger a place in which to fix its claws, nor the weapon a place to admit its point. And for what reason? Because there is in him no place of death.

CHAPTER 51

1. All things are produced by the Tao, and nourished by its outflowing operation. They receive their forms according to the nature of each, and are completed according to the circumstances of their condition. Therefore all things without exception honour the Tao, and exalt its outflowing operation.

2. This honouring of the Tao and exalting of its operation is not the result of any ordination, but always a spontaneous tribute.

3. Thus it is that the Tao produces (all things), nourishes them, brings them to their full growth, nurses them, completes them, matures them, maintains them, and overspreads them.

4. It produces them and makes no claim to the possession of them; it carries them through their processes and does not vaunt its ability in doing so; it brings them to maturity and exercises no control over them;—this is called its mysterious operation.

CHAPTER 52

1. (The Tao) which originated all under the sky is to be considered as the mother of them all.

2. When the mother is found, we know what her children should be. When one knows that he is his mother's child, and proceeds to guard (the qualities of) the mother that belong to him, to the end of his life he will be free from all peril.

3. Let him keep his mouth closed, and shut up the portals (of his nostrils), and all his life he will be exempt from laborious exertion. Let him keep his mouth open, and (spend his breath) in the promotion of his affairs, and all his life there will be no safety for him.

4. The perception of what is small is (the secret of) clear-sightedness; the guarding of what is soft and tender is (the secret of) strength.

5.
> Who uses well his light,
> Reverting to its (source so) bright,
> Will from his body ward all blight,
> And hides the unchanging from men's sight.

CHAPTER 53

1. If I were suddenly to become known, and (put into a position to) conduct (a government) according to the Great Tao, what I should be most afraid of would be a boastful display.

2. The great Tao (or way) is very level and easy; but people love the by-ways.

3. Their court(-yards and buildings) shall be well kept, but their fields shall be ill-cultivated, and their granaries very empty. They shall wear elegant and ornamented robes, carry a sharp sword at their girdle, pamper themselves in eating and drinking, and have a superabundance of property and wealth;—such (princes) may be called robbers and boasters. This is contrary to the Tao surely!

CHAPTER 54

1.
> What (Tao's) skilful planter plants
> Can never be uptorn;
> What his skilful arms enfold,
> From him can ne'er be borne.
> Sons shall bring in lengthening line,
> Sacrifices to his shrine.

2.
> Tao when nursed within one's self,
> His vigour will make true;
> And where the family it rules
> What riches will accrue!
> The neighbourhood where it prevails
> In thriving will abound;
> And when 'tis seen throughout the state,

> *Good fortune will be found.*
> *Employ it the kingdom o'er,*
> *And men thrive all around.*

3. In this way the effect will be seen in the person, by the observation of different cases; in the family; in the neighbourhood; in the state; and in the kingdom.

4. How do I know that this effect is sure to hold thus all under the sky? By this (method of observation).

CHAPTER 55

1. He who has in himself abundantly the attributes (of the Tao) is like an infant. Poisonous insects will not sting him; fierce beasts will not seize him; birds of prey will not strike him.

2. (The infant's) bones are weak and its sinews soft, but yet its grasp is firm. It knows not yet the union of male and female, and yet its virile member may be excited;—showing the perfection of its physical essence. All day long it will cry without its throat becoming hoarse;—showing the harmony (in its constitution).

3.
> *To him by whom this harmony is known,*
> *(The secret of) the unchanging (Tao) is shown,*
> *And in the knowledge wisdom finds its throne.*
> *All life-increasing arts to evil turn;*
> *Where the mind makes the vital breath to burn,*
> *(False) is the strength, (and o'er it we should mourn.)*

4. When things have become strong, they (then) become old, which may be said to be contrary to the Tao. Whatever is contrary to the Tao soon ends.

CHAPTER 56

1. He who knows (the Tao) does not (care to) speak (about it); he who is (ever ready to) speak about it does not know it.

2. He (who knows it) will keep his mouth shut and close the portals (of his nostrils). He will blunt his sharp points and unravel the complications of things; he will attemper his brightness, and bring himself into agreement with the obscurity (of others). This is called 'the Mysterious Agreement.'

3. (Such an one) cannot be treated familiarly or distantly; he is beyond all consideration of profit or injury; of nobility or meanness:—he is the noblest man under heaven.

CHAPTER 57

1. A state may be ruled by (measures of) correction; weapons of war may be used with crafty dexterity; (but) the kingdom is made one's own (only) by freedom from action and purpose.

2. How do I know that it is so? By these facts:—In the kingdom the multiplication of prohibitive enactments increases the poverty of the people; the more implements to add to their profit that the people have, the greater disorder is there in the state and clan; the more acts of crafty dexterity that men possess, the more do strange contrivances appear; the more display there is of legislation, the more thieves and robbers there are.

3. Therefore a sage has said, 'I will do nothing (of purpose), and the people will be transformed of themselves; I will be fond of keeping still, and the people will of themselves become correct. I will take no trouble about it, and the people will of themselves become rich; I will manifest no ambition, and the people will of themselves attain to the primitive simplicity.'

CHAPTER 58

1.
The government that seems the most unwise,
Oft goodness to the people best supplies;
That which is meddling, touching everything,
Will work but ill, and disappointment bring.

Misery!—happiness is to be found by its side! Happiness!—misery lurks beneath it! Who knows what either will come to in the end?

2. Shall we then dispense with correction? The (method of) correction shall by a turn become distortion, and the good in it shall by a turn become evil. The delusion of the people (on this point) has indeed subsisted for a long time.

3. Therefore the sage is (like) a square which cuts no one (with its angles); (like) a corner which injures no one (with its sharpness). He is straightforward, but allows himself no license; he is bright, but does not dazzle.

CHAPTER 59

1. For regulating the human (in our constitution) and rendering the (proper) service to the heavenly, there is nothing like moderation.

2. It is only by this moderation that there is effected an early return (to man's normal state). That early return is what I call the repeated accumulation of the attributes (of the Tao). With that repeated accumulation of those attributes, there comes the subjugation (of every obstacle to such return). Of this subjugation we know not what shall be the limit; and when one knows not what the limit shall be, he may be the ruler of a state.

3. He who possesses the mother of the state may continue long. His case is like that (of the plant) of which we say that its roots are deep and its flower stalks firm:—this is the way to secure that its enduring life shall long be seen.

CHAPTER 60

1. Governing a great state is like cooking small fish.

2. Let the kingdom be governed according to the Tao, and the manes of the departed will not manifest their spiritual energy. It is not that those manes have not that spiritual energy, but it will not be employed to hurt men. It is not that it could not hurt men, but neither does the ruling sage hurt them.

3. When these two do not injuriously affect each other, their good influences converge in the virtue (of the Tao).

CHAPTER 61

1. What makes a great state is its being (like) a low-lying, down-flowing (stream);—it becomes the centre to which tend (all the small states) under heaven.

2. (To illustrate from) the case of all females:—the female always overcomes the male by her stillness. Stillness may be considered (a sort of) abasement.

3. Thus it is that a great state, by condescending to small states, gains them for itself; and that small states, by abasing themselves to a great state, win it over to them. In the one case the abasement leads to gaining adherents, in the other case to procuring favour.

4. The great state only wishes to unite men together and nourish them; a small state only wishes to be received by, and to serve, the other. Each gets what it desires, but the great state must learn to abase itself.

CHAPTER 62

1.

Tao has of all things the most honoured place.
No treasures give good men so rich a grace;
Bad men it guards, and doth their ill efface.

2. (Its) admirable words can purchase honour; (its) admirable deeds can raise their performer above others. Even men who are not good are not abandoned by it.

3. Therefore when the sovereign occupies his place as the Son of Heaven, and he has appointed his three ducal ministers, though (a prince) were to send in a round symbol-of-rank large enough to fill both the hands, and that as the precursor of the team of horses (in the court-yard), such an offering would not be equal to (a lesson of) this Tao, which one might present on his knees.

4. Why was it that the ancients prized this Tao so much? Was it not because it could be got by seeking for it, and the guilty could escape (from the stain of their guilt) by it? This is the reason why all under heaven consider it the most valuable thing.

CHAPTER 63

1. (It is the way of the Tao) to act without (thinking of) acting; to conduct affairs without (feeling the) trouble of them; to taste without discerning any flavour; to consider what is small as great, and a few as many; and to recompense injury with kindness.

2. (The master of it) anticipates things that are difficult while they are easy, and does things that would become great while they are small. All difficult things in the world are sure to arise from a previous state in which they were easy, and all great things from one in which they were small. Therefore the sage, while he never does what is great, is able on that account to accomplish the greatest things.

3. He who lightly promises is sure to keep but little faith; he who is continually thinking things easy is sure to find them difficult. Therefore the sage sees difficulty even in what seems easy, and so never has any difficulties.

CHAPTER 64

1. That which is at rest is easily kept hold of; before a thing has given indications of its presence, it is easy to take measures against it; that which is brittle is easily broken; that which is very small is easily dispersed. Action should be taken before a thing has made its appearance; order should be secured before disorder has begun.

2. The tree which fills the arms grew from the tiniest sprout; the tower of nine storeys rose from a (small) heap of earth; the journey of a thousand li commenced with a single step.

3. He who acts (with an ulterior purpose) does harm; he who takes hold of a thing (in the same way) loses his hold. The sage does not act (so), and therefore does no harm; he does not lay hold (so), and therefore does not lose his hold. (But) people in their conduct of affairs are constantly ruining them when they are on the eve of success. If they were careful at the end, as (they should be) at the beginning, they would not so ruin them.

4. Therefore the sage desires what (other men) do not desire, and does not prize things difficult to get; he learns what (other men) do not learn, and turns back to what the multitude of men have passed by. Thus he helps the natural development of all things, and does not dare to act (with an ulterior purpose of his own).

CHAPTER 65

1. The ancients who showed their skill in practising the Tao did so, not to enlighten the people, but rather to make them simple and ignorant.

2. The difficulty in governing the people arises from their having much knowledge. He who (tries to) govern a state by his wisdom is a scourge to it; while he who does not (try to) do so is a blessing.

3. He who knows these two things finds in them also his model and rule. Ability to know this model and rule constitutes what we call the mysterious excellence (of a governor). Deep and far-reaching is such mysterious excellence, showing indeed its possessor as opposite to others, but leading them to a great conformity to him.

CHAPTER 66

1. That whereby the rivers and seas are able to receive the homage and tribute of all the valley streams, is their skill in being lower than they;—it is thus that they are the kings of them all. So it

is that the sage (ruler), wishing to be above men, puts himself by his words below them, and, wishing to be before them, places his person behind them.

2. In this way though he has his place above them, men do not feel his weight, nor though he has his place before them, do they feel it an injury to them.

3. Therefore all in the world delight to exalt him and do not weary of him. Because he does not strive, no one finds it possible to strive with him.

CHAPTER 67

1. All the world says that, while my Tao is great, it yet appears to be inferior (to other systems of teaching). Now it is just its greatness that makes it seem to be inferior. If it were like any other (system), for long would its smallness have been known!

2. But I have three precious things which I prize and hold fast. The first is gentleness; the second is economy; and the third is shrinking from taking precedence of others.

3. With that gentleness I can be bold; with that economy I can be liberal; shrinking from taking precedence of others, I can become a vessel of the highest honour. Now-a-days they give up gentleness and are all for being bold; economy, and are all for being liberal; the hindmost place, and seek only to be foremost; — (of all which the end is) death.

4. Gentleness is sure to be victorious even in battle, and firmly to maintain its ground. Heaven will save its possessor, by his (very) gentleness protecting him.

CHAPTER 68

He who in (Tao's) wars has skill
Assumes no martial port;
He who fights with most good will
To rage makes no resort.
He who vanquishes yet still
Keeps from his foes apart;
He whose hests men most fulfil
Yet humbly plies his art.

Thus we say, 'He ne'er contends,
And therein is his might.'
Thus we say, 'Men's wills he bends,
That they with him unite.'
Thus we say, 'Like Heaven's his ends,
No sage of old more bright.'

CHAPTER 69

1. A master of the art of war has said, 'I do not dare to be the host (to commence the war); I prefer to be the guest (to act on the defensive). I do not dare to advance an inch; I prefer to retire a foot.' This is called marshalling the ranks where there are no ranks; baring the arms (to fight)

where there are no arms to bare; grasping the weapon where there is no weapon to grasp; advancing against the enemy where there is no enemy.

2. There is no calamity greater than lightly engaging in war. To do that is near losing (the gentleness) which is so precious. Thus it is that when opposing weapons are (actually) crossed, he who deplores (the situation) conquers.

CHAPTER 70

1. My words are very easy to know, and very easy to practise; but there is no one in the world who is able to know and able to practise them.

2. There is an originating and all-comprehending (principle) in my words, and an authoritative law for the things (which I enforce). It is because they do not know these, that men do not know me.

3. They who know me are few, and I am on that account (the more) to be prized. It is thus that the sage wears (a poor garb of) hair cloth, while he carries his (signet of) jade in his bosom.

CHAPTER 71

1. To know and yet (think) we do not know is the highest (attainment); not to know (and yet think) we do know is a disease.

2. It is simply by being pained at (the thought of) having this disease that we are preserved from it. The sage has not the disease. He knows the pain that would be inseparable from it, and therefore he does not have it.

CHAPTER 72

1. When the people do not fear what they ought to fear, that which is their great dread will come on them.

2. Let them not thoughtlessly indulge themselves in their ordinary life; let them not act as if weary of what that life depends on.

3. It is by avoiding such indulgence that such weariness does not arise.

4. Therefore the sage knows (these things) of himself, but does not parade (his knowledge); loves, but does not (appear to set a) value on, himself. And thus he puts the latter alternative away and makes choice of the former.

CHAPTER 73

1. He whose boldness appears in his daring (to do wrong, in defiance of the laws) is put to death; he whose boldness appears in his not daring (to do so) lives on. Of these two cases the one appears to be advantageous, and the other to be injurious. But

When Heaven's anger smites a man,
Who the cause shall truly scan?

On this account the sage feels a difficulty (as to what to do in the former case).

2. It is the way of Heaven not to strive, and yet it skilfully overcomes; not to speak, and yet it is skilful in obtaining a reply; does not call, and yet men come to it of themselves. Its demonstrations are quiet, and yet its plans are skilful and effective. The meshes of the net of Heaven are large; far apart, but letting nothing escape.

CHAPTER 74

1. The people do not fear death; to what purpose is it to (try to) frighten them with death? If the people were always in awe of death, and I could always seize those who do wrong, and put them to death, who would dare to do wrong?

2. There is always One who presides over the infliction of death. He who would inflict death in the room of him who so presides over it may be described as hewing wood instead of a great carpenter. Seldom is it that he who undertakes the hewing, instead of the great carpenter, does not cut his own hands!

CHAPTER 75

1. The people suffer from famine because of the multitude of taxes consumed by their superiors. It is through this that they suffer famine.

2. The people are difficult to govern because of the (excessive) agency of their superiors (in governing them). It is through this that they are difficult to govern.

3. The people make light of dying because of the greatness of their labours in seeking for the means of living. It is this which makes them think light of dying. Thus it is that to leave the subject of living altogether out of view is better than to set a high value on it.

CHAPTER 76

1. Man at his birth is supple and weak; at his death, firm and strong. (So it is with) all things. Trees and plants, in their early growth, are soft and brittle; at their death, dry and withered.

2. Thus it is that firmness and strength are the concomitants of death; softness and weakness, the concomitants of life.

3. Hence he who (relies on) the strength of his forces does not conquer; and a tree which is strong will fill the out-stretched arms, (and thereby invites the feller.)

4. Therefore the place of what is firm and strong is below, and that of what is soft and weak is above.

CHAPTER 77

1. May not the Way (or Tao) of Heaven be compared to the (method of) bending a bow? The (part of the bow) which was high is brought low, and what was low is raised up. (So Heaven) diminishes where there is superabundance, and supplements where there is deficiency.

2. It is the Way of Heaven to diminish superabundance, and to supplement deficiency. It is not so with the way of man. He takes away from those who have not enough to add to his own superabundance.

3. Who can take his own superabundance and therewith serve all under heaven? Only he who is in possession of the Tao!

4. Therefore the (ruling) sage acts without claiming the results as his; he achieves his merit and does not rest (arrogantly) in it:—he does not wish to display his superiority.

CHAPTER 78

1. There is nothing in the world more soft and weak than water, and yet for attacking things that are firm and strong there is nothing that can take precedence of it;—for there is nothing (so effectual) for which it can be changed.

2. Every one in the world knows that the soft overcomes the hard, and the weak the strong, but no one is able to carry it out in practice.

3.
> *Therefore a sage has said,*
> *'He who accepts his state's reproach,*
> *Is hailed therefore its altars' lord;*
> *To him who bears men's direful woes*
> *They all the name of King accord.'*

4. Words that are strictly true seem to be paradoxical.

CHAPTER 79

1. When a reconciliation is effected (between two parties) after a great animosity, there is sure to be a grudge remaining (in the mind of the one who was wrong). And how can this be beneficial (to the other)?

2. Therefore (to guard against this), the sage keeps the left-hand portion of the record of the engagement, and does not insist on the (speedy) fulfilment of it by the other party. (So), he who has the attributes (of the Tao) regards (only) the conditions of the engagement, while he who has not those attributes regards only the conditions favourable to himself.

3. In the Way of Heaven, there is no partiality of love; it is always on the side of the good man.

CHAPTER 80

1. In a little state with a small population, I would so order it, that, though there were individuals with the abilities of ten or a hundred men, there should be no employment of them; I would

make the people, while looking on death as a grievous thing, yet not remove elsewhere (to avoid it).

2. Though they had boats and carriages, they should have no occasion to ride in them; though they had buff coats and sharp weapons, they should have no occasion to don or use them.

3. I would make the people return to the use of knotted cords (instead of the written characters).

4. They should think their (coarse) food sweet; their (plain) clothes beautiful; their (poor) dwellings places of rest; and their common (simple) ways sources of enjoyment.

5. There should be a neighbouring state within sight, and the voices of the fowls and dogs should be heard all the way from it to us, but I would make the people to old age, even to death, not have any intercourse with it.

CHAPTER 81

1. Sincere words are not fine; fine words are not sincere. Those who are skilled (in the Tao) do not dispute (about it); the disputatious are not skilled in it. Those who know (the Tao) are not extensively learned; the extensively learned do not know it.

2. The sage does not accumulate (for himself). The more that he expends for others, the more does he possess of his own; the more that he gives to others, the more does he have himself.

3. With all the sharpness of the Way of Heaven, it injures not; with all the doing in the way of the sage he does not strive.